T0206675

"The editors of this remarkable collection as[...] ...d remember the dead?' Their answer, and that of their dozens of writers, poets, journalists, and analysts, is "We will." We, they said, Palestinians of Gaza who survived the slaughter, we Palestinians from elsewhere in Palestine and refugees in far-flung exile, we allies and friends from around the world, we will not let the world forget. During the 50 days of Israel's 2014 assault on Gaza, Tel Aviv's best efforts to keep the world in the dark and to keep the West believing the lie of self-defense, all failed. They failed because Palestinians did not all die, and those who lived were determined to tell their story in their own voices: their poetry, their memories, and their children. This extraordinary book joins the narrative of Palestine's witness—of oppression, brutality, and death, but also of life reaffirmed and resistance reclaimed."

—PHYLLIS BENNIS
Institute for Policy Studies

"Readers will find this rich anthology highly informative, evocative, and inspirational. They will find in it culture, creativity, and commitment. And they will also find it painful, emotional, and overpowering, such is the unremitting cruelty with which Palestinians are treated. But read it they must.... It enables us to communicate, even more powerfully, why justice is needed and needed now, and why Israel must be brought to justice. If any book is a must-read by the Prosecutor and judges at the International Criminal Court, this book is it."

—NADIA HIJAB
Executive Director, Al-Shabaka: The Palestinian Policy Network

"*Gaza Unsilenced* is an outstanding collection of short essays that discuss different aspects of Israel's murderous assault on Gaza in the summer of 2014. Given the ability of Israel and its American defenders to propagandize and distort the historical record, it is imperative that books like this be published and widely read. Israel cannot be allowed to create a false history about the horrors it has inflicted on the people of Gaza and the Palestinians more generally."

—JOHN J. MEARSHEIMER
R. Wendell Harrison Distinguished Service Professor of Political Science,
University of Chicago

"Israel takes the hammer to Gaza, but it cannot snuff out Palestinian voices. These continue to testify to the inhumanity of the Israeli occupation. There are also silences—the book ends with a list of the names of those killed in Israel's 2014 bombing of Gaza, human beings who cannot tell us their stories. This book tries to fill that gap."

—VIJAY PRASHAD
Editor, *Letters to Palestine: Writers Respond to War and Occupation*

GAZA
UNSILENCED

Just World Books

Timely Books for Changing Times

Just World Books exists to expand the discourse in the United States and worldwide on issues of vital international concern. We are committed to building a more just, equitable, and peaceable world. We uphold the equality of all human persons. We aim for our books to contribute to increasing understanding across national, religious, ethnic, and racial lines; to share more broadly the reflections, analyses, and policy prescriptions of pathbreaking activists for peace; and to help to prevent war.

To learn about our existing and upcoming titles, to find our terms for bookstores or other bulk purchasers, or to buy our books, visit our website:

www.justworldbooks.com

Also, follow us on Facebook, Twitter, and Instagram!

Our recent titles include:

- *Baddawi*, by Leila Abdelrazaq
- *Chaos and Counterrevolution: After the Arab Spring*, by Richard Falk
- *Palestine: The Legitimacy of Hope*, by Richard Falk
- *Chief Complaint: A Country Doctor's Tales of Life in Galilee*, by Hatim Kanaaneh
- *In Our Power: U.S. Students Organize for Justice in Palestine*, by Nora Barrows-Friedman
- *Gaza Writes Back: Short Stories from Young Writers in Gaza, Palestine*, edited by Refaat Alareer
- *The Gaza Kitchen: A Palestinian Culinary Journey*, by Laila El-Haddad and Maggie Schmitt
- *On the Brink: Israel and Palestine on the Eve of the 2014 Gaza Invasion*, by Alice Rothchild
- *The General's Son: Journey of an Israeli in Palestine*, by Miko Peled

GAZA UNSILENCED

REFAAT ALAREER &
LAILA EL-HADDAD, EDS.

Just World Books
Charlottesville, Virginia

Just World Books
Timely Books for Changing Times

Just World Books is an imprint of Just World Publishing, LLC.

Front cover photo by Mohammed Asad.
Back cover photo by Alaa Shamaly.
Cover design and typesetting by Diana Ghazzawi for Just World Publishing, LLC.

Publisher's Cataloging in Publication
(Provided by Quality Books, Inc.)

Gaza unsilenced / Refaat Alareer & Laila El-Haddad, eds.
    pages cm
    Includes bibliographical references.
    LCCN 2015941455
    ISBN 978-1-935982-55-5
    ISBN 978-1-935982-57-9 (ebook)

    1. Gaza Strip--History--21st century.
2. Arab-Israeli conflict--History--21st century.
3. Palestinian Arabs--History--21st century.   I. Alareer, Refaat, editor. II. El-Haddad, Laila M., editor.

DS110.G3G398 2015   953'.1056
          QBI15-600114

To our *shuhada*, those departed souls who bear witness to the crimes against them and humanity in front of our Lord.

To the living, who insist on existing, on being, beautifully, compassionately, where there is no compassion to be found.

And to the unborn thorns of disquiet,
flag bearers of freedom and tenacity.

To the defiant.
To the brave.
To the human.

Contents

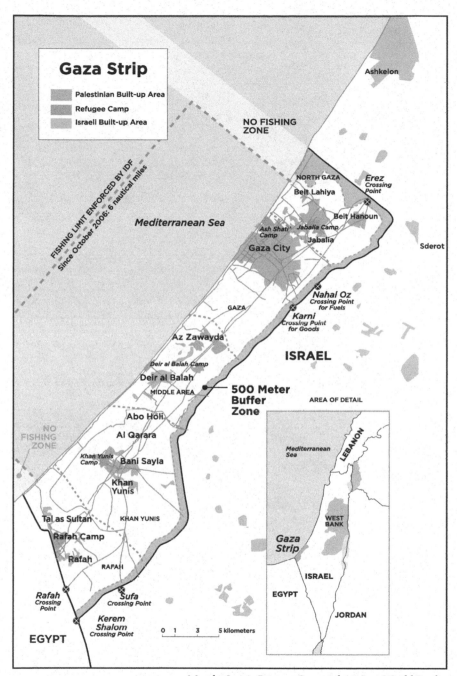

Gaza Strip

- Palestinian Built-up Area
- Refugee Camp
- Israeli Built-up Area

NO FISHING ZONE

FISHING LIMIT ENFORCED BY IDF
Since October 2006: 6 nautical miles

Mediterranean Sea

Ashkelon

NORTH GAZA

Beit Lahiya

Erez Crossing Point

Beit Hanoun

Ash Shati' Camp

Jabalia Camp

Jabalia

Gaza City

Sderot

Nahal Oz Crossing Point for Fuels

GAZA

Karni Crossing Point for Goods

Az Zawayda

ISRAEL

Deir al Balah Camp

Deir al Balah

MIDDLE AREA

500 Meter Buffer Zone

AREA OF DETAIL

Abo Holi

Al Qarara

NO FISHING ZONE

Khan Yunis Camp

Bani Sayla

Khan Yunis

Mediterranean Sea

LEBANON

WEST BANK

Tal as Sultan

KHAN YUNIS

Rafah Camp

Rafah

RAFAH

Gaza Strip

ISRAEL

Rafah Crossing Point

Sufa Crossing Point

EGYPT

JORDAN

Kerem Shalom Crossing Point

EGYPT

0   1   3   5 kilometers

Map by Lewis Rector. Copyright © Just World Books

Editors' Note

Essays and articles that previously appeared elsewhere are followed by their original source and are published here with the kind permission of their publishers.

Due to variations among writers and publishers in transliterating Arabic into English, certain names and words may appear in this volume with more than one English spelling.

Introduction

On July 7, 2014, Israel launched a colossal ground, air, and naval assault on the Gaza Strip, the tiny Palestinian coastal enclave Israel controls. This was the third, and to date the worst, such assault waged by Israel against Gaza since 2008. It was an outrageous act of premeditated aggression to which the Israeli government gave the Orwellian name "Operation Protective Edge."

In the course of fifty-one dark days, nearly 2,200 Palestinians were killed; about a quarter of them were children, many of whom were deliberately targeted.[1] One hundred and forty-two families lost three or more members. About 11,000 Gaza Palestinians were injured, maimed, or permanently disfigured. Israeli bombardment destroyed or severely damaged 18,000 housing units, displacing nearly 20,000 Palestinian families comprised of about 108,000 men, women, and children. It also flattened about 17,000 hectares of crops, and decimated the agricultural infrastructure that sustains life: irrigations systems, animal farms, and greenhouses.[2]

This relentless pummeling was directed at a population still recovering from the two preceding Israeli attacks—Operation "Cast Lead" in 2008–2009, and Operation "Pillar of Cloud" in 2012—and reeling from an illegal and debilitating seven-year-long siege and blockade that shattered livelihoods and deliberately impoverished the residents ("put them on a diet," in Israeli parlance[3]). Seventy-two percent of Gaza's residents were described by UN bodies as food insecure or vulnerable—that is, lacking access to sufficient and nutritious food to feed their families—and nearly half unemployed.[4] This same population, along with their brethren in the rest of Palestine and abroad in diaspora, had already endured sixty-six years of displacement and dispossession, almost a half century of Israeli military occupation involving continuing settler colonialism, and decades of closures and movement restrictions.

And yet, if we are to believe the popular discourse in the mainstream Western media, Gaza "had it coming," and by some perverse and morally vacuous logic, its residents "were to blame" for their own suffering. How do we make sense of all of this? Why would Israel see fit to pound Gaza over and over again, and more to the point, how can they get away with it? How can we truly understand the situation in Gaza, as a means to under-standing the situation in Palestine more broadly? How can we understand a place that is encircled from every angle, continuously and systematically assailed to rally voters (in Israel), or to "teach a lesson," or, in another ob-scene Israeli expression, to "mow the lawn"[5]—to trim those unruly, defiant hedges? Whenever Gaza is hit, it is thrust anew into the media limelight, and its residents are recast into the double roles of both victim and villain. Gaza, we fear, has been reduced to an allegory and an abstraction. We are inundated with figures and numbers attempting to depict for us what life is like in this tiniest of places. How can words convey that which num-bers and images and characters and online posts cannot, no matter how valiantly? How do you provide an accurate and humanistic—a *real* narra-tion—of the Palestinian story that is Gaza?

In *Gaza Unsilenced*, we attempt to do just this. We set out to compile a compelling collection of some of the best writing, photography, tweets, art, and poems from that harrowing time and the year that followed, to depict as truthfully and inclusively as possible what was done to Gaza, what the impact has been on both the people and the land, and how they are coping under a still existent siege.

As Palestinians from Gaza who were watching the horror unfold from abroad, we were driven by a sense of urgency, despair, and obligation to curate and edit this book, to be a conduit for voices writing from and about Gaza, as a means for changing the narrative and thereby chang-ing public opinions, which we hope can help push the long-standing U.S. policy of blind alliance with Israel in a different direction, and ultimately, let Gaza live.

Laila, an author, activist and mother of three, originally from Gaza City, was in the United States during the assault, where she makes her home along with her Palestinian husband, who is forbidden from return-ing to his native land, as are millions of other refugees. Refaat, a professor of English literature, was in the middle of his PhD program in Malaysia, where he had been obliged to travel alone because the remainder of his family was unable to leave Gaza as a result of its near hermetic closure. We first met during an early 2014 book tour of the United States for *Gaza Writes Back*, a volume of short stories written by Refaat's students in Gaza.

Besides being native Gazans, we both had another stake in this latest assault. Refaat had a deeply personal loss: his younger brother, Mohammed Alareer, 31, was killed by an Israeli missile in the presumed safety of his own home, leaving behind two young children and a wife. In his life, Mohammed was known as a loveable and somewhat mischievous character Karkour on the local television children's program *Tomorrow's Pioneers*. Refaat writes a deeply moving account of his relationship, and his brother's untimely death, in the first chapter of this book ("The Story of My Brother, Martyr Mohammed Alareer"). Refaat lost four other distant relatives (three of whom were shot at short range) and eight in-laws, and dozens of his relatives lost their houses in the battered neighborhood of Shija'ia. Laila, whose aunts and uncles reside in Gaza, learned that nine members of her extended family, including five children, had been killed in a targeted Israeli strike—on the same morning in early August 2014 on which she was scheduled to participate in a Congressional briefing. Laila's relatives were asleep inside their home when the first warning missile hit, killing half the family. They were given eight seconds to leave the house. The rest only made it as far as the outside of their house before they too were mown down.

Despite our personal losses in this ongoing ethnocide, we have been careful to avoid portraying Palestinians in Gaza as passive victims to be pitied, starving, impoverished, silenced into submission. It is our way of opening up the conversation about Gaza, of countering an Israeli narrative that has proven deadly in its ability to justify atrocities like that committed in the summer of 2014, over and over again, and of providing a forum for Gaza to speak, unsilenced and without obstruction.

Many of the pieces are new to this volume, submitted in response to a call for content, while others have been previously published on blogs and in e-zines, newspapers, and social media outlets. (For space considerations, we had to omit hyperlinks in content that was originally published online.)

Where possible, we have included photography, graphic art, and writings by Palestinians from Gaza itself—people like Dr. Belal Dabour, whose live-tweets from inside Gaza's busiest hospital kept us awake at night, or 36-year-old mother Ghadeer al Omari ("My Son Asks if We Are Going to Die Today"), who soberly concludes, "To be a Palestinian from Gaza means that you are just a postponed target, and all you can do is wait to face your destiny."

The pieces we chose deconstruct the pretexts, the untruths, used to justify this unspeakable attack. We sought to highlight Palestinian voices, whether from within the confines of Gaza or outside of it, in historic Palestine or in diaspora. We wanted to look at not only the human and institutional impact of the attacks themselves, but also the context, the bigger picture, especially as it relates to the remainder of the Palestinian people. Gaza is just a part of the Palestinian equation, after all. We also sought to explore how Palestinians and other people of conscience responded, whether by digital and creative means or by way of analysis, and finally, to look carefully at the aftermath of the 2014 military attack, as the slow asphyxiation of Gaza by other means continues to this day. We felt it vital to explore not only the immediate impact of the Israeli assault, but to go in depth and analyze the effects of the siege and blockade beyond 2014 and continuing with no end in sight, as part of an overarching and systematic Israeli policy to strip Palestinians of freedoms, livelihoods, and land.

A Brief History

Sometimes referred to as the world's largest open air prison, a modern Warsaw ghetto, or other depictions that attempt to convey the cruel reality that this small corner of the world, our home, has become by design, Gaza is a very tiny place. It has a population of just over 1.8 million that is growing at a rate of three percent yearly, the thirteenth highest growth rate in the world. Its land mass is roughly that of the city of Philadelphia's, a third of New York City, with a population density equal to that of Boston. It is a place where every space and plane is surveilled, occupied, and surrounded, where Israel's ever-buzzing drones have become a disquieting, omnipresent fixture of the likewise besieged sky. It is a place defined by political paradoxes and subject to hegemonic hypocrisy—a place where your freedom to travel, to learn, to farm, to fish, to marry, to live, to build, or to simply be are controlled by an outside power, who nevertheless claims to have relinquished that control.

The modern-day Gaza Strip was carved out of a much larger British administrative swathe known as the Gaza District, which was connected without interruption to the rest of historic Palestine, and which was approximately three and a half times the size of the modern day Gaza Strip. As part of the Egyptian-Israeli Armistice Agreement of 1949, Gaza's

A pictorial depiction of the ongoing seige of Gaza.
Graphic by Mahmoud Alarawi.

borders were redrawn to suit its eventual occupier's colonial objectives, and its inhabitants—along with the hundreds of thousands who fled there for safety from invading Zionist militias in 1948—were sealed in and prevented from returning to their homes and their land, which in many cases were only a few miles away. This influx of refugees from other parts of Palestine tripled Gaza's population overnight.

For the next 19 years, Gaza remained under Egyptian administrative rule and control. During this period, the newly established state of Israel attacked Gaza ruthlessly and repeatedly, under the guise of preventing "infiltrators" from crossing the border (Palestinians attempting to return to their homes or reclaim their property), especially under the direction of a young Ariel Sharon and his infamous Unit 101. Between 1956 and 1957, Israel briefly occupied Gaza and summarily executed more than a thousand Palestinian men and women, an event that Laila's mother, Maii El-Farra, who was 11 years old at the time, recalls vividly.[6] In the early 1970s, Sharon, by then chief of the Israeli military's Southern Command, hit Gaza hard in an attempt to crush the resistance in its refugee camps, bulldozing large blocks of entire neighborhoods to make way for army vehicles and deter future resistance, and burying alive many suspected fighters in the process.

In 1967, Israel invaded and formally occupied the entire Gaza Strip, along with the Sinai Peninsula, the West Bank, the Golan Heights, and East Jerusalem. Since then, Palestine has been suffocating under a brutally oppressive occupation. Palestinians have continually paid heavy price for refusing to succumb to an alien invasion. Tens of thousands of houses have been destroyed, almost a million trees have been uprooted, and close to a million Palestinians have spent time in Israeli military prisons.

Now, 48 years later, Gaza is bordered by an inaccessible Mediterranean to its west, by a hostile Egypt on its south, and is hemmed in on its north and east by an impermeable Israeli buffer zone, whose construction began in 1996—in the immediate aftermath, ironically enough, of the so-called Oslo "Peace Accords." During the following years, Israel fortified this buffer zone with high-tech sniper towers, sometimes equipped with robotically controlled machine guns, and more often with Israeli soldiers under vague "open fire" and "shoot to kill" orders.[7] As for those refugees from 1948, who currently make up 75 percent of the population of Gaza—they are still prevented from exercising their right, as spelled out in the 1948 Universal Declaration of Human Rights, to return to their homes and their lands.

This was the historical backdrop of the events that unfolded in the summer of 2014. What of the more immediate context? What actions preceded "Protective Edge," and more to the point, what is the context that is so sorely lacking in this discussion?

Prelude and Context

Few Westerners may have recalled, in the heat of last summer's Gaza onslaught, the shooting deaths of two Palestinian boys in Beitunia on May 15, 2014, outside of Israel's Ofer prison. Nadim Nuwara (17) and Mohammad Mahmoud Odeh Salameh (Abu Thaher, 17) were participating in Nakba Day protests, in remembrance of 66 years of forced expulsion from their homes. The demonstration they took part in also coincided with solidarity protests for hunger-striking Palestinians being held on administrative detention in Ofer. (The strike would go on for two months, believed to be the longest mass hunger strike in Israeli prisons.) Israeli authorities, as per their standard operating procedure, were quick to absolve themselves of responsibility for the two teens' deaths, going so far as

to claim that reports of their killings were fabricated, though video footage clearly showed how they were killed.[8] As Mouin Rabbani notes in his
"Institutionalised Disregard for Palestinian Life," included in this anthology, the killings, "like any number of incidents in the intervening month
where Israel exercised its right to colonize and dispossess—is considered
wholly insignificant."[9]

As far as Israel was concerned, it was the disappearance of three
Israeli teens on June 12 that required a massive military response irrespective of the identity of the perpetrators. The subsequent "bring back
our boys campaign" was a propagandized, hate-fueled effort that led to
the mass incarceration of more than 600 Palestinians in the West Bank,
to the largest military campaign there in more than a decade, and later to
the massive assault on Gaza known as "Protective Edge." This despite the
fact that, as it later emerged, the Israeli authorities knew from shortly after
the disappearance of the three Israeli youths that they were already dead
and that the action against them had not, as Israeli leaders claimed, been
a directive issued by the Hamas leadership in the Gaza Strip. But regardless of the facts, the standard "Western" narrative of that summer's events
went something like this: Hamas kidnaps three Israeli teens; teens found
murdered; Gaza is bombed.

In the weeks preceding the war, however, five more Palestinians were
shot to death. A sixth victim, 16-year-old Muhammad Abu Khudair,
was kidnapped and burned to death by Jewish vigilantes, shortly after
Netanyahu's infamous "vengeance for the blood of 3 pure youths" tweet.
(His cousin Tarek, a U.S. citizen who was visiting for the summer, was
brutally beaten by Jewish thugs in an incident that generated no discern-
ible outrage from U.S. elected officials.) As far as Palestinians were concerned, the kidnapping of the three Israeli teenagers was simply the latest
pretext used by a lawless Israeli government to "mow the grass" in Gaza
and pummel its population (and beyond Gaza, the entire Palestinian population) into submission.

So why attack Gaza, then? Officially, Israel stated its desire for deterrence and security. A more immediate target identified by some was the
desire to disrupt the Fatah-Hamas reconciliation talks, and to render Gaza
a "docile ghetto,"[10] in the words of Rashid Khalidi. More bluntly, Israel
continuously pummels Gaza just to show they can; to put Gaza and its
people in their place; and to send a stark reminder to other Palestinians of
the fate they may suffer if they choose not be willing parties in their own
imprisonment and dispossession.

It bears remembering, too, that Israeli aggression against Palestinians, and in particular Israel's violations of the 2012 truce with Palestinian factions in Gaza, were constant and continuous, though they went largely unreported by the Western media. An objective reading of the period prior to the 2014 offensive reveals hundreds of Israeli violations of the 2012 truce, ranging from shootings of farmers, to attacks on fishermen, to actual armed incursions into the Gaza Strip.

According to a study conducted by Yousef Munayyer in early 2014, "Israeli cease-fire violations have been persistent throughout and have routinely resulted in Palestinian injuries and deaths. Palestinian launches have been rare and sporadic and occurred almost always after successive instances of Israeli cease-fire violations."[11] Munayyer traced and documented more than 100 Israeli violations that preceded the 2014 offensive.[12]

British journalist Ben White has noted that in most of the Western media "a period of calm" is "exclusively defined in terms of attacks on Israelis. 'Calm' from this perspective means security for Israelis—but more dead and injured Palestinians."[13]

Misrepresentations by Western media, and Israeli misinformation and the "self-defense" pretext it uses thus continue to be major reasons why many in the West are uninformed or ill-informed about the situation in occupied Palestine. Indeed, the mainstream media in the West is complicit in the war crimes committed by Israel as its writers and editorialists continue to provide the cover and the excuses for Israel as it goes on with its brutality and human rights violations.

The Human Toll

We frequently hear Gaza explained in the context of numbers: this many dead, and that many living, in this large of an area. But what does it really mean when children are deliberately targeted while running for cover, or when entire families are wiped out as they sit for their evening Ramadan meal, or when the only survivors are too young to tell you who they are? When there are so many dead and so little electricity that little bodies are piled into ice cream trucks instead of morgues? When children under six years old have witnessed three separate assaults in their still extremely vulnerable young lives? How can we reconcile these scenes with the impenitent statements of Israeli talking heads about self-defense?

Laila's aunt, Dr. Mona El-Farra, a physician and human rights activist who was working shifts at a clinic in Gaza City during the assault, has talked in a poignant matter-of-fact way about two such child survivors,

whom she had happened upon. The realization dawned on her only gradually that she was treating unidentified children who had lost their entire families. One story stood out in particular—that of unnamed child
"Number 6":

> He was around three years old and had identifying stickers on his
> arms saying "Unknown" and "Number 6." I was shocked and im-
> mediately asked the nurses and ambulance drivers what his name
> was. They said no one knew, they'd found him in a mass of de-
> stroyed houses and he seemed to be the only surviving member
> of his family. "Doesn't anyone remember where his house was?"
> I asked. They said that where they had found him, all the build-
> ings had been destroyed and were mixed up with each other, and
> sometimes children were blasted from one place to another. So
> they didn't know where he had been living exactly.
>
> And then I realized that he was Number 6, and that means
> there were five other unidentified children before him—and prob-
> ably many more children after him.
>
> I stopped asking questions because I needed to get on with
> my work.[14]

By some estimates, Israel's use of firepower on Gaza by land, sea,
and air during Operation "Protective Edge" was equivalent to the atomic
bomb used in Hiroshima. Concretely, some 23,400 tank shells, 20,400 artillery shells, and 2.9 million bullets, or "almost two bullets for every man,
woman, and child in Gaza,"[15] were emptied out into Gaza and its people.
These tank and artillery shells were no crudely made rockets. They were
state-of-the-art, sophisticated ordnance, whose purpose is not to protect,
but to maim and kill, especially considering they were being launched into
densely populated areas.

According to a report from the United Nations Development Program
(UNDP), during the 51 days of aggression, the Israeli occupation anni-
hilated not only thousands of lives, but entire sectors of Gaza's economic and social life. Twenty-eight hospitals and clinics were destroyed,
along with 141 schools, scores of places of worship, and 60,000 homes.
"Protective Edge" also inflicted billions of dollars worth of damage on
vital civilian infrastructure such as water, sanitation, roads, electricity,
and telecommunication.[16]

It is difficult to grasp what the fallout from all this means as Gaza
struggles to rebuild: farmers without farms, students without classrooms,
workers with no factories, fathers without jobs, children without parents,

parents without children. An entire population was left reeling from severe trauma and a still unrelenting siege.

A War of Words

Gaza is a place drowning in euphemisms and the intentional semantic legerdemain that Israel uses to obscure its real intentions. Accompanying every attack, Israel rolls out a carefully considered operational name to evoke relief and comfort, even invoking the Bible: Operation Rainbow in 2004, Summer Rains in 2005, Autumn Clouds in 2006, Cast Lead in 2008, Pillar of Cloud in 2012. Spin-doctors are employed to sell these attacks to the international media in order to sustain them for as long as possible and to make them sound the only reasonable option at the disposable of a restrained and reluctant Israel.

There is no shortage of hasbarists (propagandists) and Israel apologists who invest time and money into defending the indefensible, ready to spring into action as soon as the first bombs fall.[17] Various branches of the Israeli government and military have their own interactive media teams, along with professional graphic designers, attempting to persuade audiences abroad of the righteousness of the campaign.

But imposing Israel's voice and narrative—or always finding an excuse for whatever crimes the Israeli occupation perpetrates—is not their only mission. They also work to smother and delegitimize the voices of the indigenous Palestinians. As the Palestinian political anthropologist Irene Calis explains:

> The dehumanization of native populations within a supremacist social order is not in itself sufficient to maintain an apartheid and settler-colonial regime. Such a regime also involves their criminalization for simply existing—for continuing to be present in the coveted land. This means that resistance, in any form, to the status quo is treated as a criminal offence.[18]

Israel has cultivated myths and narratives that dominate the mainstream of Western discourse, while simultaneously devaluing and delegitimizing those of the indigenous inhabitants it has for so long repressed.

The aim of Israel's propaganda is to dehumanize the Palestinians and to render their very existence questionable at best, easily disposable at worst, employing ethnocentric and outright racist tropes to make their point—some specific to this particular assault, and others recycled, employed equally against whichever Palestinian party happens to be in power. This was a defensive war, we were told. No country would tolerate rockets raining down on its citizens, we kept hearing. "We were aiming to destroy tunnels.... We do so in a way that minimizes civilian causalities, while our enemies take no such precaution.... They would kill more if they could; it's not for lack of trying.... We love our children; they use theirs as human shields. But we want a better future for everyone. Their children are victims of terrorist rulers. They store weapons in schools, or under schools, or near schools, and hospitals, and places of worship! Civilian casualties are unavoidable, but it's not our fault; it's theirs. We allow them access to our hospitals. We offer them peace, but we have no partner for peace...."

One notable example of a prominent American journalist buying Israel's line hook, line, and sinker was that of Diane Sawyer, who commented to her viewers in early July 2014, that what they were seeing on some shocking video footage showing badly pulverized homes and their distressed residents was "an Israeli family trying to salvage what they can" after "rockets rain[ed] down on Israel today as Israel tried to shoot them out of the sky." But the footage was not of Israelis or even Israel, but of the aftermath of Israeli airstrikes on Gaza, and a Palestinian family gathering belongings in the smoking debris of a missile-hit home.[19] She later apologized to viewers for the mistake—but the broader message of "vulnerable, beleaguered Israelis reeling from lethal Palestinian rockets" probably lingered. (During the 51 days of war, the Palestinian factions' generally primitive rockets caused only very limited damage to Israeli civilian structures—the degree of damage to Israeli military targets was subject to strict Israeli censorship and was never reported in the media. Six civilians died in Israel during the fighting, along with 67 members of the IDF.[20])

The Jewish-American scholar-activist Norman Finkelstein has written, "What renders Israel's abuses unique throughout the world is the relentless effort to justify that which cannot be justified."[21] We would add that it is the impunity that Israel enjoys in the West and the receptivity there to its propaganda that render Israel unique—not the fact of its propagandizing alone, since all who commit atrocities anywhere in the world are always at pains to justify them.

The Digital Battlefield

The assault of 2014 was arguably the first large-scale Israeli atrocity to unfold live on our timelines and social media feeds. During Operation Cast Lead of 2008–2009, Israel had at times imposed a complete media and telecommunications blackout of Gaza, but this was not the case during the 2014 attack.

Many have argued that social media, particularly Twitter and Facebook, was an equalizer for Palestinians, accomplishing just that, leveling out the imbalance of power, and turning traditional media hierarchy on its head—or at the very least, that it provided the besieged with alternative tools of creative resistance with which to counter Israel's bloody and fully funded offensive. On Twitter alone, for example, the hashtag #Gazaunderattack was used more than four million times in the first two weeks of the assault.

Israel, for its part, was funding digital war rooms—recruiting supporters to take to the internet and troll tweets, Facebook posts, and the like, and posting its own cartoonish propaganda graphics. Celebrities ranging from professional basketball player Dwight Howard to actress Selena Gomez and singer Rihanna and even boyband sensation Zayn Malik joined in the sometimes raucous social-media discussions—and were often quickly chastised by Israel, speedily recanting their support for Palestinians or else forced to do damage control by restricting their tweeting to something "less controversial."[22]

Within minutes of posting #FreePalestine on his Twitter account, Dwight Howard deleted the post, replacing it instead with one that read: "previous tweet was a mistake. I have never commented on international politics and never will." (The *Nation* magazine sports editor Dave Zirin later opined that we should thank Howard for exposing "how Palestinian people are imprisoned not only by walls, barbed wire, and checkpoints but also by Western hypocrisy" and that "acknowledging the humanity of the Palestinian people comes with a price."[23])

And sometimes, as in the case of Palestinian-American professor of native studies Steven Salaita, that price is your job. Salaita's previous promise of a tenured position at the University of Illinois was rescinded after he posted a series of tweets decrying Israeli actions in Gaza, some of them featured in this book. After Salaita started posting his tweets, a student and former intern with the America Israel Public Affairs Committee (AIPAC) started a petition accusing him of anti-Semitism, hate speech, and "lack of civility." Salaita countered that his tweets were "pulled out of a much larger history of tweeting and general political commentary that indicates quite strongly and clearly that I'm deeply opposed to all forms of bigotry and racism including anti-Semitism."[24]

But with information at the speed of a tweet comes, too, the risk of creating caricatured reductionist representations of Palestinians: victims to be pitied, heroes to be idolized, numbers to be quantified, but never quite real human beings with the entirety of emotions and behaviors that might involve.

This book's contributions reveal the profundity of both Palestinian culture and Palestinian voices in their insistence on life and defense of their rights to live a decent life. It is an attempt to give faces to those rendered faceless and reduced to mere numbers. It also presents other Palestinian voices or voices inspired by the steadfastness of Palestinians.

Gaza and the Palestinian Condition

There will be those who ask, Why care about Gaza? There are surely more catastrophic conflicts, after all, hungrier tummies, more desperate citizens, higher fatalities, crueler means of extermination, all vying for our divided and beleaguered attentions and increasingly desensitized consciousness—not only in the rest of Palestine but in the entire region. So why is Gaza so special?

The late great Palestinian poet Mahmoud Darwish famously said of Gaza, that it "equals the history of an entire homeland." If one wants to understand the Palestinian condition, the thinking goes, and Israel's long-term strategies and visions, then look no further than Gaza.

Israel's continuous aggression, siege, and violations of all basic human rights as well as its occupation of Palestinian land, sea, and airspace and theft of natural resources continue to be the root cause of all the trouble in occupied Palestine. Israel's continued presence as an occupying power deprives Palestinians of their freedoms.

In this sense, writes Palestinian historian Sherene Seikaly, scenes of devastation from Israel's summer assault in Gaza "do not belong to this time or this place alone. They are instances in what is now a century-long confrontation with colonialism. They are part of an archive that is the Palestinian condition. In the immediate present, to live in Gaza is to live in perpetual search for refuge,"[25] where there is no refuge to be found.

Gaza has been subject to some form of closure since the implementation of the Oslo Accords in the early 1990s,[26] when Israeli authorities cancelled the exit permit that allowed Palestinians in Gaza to travel freely to the rest of occupied Palestine. The siege, in its more current manifestation, is simply the "culmination of a process that began twenty years ago," according to Sai Bashi, the former director of the Israeli human-rights group GISHA.[27]

In 2005, Israel unilaterally dismantled its settlements and military infrastructure from within Gaza and relocated them to the occupied West

Bank and to the borders of Gaza respectively, in a move described by the advisor to then Israeli prime minister Ariel Sharon as "formaldehyde" intended to freeze the broader diplomatic process "indefinitely."[28] But it was not a withdrawal, nor was it by any stretch of the imagination (including the legal one) an "end to occupation." All of Gaza's effective markers of sovereignty—the benchmarks of a cessation of occupation[29]—remained under Israeli control: borders, airspace, maritime access, control of the West Bank, which together with Gaza, constitute a single territorial unit, and even the population registry and the taxation system.

Immediately after the Disengagement, Gaza was sealed for months on end, resulting in an unprecedented humanitarian crisis unseen in all of Gaza's then 38 years of occupation,[30] leading then Secretary of State Condoleezza Rice to observe that many Palestinians were being "deprived of basic human needs."[31]

It was the placement of what would become an ever-tightening noose around Gaza, intended to choke it of its livelihood and render it forever dependent on the powers that would continue to control it from afar. The blockade of Gaza intensified even further after the elections of Hamas's Change and Reform party in 2006 and their subsequent consolidation of power in 2007, after their defeat of CIA-funded Fatah militias led by strongman Mohammad Dahlan aimed at toppling them.

Regardless, the blockade served no real security purpose, but was rather a very calculated tool of collective punishment. GISHA reports again: "Beginning in September 2007, Israel openly stated that it would restrict the movement of goods into and out of Gaza not in order to protect against security threats stemming from the transfer, but rather as part of a policy to apply 'pressure' or 'sanctions'...."[32]

The goals of the current and continuing siege on Gaza according to a high-ranking Israeli government official in the Netanyahu government, are "no development, no prosperity, no humanitarian crisis."[33] In other words, to prevent prosperity and development by targeting the bedrock of a self-sufficient and productive economy, while preventing an all-out media outcry. In line with this calculated policy, it should come as no surprise that Israel has systematically targeted Gaza's productive sector, specifically its institutions, agricultural, and water systems and other infrastructure.[34] Twenty percent of the animal population—some 15,000 animals—were killed in the attacks, and half of Gaza's poultry perished, according to the Food and Agriculture Organization.[35]

And yet, despite all this, we seldom hear of world leaders or media citing the Palestinian need for security or the Palestinian right of self-defense. Who, after all, would tolerate thousands of tons of bombs raining down on them—not once, or twice, but three separate times within five years? Who would tolerate a siege so asphyxiating, so enduring, that it has created a situation, to quote the United Nations, of "fishing without water, farming without land"? Where young people are categorically banned from traveling to purse their higher educations? Where your freedom to live and love and prosper as a family is, too, interrupted?

In the words of Palestinian-American academic Rashid Khalidi, whose "Collective Punishment in Gaza" we include in the concluding chapter of this book:

"The pretexts change: they elected Hamas; they refused to be docile; they refused to recognize Israel; they fired rockets; they built tunnels to circumvent the siege; and on and on. But each pretext is a red herring, because the truth of ghettos…is that, eventually, the ghetto will fight back."[36]

Holding Israel Accountable

Today, Gaza is back to the untenable status quo. The challenge of writing this book alone speaks volumes about that status quo: one of us, Laila El-Haddad, is based in the United States, and is unable to return to Gaza, though she possesses a Gaza residency identity card, or *hawiya*; when she does travel, her husband, a Palestinian with refugee status who is denied his right to return to his own native land by Israel, cannot travel with her. The other, Refaat Alareer, returned to Gaza shortly after the end of "Protective Edge"—but he has been unable to leave Gaza to resume his studies in Malaysia. Thusly, the fragmentation of the Palestinian people continues to be actively enforced by Israel. It took months of coordinating over Skype during three-hour windows of electricity due to rotating power outages there, for us to pull this book together. Between January 1 and June 3, 2015, Gaza's Rafah Crossing into Egypt has been open only five days, and only a select few of the roughly 60,000 travelers waiting to leave or enter Gaza have been allowed to pass through.

As for reconstruction efforts, only a fraction of the $3.5 billion in aid pledged to "rebuild" Gaza in the fall of 2014 has actually materialized. And what little cement has made it through is unaffordable to the vast majority of the population dependent on aid handouts. Oxfam International, which blamed Israeli restrictions on imports of construction materials into the Gaza Strip, lamented that around 100,000 people are still homeless after the 2014 summer assault. Oxfam has warned that it could take 100 years to rebuild Gaza and that "only an end to the blockade of Gaza will ensure that people can rebuild their lives." Nearly a year after the Gaza onslaught, the UN reports, "not a single totally destroyed home has been rebuilt."[37]

But the question we should all be asking is what good will it do to rebuild the laboratory, the holding pen, the ghetto that has become Gaza, if the overriding cause of its suffering, and the power structures that keep this misery in play, are not put in check? Should we not, then, work together to end injustice, oppression, and occupation in Palestine? Certainly that would contribute to peace throughout the whole Middle East.

By now, it should be clear that this story is not simply the story of a 51-day attack. Nor is it one about 2,200 people killed during the attack. It is not even a story of an Orwellian world where war is peace and victims are villains. It's a story of what happens when, despite the ability to do so, powerful nations choose to remain silent or, worse, are complicit through financing the crimes being committed in the name of their taxpayers.

Gaza is the example, and continues to be the example, time and again, for what happens when we fail to hold our leaders accountable for their actions and complicity. It is the story of steadfastness and resilience, of decades-long dispossession and an insistence on surviving and existing with dignity despite calculated efforts to rid Palestinians of their humanity and existence. And if we aren't moved to act in solidarity, or at the very least, speak out, then we have lost everything.

1

Everyone Is a Target: The Human Toll

Among other unscrupulous objectives, Israel's 2014 summer onslaught against Gaza intended to sow despair and anguish among Palestinians and to bring them to their knees. Shrill propaganda by Israeli spokespeople and their media supporters was designed to whitewash this catastrophe, but the scale of the devastation made that an impossible task. This chapter gives a selection of personal accounts, reflections, and reports of what actually took place. This was not a war on Hamas, as the conventional discourse would have us believe, and it had little to do with tunnels or rockets. Neither was it related to Israel's security, which was never threatened by children playing on the beach or on rooftops or in a UN school—all easily identifiable by Israel's precision-guided munitions. Families crammed in their living rooms in the middle of the night, or huddled around a candle to break their day-long fast, or escaping after a "knock on the roof" chased them from their beds were knowingly and purposefully eviscerated in their entirety by the most heavily armed and highly financed power in the Middle East.

The Story of My Brother, Martyr Mohammed Alareer

Refaat Alareer

My brother Mohammed Alareer, 31, a father of two, was killed by an Israeli airstrike while he was at home. While he was at home.

No one knows yet if he bled for three days or if he died of the shockwaves from the explosion, or the sound, or the debris, or the shrapnel, or the fire or by them all.

But my brother Mohammed is gone.

His two very beautiful children—Raneem, four, and one-year-old Hamza—are without a father forever. And our big house of seven flats is gone.

A house of four floors but thousands of stories is no more. The stories, however, will live to bear witness to the most brutally wild occupation the world has ever known.

Hamada

I am the second of fourteen children. Mohammed is number five after three boys and one girl. Of all my early memories in life, the birth of Mohammed is the most vivid. I was only four then.

When I heard they wanted to name my new brother Mohammed, I started crying and shouting, "I don't want you to name him Mohammed. I want you to name him Hamada! I want Hamada!"

I used to scream my lungs out every time someone called him Mohammed until no one dared do so. He was then known to all as Hamada (which is a pet name for Mohammed). Everyone called him Hamada except, to my disappointment, my dad, who always used his official name, Mohammed.

Ever since, I felt a very strong connection towards Hamada. It was like he was my son, like I owned him, like I had to take care of him and to make sure his name remained Hamada.

Born in 1983, Hamada was timid but humorous and adventurous. He would be silent most of the time, but when he did speak, he was usually seeking to go beyond the boundaries of the given.

The second intifada in the early 2000s gave him his real, life-changing experiences as some of his school friends were killed by Israel and he took leading roles in their funeral processions.

Hamada went to college and finished a two-year degree in public relations, which equipped him with skills to reach out to people. At the beginning of the second intifada, in a matter of two years, people from all over the Gaza Strip started asking me if Hamada was my brother.

Surprised, I would smile and nod. And in my mind I would wonder what made him rise to fame. I realized later that my shy brother had started leading demonstrations and reciting poetic chants to mobilize the masses protesting an Israeli attack on Jerusalem, or he would lead nationalistic chants at the many funerals of martyrs we had in Shuja'iya (locally, we pronounce it "Shijaiya") and elsewhere.

Creative

Of all our fourteen brothers and sisters, Hamada was the most distinguished and creative. As he began his twenties, he became a totally different person, with many friends and many connections. As he became more outgoing, he also became even more creative and proactive.

Every time he told us about what he was doing, I would think of shy little Hamada who never looked at a camera until he was a teenager.

His newly developed public speaking and acting skills won him the role of Karkour, the most famous television character in the Gaza Strip. Karkour, a mischievous chicken, was the star of Al-Aqsa TV's program "Tomorrow's Pioneers," which hosted children from all over the Gaza Strip.

Hamada's character attracted an audience from all over Palestine and even the Arab world, where kids would call to protest Karkour's jaywalking, shouting over the telephone, and other such annoying behaviors, and suggest to him more well-behaved alternatives.

Early this year, Hamada won a small role in another TV show that started airing this Ramadan but was stopped due to the ongoing Israeli onslaught.

The death of my brother will come as a shock to the large numbers of children whose favorite part of Friday was watching Karkour misbehave and helping him change into a better Karkour, thanks to their advice, only for him to relapse at the start of the next episode into other anti-social behavior.

By killing my brother, Israel has surely killed a promising talent, and deprived thousands of children of a funny and educational program.

Martyr Number 26

Hamada got married five years ago and had two children, Raneem and Hamza. And everyone, his wife and kids included, still called him Hamada. He was still living in my parents' place after he got married; he worked very hard to build his own flat in the same building, which he finished last year.

He was never able to move up to it, however, because the siege on Gaza, which became even tighter over the past year, made it very difficult for him to furnish the apartment.

Like all Palestinian victims who fell to Israeli terror and aggression, Hamada leaves behind a loving family. My brother will be martyr number 26 in my extended family; five of them were killed last week and had their bodies dug out of the rubble during Saturday's twelve-hour "humanitarian ceasefire."

When I spoke to my mother, who lost two nephews years ago, she was stronger than I ever imagined. My father was calmer than ever before.

They both told me about the tremendous destruction Israel left in Shuja'iya—whose name means "the land of the brave." They told me about the families that lost five, ten and even twenty members.

"We Are Steadfast"

Hearing my parents' reaction, I breathed a sigh of relief. I know how devastating it will be for them to lose a dear son. But their resilience, among so many other bereaved families, did not come as a surprise to me.

When I heard about the twelve-hour lull, I was afraid people, seeing the total destruction Israel left everywhere, would be shocked and give up their support for resistance, undoubtedly a goal of Israel's merciless attack. But I was wrong.

Israel intended to bomb people to surrender by randomly destroying houses and killing people in the streets. But to the contrary, what Israel's actions are doing is bringing Palestinians in Gaza to a position of "we have nothing to lose."

"We are patient. We are steadfast. We are believers. God will surely end this aggression," Mom kept assuring me.

"They can't beat Shuja'iya. They just can't," my father told me.

We now live at a time in Palestine when a son lost, two kids orphaned, a young wife widowed must be compared to those who have lost ten or twenty family members at once. There is a clear attempt to ethnically cleanse Palestine, to make us leave and never come back.

Wild Rhino

Israel has been acting like a wild rhino let loose in a field of lavender. Palestinians have been acting as they should: resilient, steadfast, and even more determined.

We understand that we are not only fighting our own battle but also fighting a universal battle for justice and human rights against barbarity and occupation.

And now, like hundreds of kids who survived the horror of Israel killing either or both of their parents, Raneem and Hamza will be without a father for life. Nothing we can do will replace the warmth and the love of the father they had to lose because Israel wanted Hamas leaders to see the destruction of Gaza.

Raneem and Hamza will live to be witnesses to Israel's war on civilians. They will live and grow in an unjust world where their father can be killed because he is in his own house and the killer will not even be brought to justice because he is an Israeli soldier.

But before that happens, we will continue the struggle against Israeli ethnic cleansing of Palestinians, in the hope that before Hamza and Raneem are old enough, Israeli apartheid will be abolished forever.

Live Forever

When my brother passed away, everyone was lamenting the death of "Mohammed." No one called him Hamada. He is again Mohammed.

But I didn't shout at them. I came to the realization that I have to finally let go and let Hamada grow into Mohammed.

Israel's barbarity to murder people in Gaza and to sever the connections between people and people, and between people and land and between people and memories, will never succeed. I lost my brother physically, but the connection with him will remain forever and ever.

His memories, his tales, his jokes, his innocent smile will live forever through us, through his two beautiful children, and through the thousands of children who loved him on TV and in real life.

The Electronic Intifada, July 28, 2014, http://bit.ly/1zmMreE

The Boy Who Clung to the Paramedic: The Story Behind the Photo
Belal Dabour

Thursday night, July 17, was the heaviest yet since Israel's bombardment of Gaza began almost two weeks ago.

Dozens of people arrived to Gaza City's al-Shifa hospital, where I was on shift that night. Some arrived torn to pieces, some beheaded, some disfigured beyond recognition, although still alive and breathing.

Seemingly indiscriminate artillery fire, a new element in Israel's assault, had exacted a heavy toll on civilians.

The medical staff were lucky to get a break of less than half an hour. Some spent it watching the flares and bombs Israel was raining on the eastern neighborhoods of Gaza City, while others refueled with coffee or lay down for a few moments.

The relative calm did not last long. At around 3 a.m., about eight or nine casualties arrived at the emergency room all at once. The last to come in were four siblings—two of them little children, both about three years old, with relatively superficial wounds. But it was clear they were pulled from under rubble, their faces and clothes covered in dirt and dust.

Then came the older of the four siblings, a boy in his early teens. His head and face were covered in blood and he was pressing a rag to his head to stanch the flow. But his focus was on something else: "Save my little brother!" he kept screaming.

The last to arrive was his brother, the child in the photo (opposite) that circulated around the world. "I want my father!"

He was carried in by a paramedic and immediately rushed to the intensive care unit, which is right next to the ER. He clung to the paramedic, crying, "I want my father, bring me my father!" until he had to be forced to let go.

As I stood by, alert for orders, a group of four medical personnel immediately started to treat the boy. But he kept kicking and screaming and calling for his father.

His injuries were serious: a wound to the left side of his head, which could indicate a skull fracture and a large piece of shrapnel in his neck. Another piece of shrapnel had penetrated his chest and a third had entered his abdomen. There were many smaller wounds all over his body.

Immediate measures had to be taken to save his life; he was sedated so the medics could get to work.

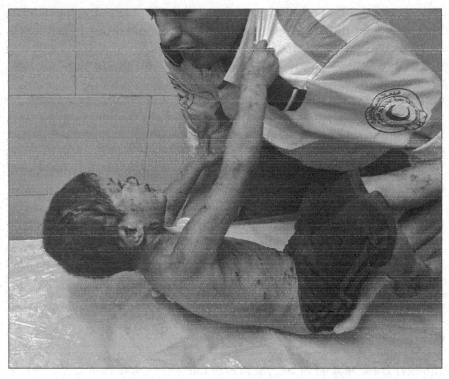

Severely injured child screaming for his father.
Photo by Ezz Al Zanoon.

Upon carefully examining the wounds, it appeared that the explosion from the artillery round sent flying small pieces of stone from the walls of his house, and that some of his wounds were caused by these high-velocity projectiles.

He was extremely lucky: his neck injury was just an inch away from a major artery, his chest injury penetrated all the way through but failed to puncture his lung, and his abdomen was struck by shrapnel that just missed his bowel.

Luck

He had a stroke of luck denied to many that night.

The medics performed heroic measures in a remarkably short time, and the little boy's life was saved.

Meanwhile in the emergency room, the elder brother was stitched up and the younger two siblings were washed and thoroughly examined for possible hidden injuries.

Somehow, despite the horror and the pain, they were sleeping. I don't know how they did it, but I felt envious and grateful for the divine mercy that found its way to them.

Their brother with the most serious wounds will almost certainly survive, but with many scars and a difficult recovery period, both physical and psychological.

Too many casualties came in that night, too many for me to get this boy's name, to know whether he was reunited with his father, or even what became of the rest of his family.

But there's one thing that I know for sure, which is that hundreds of children just like him suffered similar or worse injuries, and up to the moment of this writing, nearly eighty children just like him have been killed as Israel's merciless attack goes on.

The Electronic Intifada, July 20, 2014, http://bit.ly/1yJFvYG

My Son Asks if We Are Going to Die Today
Ghadeer al Omari

Ghadeer is the mother of two small boys and works as a media officer for a human rights organization in Gaza City. Hikmat (8) is now living through his third offensive on Gaza. Ahmad (6) was born shortly after "Operation Cast Lead." In conversation with Voices of Gaza this morning, Ghadeer expressed deep anxiety about the ongoing attacks, saying, "Things are getting worse and worse here. Last night was the worst ever. Wallah, I'm speechless." Below, she describes the impact of the situation on her children.

Inside our weary bodies and souls, something will stay broken.

I'm a mother of two little boys, Hikmat (8) and Ahmad (6). Like any normal mother in this world, all I want is to keep my boys safe and happy but, unfortunately, it seems that this wish is just impossible. Why? Simply and briefly, because I'm a Palestinian and I live in Gaza.

To be a Palestinian from Gaza means that you can be under attack from Israel at any time. It means that you are just a postponed target, and all you can do is wait to face your destiny. This is how we live in Gaza, both with and without war. I have experienced three wars in the last six years. During the first war on Gaza, in 2008–2009, my apartment was destroyed when the Israeli occupation forces targeted the Palestinian government complex. At the time, I was seven months pregnant, and I had been decorating my baby's room! In the second war, which took place in November 2012, I learned exactly what being homeless really means. Israel targeted the building where my family was living and in which I was staying. We evacuated the building and went to stay at my sister's house.

During war, the days are too long. Every single hour that passes feels like a whole year. Since the beginning of this war, I'm living the worst days and nights ever, as the peaceful moments are so few. As we are fasting, every day we have our morning and evening meals, listening to the bombing outside and asking God to keep us and the people of Gaza safe. Israeli airplanes are shelling houses. Many houses have been destroyed over the heads of children and women. These children and women are human beings. They have names, dreams, and beloved ones. The photographs of those victims are heartbreaking, and I can't stop my mind from drawing awful pictures of me and my family with our house over our heads just like them.

Our bodies shake and our hearts sink with every single airstrike. I try not to freak out so my two little boys won't either but sometimes I'm just a big failure! During daylight hours, all of us gather together in the same place, a room, or a corner, listening to the shelling, trying to figure out which are the targeted areas, and following the news second by second. I keep the boys inside the house all the time. I can't even let them go out into the backyard or to the rooftop. I'm doing my best to keep them away from this insanity, but how can I when it's everywhere?! I wish I could cover their ears so they wouldn't hear the sound of bombing. I feel like I'm dying, as I see the fear in their eyes.

At night, things are much harder. I spend every night moving my boys from one room to another, looking for safety. I'm too frightened to sleep, not only because of the loud noises caused by the continuous bombing, but also because I think I need to be awake, monitoring the situation around in order to decide, according to the sounds of the shelling, whether to keep my boys in this room, or to move them to another one. We have had no electricity for three days now and I guess you can imagine how it feels without electricity in circumstances like those we are facing in Gaza during this war.

The Israeli crimes committed against civilians in Gaza undermine my faith in international law and international bodies. It seems like these bodies were created to defend Israel and cover up its crimes against the innocent people of Palestine. A massacre was committed last night in Al-Shuja'iya neighborhood, in the east of Gaza. The reality here is so bloody and what is happening is so much more than any human can bear. Hundreds of artillery shells are falling on houses even at this very moment. The photographs of the victims are more than horrendous. People are running out of their houses, dead bodies are in the streets, and ambulances can't reach those who have been murdered. Every single picture reminds me of the Nakba.

I guess that we Palestinians should only believe in the law of power. We face death every moment of every day, and the whole world is silent. When they speak, they tell us about Israel's right to self-defense! Why? I need someone wise to tell me why. We are under occupation and Israel is the occupying force. These are not two equal sides.

This morning, Hikmat and Ahmad woke up to the sound of a huge explosion. I hugged their shaking bodies, asking them not to be afraid. Hikmat, who is 8, said, "I hate Israel. I hate all the Israeli people." I asked him, "Why, sweetheart?" He answered, "Don't you know why, Mum? Don't you see what they are trying to do? They want to kill us."

The Israelis claim that we teach our kids hate, but we don't. This is how Palestinian children start to feel hatred toward Israel. After 13 days of war, my two boys are able to know the difference between F16s and Apache helicopters, and they play guessing games together, distinguishing between tank shelling and airstrikes. This is how our kids spend their summer!

Ahmad, my younger boy, asks me every morning, "Mum, we are not going to die today, are we?" Hikmat answers, saying, "Don't worry, Ahmad. Mum and Dad will protect us." This sentence makes me speechless. I don't know what to say or what to tell them. I would die for my kids but I'm afraid because I know that I am helpless. There is no way to protect my boys and, except God, no one knows what will happen in the next second. The war is still taking place over the Gaza Strip. There will be an end, but inside our weary bodies and souls something will stay broken.

Voices of Gaza, July 20, 2014, http://bit.ly/1oYySuE

"Wake Up, My Son!" None of Gaza's Murdered Children Are Just Numbers

Ali Abunimah

Sahir Salman Abu Namous was just four years old, soon to turn five.

"Everyone who saw him loved him because he was always smiling," his first cousin Diaa Mahmoud recalls in an email he sent me from Gaza.

"One month before Sahir died, his father was sitting and talking to the boy's aunt," Mahmoud says. "He looks so clever," Mahmoud remembers the boy's proud father saying, "even more clever than his siblings."

Sahir was killed on Friday afternoon when an Israeli warplane bombed his family home in the Tal al-Zaatar neighborhood in northern Gaza

"He was playing and smiling next to his mother when missile shrapnel divided his head," Mahmoud writes.

"His father took him to the hospital screaming 'Wake up, my son! I bought toys for you, please wake up!'"

The photo that Mahmoud sent of Sahir with little left of his head, cradled in the arms of his anguished father, Salman Abu Namous, is too graphic to show here.

But Mahmoud sent me some other photos of his cousin Sahir in happier times.

"He was just a kid who wanted to play and be happy," Mahmoud says, "he wasn't just a number."

Since Monday, Israel has targeted hundreds of private homes, banks, social institutions and mosques with relentless bombardment.

Sahir Salman Abu Namous was one of 21 children who had been killed in the onslaught by Friday.

Two Disabled Women Among Dead in Unrelenting Massacre

By Saturday, the toll had exceeded 130 people killed and more than 1,000 injured, almost 80 percent noncombatant civilians.

In a particularly horrifying attack, Israeli warplanes last night bombed a home for people with disabilities in northern Gaza, killing two women, Suha Abu Saada, 47, and Ola Wishaa, 30.

Residents of the home "were barely mobile," neighbors told the *Guardian*, "spending their time in bed or in wheelchairs, and could not escape the building."

None of them are just numbers.

The Electronic Intifada, July 12, 2014, http://bit.ly/1q6ivCG

Devastated Family Remembers Cheerful Boy Cut Down by Israeli Fire on Gaza Beach

Rami Almeghari

The day before he was killed, "Ismail came home carrying fresh fish and began joking with his brothers and sisters. He seemed unusually cheerful and happy," his mother Sahar Baker told the *Electronic Intifada* at her home in Gaza's Beach Camp just twenty-four hours after her son's brutal slaying.

"I asked him, my son, why did you go to the beach while the situation is dangerous? He answered, we were playing as we wanted to play, why should we be afraid?" Sahar said.

Ismail Muhammad Baker, nine years old, was killed along with his cousins Ahed Atif Baker and Zakaria Ahed Baker, both ten years old, and eleven-year-old Muhammad Ramiz Baker when Israeli fire targeted them on a beach near Gaza City's seaport on July 16.

The massacre, witnessed by international journalists at the nearby Al-Deira hotel, caused outrage around the world and drew attention to the horrifying death toll among Gaza's children.

As of Saturday, more than sixty children were among the 339 people who have been killed since Israel began its round-the-clock bombardment of Gaza on July 7. The death toll rose sharply since Friday, when Israeli forces began a ground invasion in parts of Gaza.

Deeply distraught and surrounded by mourners and relatives, and joined by Ismail's father, Muhammad, Sahar Baker said she hoped God would punish Israeli Prime Minister Benjamin Netanyahu and his government for "stealing my dear son. We raise our children and all of a sudden they steal them from us."

A Cheerful Boy

A mother of six other sons and three daughters, Sahar recalled that Ismail was always helpful to her and acted more mature than his age.

Ismail had recently started selling tea at the seaport to earn a few shekels to help the family out, his father said. "This newly-built house will not see Ismail grow up," Muhammad added.

Ismail's father was also deeply distraught and emotional when he spoke to the *Electronic Intifada*. He is unemployed like so many others in

Grieving parents of Ismail, Ahed, Zakaria, and Mahammad Baker, who were killed on July 16 by shelling from an Israeli gunboat as they played soccer on a Gaza beach. Photo by Alaa Shamaly.

Gaza's dire economic situation, but the family home was recently rebuilt thanks to a grant from the Qatari government.

"Hours before I heard news of his death, Ismail asked me to prepare him some food, which I did," Sahar recalled. "As we heard loud explosions, I felt so worried for him. Then later I saw his body dismembered, his abdomen, his back, his limbs...."

Samara, Ismail's twelve-year-old sister, stood in the corner crying. "Ismail was such a kind brother. Everyone loved him," she said. She remembered how he would take younger children to the store to buy them treats.

"I used to have seven brothers, but now I only have six," she said, embracing her father for support.

"What Did He Do?"

"Ismail was so tender and kind," his maternal grandmother, Um Said, told the *Electronic Intifada*. "Why did they kill him? What did he do?"

"Was my son one of the targets in Israel's target bank?" his father Muhammad asked.

Preparing to bury the four Baker boys, who were killed on July 16, 2014,
by shelling from an Israeli gunboat as they played football on a Gaza beach.
Photo by Alaa Shamaly.

"I call on [Prime Minister Recep Tayyip] Erdogan of Turkey to help bring justice to the Turkish victims of Israel's attack on the flotilla," Muhammad said, noting that there is a memorial at Gaza port to the ten victims of Israel's May 2010 attack on the *Mavi Marmara*.

"And I call on Erdoğan to help bring justice for my slain son," Muhammad added.

The Electronic Intifada, July 19, 2014, http://bit.ly/1p58oMi

Gaza: Israel Puts Paramedics in Its Crosshairs
Mohammed Suliman

Twenty-eight-year-old Ayed al-Buraey was a Palestinian paramedic from northern Gaza. After he finished his shift, Ayed would normally call his wife to assure her that he was safe. This time however, he did not call.

Ayed was killed on July 25 when Israeli forces shelled the ambulance he was in while he and his crew were on their way to evacuate the injured in Beit Hanoun. The shells struck the ambulance and set it on fire.

Hatem Shahin, a volunteer paramedic, was with the crew when the ambulance vehicle was shelled. He was injured in the attack but managed to get out of the ambulance and, with the help of few young men, walked to Beit Hanoun Hospital, where he was then taken to al-Awda Hospital in Jabaliya.

"We were heading to al-Masreyyeen Street to evacuate a few injured people stuck there. Once we entered the street, a shell hit our ambulance. I started shouting but couldn't hear anything. The vehicle was ablaze. I crawled out of it and walked away," 38-year-old Shahin told *Al-Akhbar*.

"When I arrived at the hospital, I was told that Jawad Bdeir [the ambulance driver] was also injured and that Ayed was killed. I was shocked," Hatem said.

Since the start of its most recent onslaught on Gaza on July 8, Israeli forces have on several occasions attacked medical personnel, rescue teams and ambulances. According to the Palestinian Center for Human Rights in Gaza, Israeli forces have killed seven medical personnel and injured 16 others so far. Nearly 20 ambulance vehicles have been completely destroyed during the same period.

Israeli forces have also attack hospitals and medical staff such as Balsam hospital, Beit Hanoun hospital in Beit Hanoun, the Algerian hospital in Khan Younis and al-Wafa hospital, which finally collapsed after Israeli warplanes bombarded it several times.

"I Came Home to Tell You I'm Safe"

As the Palestinian death toll increased day by day, Ayed would rarely come back home to see his wife and two little children. On the few occasions he did manage to come back, he would take his four-month-old baby in his arms and fall asleep.

"I was always worried to death about him," Reham said tearfully. "It was like I knew something wrong would happen to him. We rarely saw him, he came home only three times since the start of this war."

"When I asked him about his work, he couldn't even reply because of how tired he was. He only hugged the children and slept. He used to tell me, 'I came back to tell you I'm safe, so don't worry about me.'"

The ambulance vehicle in which Ayed was killed belonged to the Palestinian Red Crescent Society. It was then removed from the street by an Israeli armored bulldozer, which put it on the side of the street. Shortly afterwards, another ambulance arrived at the scene in order to evacuate Ayed's body. This time, the International Committee of the Red Cross coordinated its access to the area, but as soon as it came into the street, it was fired upon by the Israeli army and another medic was moderately injured.

In another incident, Israeli forces opened fire on medical personnel as they were evacuating a handicapped person from al-Qarara area in Khan Younis. They killed one paramedic. Al-Mezan Center for Human Rights in Gaza reports: "As a result of the attack, a medic, Mohammed Hassan al-Abadla, 32, was injured when he was outside the vehicle. Under the fire, the ambulance driver drove away. Communication with the injured medic was cut and he stayed in the area for half an hour, during which he bled to death. The ICRC had to coordinate again for his fellow medics to reach him. They found him dead."

Jihad Saleem, 43, is an ambulance officer from Gaza. He says although this has been his job for years, every time he receives a call informing him of a body to be picked up or an injured person to be rescued or a group of people to be evacuated, he feels his heart beat as if it was his first time all over again.

"When I see bodies torn to pieces, sometimes disemboweled, I think of them as my own family," he told *Al-Akhbar*.

"We're always stressed because of what we see and what we have to deal with. We always imagine this is our own family we're going to save," he explained, adding that it actually happened to one of his colleagues. "He went to save a group of people only to find out it was his brother's house and four of the dead were his own nephews."

Another paramedic, Ahmed Musallam, was injured while he was evacuating residents from a building that was going to be bombed. Even though Ahmed was hit by shrapnel in his leg, he refuses to let his injury stop him from doing his job.

"I just couldn't sit at home despite the pain in my leg. It pains me much more to see these little children dying under the rubble and hear their mothers mourn over them. I had to come back here," the 30-year-old told *Al-Akhbar*. "This is where I belong, and my people need me here."

Israeli attacks on medical personnel, particularly paramedics, as well as the obstruction of medical access to the injured have been condemned by various human rights organizations in Gaza and described as "a serious violation of the international humanitarian law that may amount to war crimes."

*In Shija'ia, ambulances were not off limits (July 26). By the end of the assault,
at least 36 had been damaged by Israeli firepower.[1]
Photo by Mohammed Asad.*

Today Reham is completely distraught over Ayed's loss. She described him as stubborn, saying he always refused sit at home. "He used to tell me, 'If we all sat at home and didn't go to work, who will save all these people?'"

"But now he's [the one who] died and no one came to save him. My children and I will never see him again," she said.

Al-Akhbar English, July 28, 2014, http://bit.ly/1BNIhMx

Losing a Good Friend
Mu'taz Hilal Muhammad al-'Azayzeh

Mu'taz Hilal Muhammad al-'Azayzeh, 15, is a grade 11 student. He lives in Deir al-Balah. His testimony was taken by Khaled al-'Azayzeh on October 26, 2014.

I'm a grade 11 student in 'Abd al-Karim al-'Akluk School in Deir al-Balah and live there with my family.

I used to go to Rudolph Walter School, on Salah al-Din St. on the eastern side of Deir al-Balah. There, I was close friends with 'Alaa Abu Dahruj. We studied together from Grade 6 through Grade 10 and spent all our time together, in class, during recess and after school. 'Alaa was a very good soccer player and played for the Deir al-Balah club and other clubs. He wore sports clothes all the time. I played with him and we spent most of our free time practicing soccer. 'Alaa told me a few times that he couldn't go a whole day without playing.

At the beginning of last summer, we got together all the time, sometimes at the soccer club and sometimes at the mosque. 'Alaa lived a 10-minute walk from my house. During the war, we saw each other three times, once in town, once at the mosque and the third time, he came to visit me at home. We sat on the sidewalk across from my house with another friend, Muamen Abu Sha'ar. We heard the explosions and talked about the war. 'Alaa said he wasn't afraid to die and told us he was still playing soccer outside, by his house.

On July 21, 2014, we fled from our home, which is located in an area that was shelled all the time. We went to my grandfather's house in downtown Deir al-Balah. This was during the month of Ramadan. On that day, at 3:30 p.m., a friend of mine from school phoned and told me it had been reported on television that a person named 'Alaa Abu Dahruj had been killed, but he wasn't sure whether this was our friend 'Alaa, because the report did not give the father's name.

I phone a mutual friend of mine and 'Alaa's and asked him. He told me 'Alaa had been killed in the bombing on Shuhadaa al-Aqsa Hospital. 'Alaa and his family had left their home when the bombardment began and fled to the hospital to take cover, but shells hit the hospital and 'Alaa was hit by shrapnel in the abdomen and killed.

I started crying and walked out of my grandfather's house despite the bombing and war. I headed towards the hospital to see him. I wasn't afraid and I didn't care about the shelling because I wasn't aware of anything happening around me. I was thinking only of 'Alaa and what had happened to him. I recalled our walks together, and the time we'd spent together. My father met me along the way and kept me from going to the hospital because it was dangerous there. The next day, 'Alaa was buried in the Deir al-Balah cemetery and I didn't go to the funeral because my father wouldn't let me leave the house. That afternoon, I went to the cemetery and sat by his grave. I read the el-Fatiha prayer and prayed for him, and I took photos of the grave. The cemetery was empty because there were was still some occasional shelling and air strikes.

Since the school year began, I've gone into the cemetery most days on my way to class. I visit 'Alaa's grave for a few minutes, remembering stuff we used to talk about. I pray for him and continue on my way to school. My school friends and I get together almost every day and remember 'Alaa and all kinds of things we did and saw together.

'Alaa really liked me. Once, he stood up to the teacher and defended me when another student wrongly complained about me. 'Alaa said the other student was lying. Sometimes, we quarreled for a day or two but then we'd make up because we missed each other.

B'Tselem, *Testimonies*, http://bit.ly/1ClcPTY

In Gaza's al-Shuja'iya: "I Just Survived a Massacre"
Mohammed Suliman

"A massacre, a massacre!" were the words my brother, who works as a doctor at Gaza's al-Shifa Hospital, said as he yelled over the phone urging me to come to Gaza's main hospital immediately. "Come witness the massacre," he said.

At first light, as I readied myself to go to the hospital, I heard knocks on my door. Three young men in tattered, seemingly burned clothes stood there. They asked me if I knew of any flats in the area they could rent. They were survivors of the yet unfinished massacre. "We've just fled from Shuja'iya, there's a massacre there," they told me before they walked away.

On my way to al-Shifa, I saw scores of people roaming the streets, some barefoot, others weeping. They had fled the "Death Zone." Drones were still buzzing overhead, warships shelled sporadically, and Israeli jet fighters roared intimidatingly before the roaring soon faded into the distance. But it all somehow felt so quiet.

I soon arrived at al-Shifa. Flabbergasted, I made my way through the crowds of people who had already gathered there seeking shelter with their families and children. Some lay on the ground, and others wailed the death of their children and relatives. Some stood by the morgue looking for their lost family members. These were some of the survivors of the Shuja'iya massacre.

"We were sitting at home after iftar when suddenly shells started raining down on us," 42-year-old Fatima al-Dib told *Al-Akhbar*. Fatima and her family hid under the stairs and were stranded for nearly 10 hours unable to escape while Israeli mortar shells fell on and around their house.

"There was a blazing fire outside," Fatima, a mother of two boys and three girls, recalled the past night. "My daughter was injured, so we carried her and hid under the stairs. We stayed there all night long from 8:30 in the evening until 6:00 in the morning as we heard the Israeli artillery fire shells in our direction nonstop," she told us tearfully, her daughter in her arms.

Surviving a Massacre

On their way out, Fatima saw houses left in ruins, glass shattered, corpses strewn on the sidewalks, some disfigured and others ripped apart. "They must have been trying to flee when they were killed.... When I got to al-Shifa, I realized I have just survived a massacre," Fatima commented.

On July 19, Israeli forces perpetrated a vicious massacre against residents of Shuja'iya area, east of Gaza City. When night came, Israeli artillery intensified its bombardment of Shuja'iya throughout the night. Ambulances and civil defense forces were prevented from entering the targeted areas to evacuate the dead and injured. Houses were destroyed with their residents trapped inside, and other houses burned all night long. Corpses were buried under the rubble, and the injured bled to death. Children screamed for their lives. More than 70 have been killed, and more than 250 others were injured, the vast majority of them civilians. Over half of them are women and children.

Abu Mohammed al-Helo and his family were some of the survivors. Abu Mohammed came to al-Shifa and was frenetically looking for his brother Jihad and his family. Neighbors told him that Jihad's house was shelled but that he was still alive. "My brother and his family are trapped under the rubble," he told us. "Neighbors say they heard them shouting for help as they escaped the area but couldn't rescue them because of the strikes,. With tears welling up in his eyes, he walked away, looking for help.

As I stood by the morgue to meet some of the families of the victims, very few people came to see the corpses and identify their relatives. It was simply unclear who was dead and who was still alive. Some were also completely disfigured that it was impossible to identify them. Most of the families were either still stranded in Shuja'iya or just unaware that their family members have been killed. They were instead waiting for them to join them at UNRWA schools where families sought shelter.

The International Committee of the Red Cross has come under fire for failing to intervene and rescue the injured and evacuate residents of Shuja'iya whose calls went unanswered.

Ahmed Jindiyya lost his brother Mohammed after a missile landed on his house. He called the Red Cross, which told him they would come to their rescue but never really turned up. "We were at home when our neighbor's house was bombed. We tried to escape but the shells soon hit our house," Ahmed told Al-Akhbar.

"As the shells hit around us, I hugged my children and tried to calm them down. But the shelling got closer and closer, so we covered our heads with pillows and a mattress. Then a missile hit our house. Mohammed [Ahmed's brother] got killed, and some others were injured"

An ambulance finally arrived, and the injured were picked up. Ahmed, whose family is comprised of five sons and three daughters, escaped with his family in the middle of the night. According to Ahmed, a family including women and children was running away ahead of them when a shell hit and killed them.

"We decided to hide by walking on the sidewalk close to the wall," Ahmed narrated how he and his family barely escaped death as mortars fell near them. "My children were crying and we walked as fast as we could till we got to Shuja'iya Square where ambulances picked us up."

When they got to al-Shifa hospital, Ahmed was reunited with the rest of his family. He saw his dead brother for only a short time as bodies were being piled on top of each other as new ambulances arrived.

Hamada al-Ghafeer described his and his family's survival as "a miracle." As bombs fell down, he and his family hid under the stairs, broken glass showering over them. "I prayed that I'd die before my kids and not live to see them torn and burnt in front of my eyes," 39-year-old Hamada said.

"They were bent on obliterating all of Shuja'iya. I can't believe we outlived this massacre. It's a miracle, a rebirth."

Al-Akhbar English, July 22, 2014, http://bit.ly/1nBHnAh

An Eyewitness to Genocide:
A Night in Khuza'a

Sarah Algherbawi

Khuza'a is a 4,000-acre town that lies east of Khan Yunis city in the southern area of Gaza, with a population of almost 11,000 people. On Monday night, July 21, Israeli forces started to bomb Khuza'a heavily, with the aim of destroying it. Before the operation started, the Israeli army ordered the residents of Khuza'a to evacuate their homes; almost 70 percent of the residents left their homes to UN shelters or relatives' houses in relatively safe areas, while around 3,000 people decided not to leave.

Mahmoud Ismail, one of the eyewitnesses of the massacre, explained the reasons behind 3,000 people not leaving their homes in response to the IDF orders, saying: "Neglecting Israel's orders of evacuating our homes was a decision that each of us has made individually, and not at all heroic! It is just that many of us did not have the emotional capacity to sleep away from home, others thought the operation would be over very fast and it wasn't worth the effort of evacuation, while the majority like me didn't expect, even in the worst case scenario, that we will witness the worst nightmare of our lives in the coming few hours."

At first, a bomb cut the main road that linked Khuza'a with Khan Yunis, another one then destroyed the power transformers, another damaged the mobile networks, and a fourth destroyed the landlines! Leaving Khuza'a with no electricity, Internet, mobiles, or telephones, completely disconnected.

People spent the whole night in complete darkness; they heard nothing but the noise of shelling, warplanes buzzing, and the falling glass of windows. Fragments of bombs hailing down reached everywhere. Danger surrounded every corner of the house and everybody.

Mahmoud's mind was besieged with ideas and scenarios that would happen, just as black as the darkness around. He was counting the number of shells, foretelling where they'd fall, whose house that was bombed, is it coming to ours? Which mosque? What kind of bombs are they using? Is it tanks or F16s...? Countless questions with no answers, just the sound of bombs.

The next morning, the ICRC (International Committee of the Red Cross; after hundreds of appeals by residents to save the lives of people, evacuate the injured, and pull out the dead) told them to leave their homes to the entrance of the town to secure their exit. The trapped 3,000 people left their homes in a legion similar to their predecessors, 66 years ago. They reached the entry point with extreme difficulty, but were surprised with Israeli tanks instead of ICRC ambulances, that started to shell and shoot every moving body! People rushed back in the opposite direction; in the meantime, many were killed and injured.

Mahmoud, his family, and other people who he didn't even know, were able to reach a house that contained 50 people, they distributed themselves into three rooms; believing that this way they might lessen the death toll.

The second night was more horrific, children were crying and screaming, they were terrified and thirsty; as the IDF bombed the town's water tanks, leaving residents with no water to drink. Mahmoud and many others were waiting for the morning light, hoping that the light would shed some hope.

The light came up, along with a sound of a bomb that hit the shelter. What was even worse than the sound of a bomb was the silence that followed. Everything was hit, and grey is all you see. Moments after, the grey turned into RED! Mother, brother, still alive? He wondered. He checked if he still had his feet, his only way to survive.

Run, he told himself; minutes passed and he reached his house. Once he arrived, the house was hit with yet another bomb. He ran again with hundreds of people in different directions, as they came to realize the direction of shelling. On the streets they were stepping on dead bodies and injured people left to bleed. Many faces were familiar to Mahmoud, but they had no choice but to jump over bodies to save their own lives, until they were finally away from Khuza'a.

Why and how Mahmoud, his family, and a number of other families survived, he doesn't know, it's luck and nothing more than luck. They left people behind, and until this moment the actual number of martyrs in Khuza'a is unknown; the only thing Mahmoud knows for sure is that a lot of bodies are still under the rubble.

International Solidarity Movement, July 31, 2014,
http://bit.ly/1m4lnbX

Israeli Army Uses Gaza Children as Human Shields

Rania Khalek

Since the assault on Gaza began, Israeli leaders and their supporters have repeatedly accused Hamas of using Palestinian civilians as human shields in an attempt to absolve Israel of responsibility for deliberately killing more than 1,600 Palestinian civilians in the besieged Gaza Strip.

Despite there being no evidence to prove this libelous claim, it has been unquestioningly echoed in major media outlets and invoked by U.S. officials to blame Palestinians for their own slaughter. It has even been used to justify genocide against Palestinians in a newspaper ad created by anti-Palestinian extremists Shmuley Boteach and Elie Wiesel.

But the available evidence demonstrates that it is the Israeli army, not Hamas, that has been using Palestinians as human shields in Gaza.

In video testimony released by the Euro-Mid Observer for Human Rights, Ramadan Muhammad Qdeih recounts how Israeli forces stormed his home in Khuza'a, where some sixty members of his extended family were sheltering in the basement on July 25, and forced them to act as human shields.

First, the Israeli soldiers shot dead his 65-year-old father Muhammad Odeih near the entrance of the home as he tried to alert the soldiers to the presence of women and children while carrying a white flag.

Next, says Qdeih, the soldiers forcibly positioned members of his family, including the children, at the windows of his home and proceeded to fire from behind them.

"They ordered us to take off our clothes and tied our hands up," says Qdeih. "They took us to one of the rooms and used us as shields, making us stand at the windows as if we were looking outside. I was at one window and three children from my family at another. The soldiers then began firing around us."

For eight hours, Qdeih's relatives were denied food and water as they were shuffled from one room to another with their hands restrained behind their backs and forced to stand in front of open windows as Israeli soldiers fired from behind their bodies.

Hiding Behind Children

Qdeih's family members weren't the only Palestinian civilians Israeli soldiers hid behind in Gaza. According to Euro-Mid, for five days Israeli forces used a Palestinian teen as their own personal human shield:

> In another incident, on July 23, 17-year-old Ahmad Jamal Abu Reeda says he was restrained by Israeli troops who threatened to kill him. After harshly interrogating and beating him, the troops ordered Abu Reeda to walk ahead of them at gunpoint, accompanied by police dogs, as they searched houses and other buildings. Several times, they demanded that he dig in places they suspected tunnels to exist. Abu Reeda was forced to remain with the Israeli forces for five days.

This procedure is not new. During Operation Cast Lead, Israel's three-week bombardment of the Gaza Strip in the winter of 2008-2009, Israeli soldiers used an eleven-year-old Palestinian boy as a human shield, forcing him to walk in front of them at gunpoint and enter potentially booby-trapped buildings to check for explosives.

And these are not isolated cases. Israel has a well-documented history of systematically using Palestinian civilians as human shields, particularly children.

Ethnic Cleansing

From summary executions to deliberately murdering fleeing civilians carrying white flags and using civilians as human shields, there is no shortage of atrocities committed by the Israeli army in Khuza'a, which was completely flattened by non-stop Israeli shelling in what has been described as a massacre.

After visiting Khuza'a and speaking with survivors, Jaber Wishah, the deputy director of the Palestinian Centre for Human Rights in Gaza, told Gaza-based journalist Mohammed Omer that he believes Israel's intention was to ethnically cleanse Khuza'a in an effort to split the Gaza Strip in two, north and south, to make it easier to control.

As more information about Israeli criminality in Gaza comes to light, it has become increasingly clear that Israel is spreading lies about Palestinians.

Israel is the one using Palestinian children as human shields. Israelis are the ones celebrating death in Gaza. Israeli officials are the ones declaring a "holy war." And Israeli leaders are the ones calling for genocide.

The Electronic Intifada, August 11, 2014, http://bit.ly/1uhXpIG

Psychological Damage of Gazan Children Will Have Long-term Consequences

Lynda Franken

Hassan al-Zeyada, 50, works as a psychologist at the Gaza Community Mental Health Program's center in Gaza City. He treats several residents who suffer from psychological trauma due to Israeli military operations in the coastal enclave. When his own home was shelled on July 20, killing six of his family members, he found himself with the difficult job of having to treat himself.

No Safety

Tackling the psychological problems in Gaza stemming from the aftermath of Israel's Operation Protective Edge, during which nearly 2,000 people in Gaza were killed, will be a huge challenge. UN statistics presented today show that approximately 335,000 people are displaced and live in shelters, schools, or with family. These numbers only include persons that registered through local or international NGOs. The real number of displaced people is therefore likely to be higher and is also "expected to rise again if hostilities resume."

With the Israeli military attacking UN shelters, schools and mosques alike, safety is nowhere to be found in the Gaza Strip—a worry al-Zeyada feels quite acutely. "They may hit at any time. There is no safe place. Psychologically, that is the problem," he told the *New York Times*.

Even with the 72-hour truce entering its third day, many residents of the Gaza Strip do not feel secure enough to permanently move back to their hometowns. Keeping in mind the failure of extending the previous 72-hour truce, former Beit Lahiya resident Hikmat Atta said he is not taking any chances. "We're just going back for the day, at night we'll come back (to the UN shelter)," he told *Al-Jazeera* yesterday.

Children Are the Main Victims

With half of the Gazan population under the age of 14, children have been the main victims of the latest Israeli military operation. The UN Office for the Coordination of Humanitarian Affairs (OCHA) estimates that 373,000 children in Gaza are in need of direct and specialized psychological support.

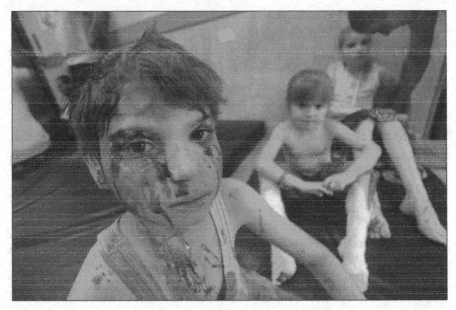

Child injured when his neighbor's home was hit by an F-16 missile (August 17).
Photo by Mohammed Asad.

High levels of stress felt by worried Gazan parents have a negative influence on their children, argues Dr. Jennifer Leaning, director of FXB Center for Health at Harvard University. "I would say that in all studies of disaster and in war crisis, the fundamental feature that protects children from serious psychological stress is their certainty...that their parents or grandparents will be able to protect and hold them."

She adds however that: "The parents and grandparents...are in no psychological position to be able to convey that umbrella of hope and safety for their children."

The Aftermath of Operation Cast Lead

In 2010, a report presented by the United Nations Educational, Scientific and Cultural Organization (UNESCO) showed that both teachers and students in Gazan schools faced psychological problems in the aftermath of 2008–2009 Operation Cast Lead.

Seventy-seven percent of the teachers saw a decline in their students' performance levels. Teachers themselves were struggling to maintain order and 57 percent of all teachers did not feel safe in their own school.

"If you don't feel safe, you can't help students feel safe," one teacher remarked in the UNESCO-report.

One of the main problems after Operation Cast Lead was the increasing dropout rate of students. A UNESCO survey among 6,000 students showed that many of them had to work to provide for their families after the death of family members who used to provide for them, or to fill in for family members that became unemployed due to the military operation. Some students managed to work during the night while attending school during the day, but they underachieve because they lack the time to properly study and rest.

"I began working...one year ago during the war because there was no other source of income for my family. I work 6 p.m. to 6 a.m., sleep, then go back to school at 11 a.m. There is no time to study," a preparatory student remarks in the UNESCO report.

Problems Ahead

The Israeli NGO B'Tselem puts the Palestinian death toll after Israel's three-week 2008 Operation Cast Lead campaign at 1,385. Operation Protective Edge, which has lasted for 36 days thus far, has a running death toll of 1,962. The main difference between the two operations is the amount of civilian casualties. During Cast Lead, half of the casualties were civilians, whereas UN statistics show that 71 percent during Protective Edge have been civilians.

The high number of civilian casualties in the 2014 operation is expected to correlate with an increasing number of children affected by psychological problems. Bassema Ghamen, a counselor worker for the UN agency for Palestinian refugees (UNRWA), stated that counselors have already noticed "serious behavioral changes in children, such as aggression, anger, nervousness and restlessness. Children cannot sleep or fall asleep only to wake up screaming in the middle of the night, clinging to their parents."

The psychological damage faced by Gazan children will also affect future peace negotiations, argues Dr. Jesse Ghannam, a clinical psychiatrist working for UNRWA.

"When we are talking about creating a solution for the Palestinian-Israeli conflict...they aren't growing up interested in peace and wanting to make things better. They just grow up deeply traumatized and very distraught and angry."

Palestine Monitor, August 13, 2014, http://bit.ly/1EW1P2r

A Gaza Mother amid the Airstrikes
Eman Mohammed

As a photojournalist, stepping into war isn't a dilemma for me. It is my instinct to grab my cameras and run out to document the man-made misery, the horrors of war, each and every time hoping humanity will get the lesson.

But nothing prepared me to understand how to raise children in a war zone—not even having been a child in one myself.

I grew up in Gaza. When I was in school, I spent my days walking to and from class, avoiding the streets that were normally targeted by airstrikes. On my summer holiday, I stayed indoors for fear of meeting the same fate as the families who dared to visit the beach and were killed by missiles while they enjoyed their barbecue.

Despite my best efforts to give my daughters a different life, I have found myself in the exact same situation my mother was in 16 years ago when airstrikes hit Gaza. I was 10 years old, and the strikes haven't really stopped since.

After covering two wars in Gaza, I shifted my whole life. I moved with my American husband to the United States, to try to give my two daughters—Talia, who is three, and Lateen, who is one — the universal dream of peace. But as I drifted into a suburban life, I also longed for my sweet mother and my home. I longed to smell the roses while walking on the beach. So I took my daughters back to Gaza to visit their grandmother, and now I find myself again at ground zero, trapped between airstrikes and the unknown.

Now, seeing my two daughters staring at me in shock, calling my name in fear, asking to come with me when I leave on assignment to photograph the airstrikes or their aftermath, my heart refuses to believe I could have possibly risked the lives of my two angels by bringing them here. They don't understand why their little adventure to see grandma escalated into war so quickly and so dramatically, or why they can't get a hug from daddy, but only get to see his face through the cold laptop screen.

The ones who write the rules of war are the ones who never experience it. If you haven't tasted the pain of losing a loved one, the urge to run away when there is no way out, or the need to jump out of bed to hold your kid and cover her ears because a war plane just offloaded its rockets around your house—then you have no idea what life in Gaza is like.

Talia is convinced that an angry, bad bird is making the noises. Each time she hears an explosion, she yells back, telling the bird to go home. My younger daughter doesn't understand what's happening. Sometimes she cries. Sometimes she is quiet and looks around. My mother is a pharmacist and these days she is on the emergency schedule, working every day. When I am out covering the funerals and the bombings, I leave the girls with her. I try to leave very early in the morning so I can come back early and spend time with them. Or I leave late so I can spend time with my daughters before I go out.

In the field, I capture a mother mourning her three-year-old girl. It fills me with pain—the daughter is the same age as my baby—but the mother lost her child and I am able to go back home and hold mine.

As a photojournalist, there was distance between my subject and me. Now, as a mother, when I turn on the TV and see a mother in another war zone crying her heart out, or an anxious mother in Israel, I can only wonder: Whose war is this? When things get darkest, I wonder: Will I be next? Will I be the next mother crying over the dead body of her baby? My trust in humanity fades away, and I sink into tears of rage and weakness.

I don't fear for my life in the same way as I do for my daughters' lives. They didn't choose this. They deserve decades of happiness, life and joy. I was pregnant with Lateen when I covered the 2012 Gaza war, hoping it would be the last one.

My daughters have no shelters to run to. Israelis hide in shelters in Jerusalem, Tel Aviv, Jaffa, and Haifa. But Gazans have none; Israel has banned cement from entering, with minor exceptions, since the siege was imposed on the Strip seven years ago. Gazans succeeded in smuggling some through underground tunnels from Egypt. But it was barely enough to rebuild their destroyed houses.

Meanwhile, Talia's bad birds keep flying. I'm torn between spending time with my children and documenting mothers grieving their losses, waiting like thousands of other peaceful civilians for a glimpse of hope from underneath the rubble.

The Jewish Daily Forward, July 15, 2014, http://bit.ly/1Dg7TGw

Gaza: A Human Tragedy
Sarah Ali

What is it like to live in Gaza under Israeli offensive?

Boom! It's 3:05 a.m. We wake up for suhour, the pre-dawn meal in Ramadan, after a long and horrifying night made worse by the thick presence of Israeli surveillance drones in Gaza's sky. Friends on my Facebook newsfeed complain of sleep deprivation and continuing Israeli air strikes around them. The radio has a bad signal, so I turn it off. My two-and-a-half-year-old niece flinches as a deafening explosion strikes a nearby area. Her forefinger pointed upwards, she exclaims, "wawa!" (a colloquial Arabic word babies use to say they are in pain).

On July 7, Palestinians found themselves in the throes of yet another Israeli aggression. Thirteen days into the Israeli onslaught on Gaza, over 400 Palestinians have been killed, most of them civilians. At least 77 children are among the dead. Thousands of people have been injured and over 50,000 displaced. Some 15,000 houses have been destroyed or severely damaged, and dozens of fishing boats have been burned, destroyed or partially damaged.

The main water line for al-Shati refugee camp in Gaza was bombed and damaged, while 50 percent of sewage pumping and treatment centers are no longer operating. A home for the disabled run by a charitable center was destroyed, killing two women and injuring others. A kindergarten was hit and damaged. A rehabilitation hospital was targeted. The house of police chief Tayseer Al-Batsh was hit by two Israeli bombs, critically injuring him and killing 17 people of Al-Batsh family. Four children playing on the beach were slain as an Israeli gunboat targeted them in broad daylight. Another three children were killed while playing on the rooftop of their house. The list goes on and on.

In response to Israel's occupation and illegal blockade of the Gaza Strip (with Egypt's complicity), its wreaking havoc across the West Bank, its constant human rights violations and arrests, shooting at Palestinian fishermen and farmers, and frequent bombing of Gaza—Palestinian armed groups have fired a barrage of rockets into Israeli territory. Sirens go off in Jerusalem, Sderot, Tel Aviv, Isdoud, Beer Saba', and other areas, forcing Israeli citizens into shelters. So far there have been two civilian deaths in Israel and five Israeli soldiers have been killed in clashes with Palestinian fighters.

In late afternoon on July 16, the house of my deceased grandparents—home to four families and 12 people in East Gaza—was bombed. My uncles and cousins received no phone call, no messages, nothing (not that a phone call telling you "we'll bomb your house" makes it any better). The distance between their house and that of their neighbors is less than a meter. No rocket could have possibly been fired from their house into Israel. And, yet, an Israeli "targeted" strike hit them. When the first missile fell, they ran out of the house. My uncle and 70-year-old aunt sustained injuries, but they all miraculously survived.

Homeless, in every sense of the word, they are now split into relatives' homes. Their house has been completely destroyed. Most of their belongings remain in the street; they visit every morning, trying to find and pull out of the rubble anything still fit for use. My uncle's wife, an agriculture engineer and a lifelong embroidery enthusiast, laments, "How did I not take my embroideries? Why did I leave without them?"

We are still in the holy month of Ramadan, a time of spirituality, reflection, and religious devotion, when people socialize outside and at home with family and friends. Mornings and evenings of Ramadan are no longer the same, though. Most workplaces are closed. People do not go to school or work. They are careful not to go out a lot, although many Palestinians still venture out to get food and perform Taraweeh—evening prayers. At night, most people, except for medical staff and journalists, remain indoors.

War is horror. War is our vulnerability and helplessness. It is our inability to protect family and friends. It is deciding not which area in Gaza is safer, but which one is less dangerous. It is packing official papers, a bottle of water, life savings, a mobile with a dead battery, and, above all, memories into one small "emergency bag" and forgetting the bag altogether once your house is shelled. War is having no time to say goodbye to your window, or the stickers on your wall, or a piece of embroidery, or that crack in the door you always hated. War is leaving your house barefoot. War is your grief aired live on TV. War is humiliation. War is remorse for things you have not done. War is traumatized children and traumatized adults. War is broken hearts and scars that do not heal.

War is the painful abruptness of loss. All it takes is a minute, or perhaps less than a minute. A sky lantern lights up the whole area around the "target," guiding the Israeli apache or F16 through the dark strip. A terrifying whoosh accompanies the missile as it falls upon the house. Screams and silent tears. A last declaration of faith in Allah and His messenger.

A last breath. The sky lights up again. A massive explosion is heard outside. Smoke clouds the area and the air around smells of death. Flames erupt. The explosion echoes in your ear. In seconds, someone's memories are buried under the rubble of their home. Someone's loved ones are gone forever.

It is 3:30 a.m. I hear the third boom in a span of only a few minutes as a reminder of the war. War is waking up for suhour not by an alarm clock, but by a blast. Faces are pale and food is tasteless. Time is meaningless. Power is now off and there is no way I can make sure my friends are alive. My niece, still crying and terrified by the sounds of bombing yawns, her tears lulling her to sleep. I turn on the radio again only to hear about Western leaders staunchly asserting, from the comfort of their countries, the right of our oppressor to "defend" itself, while simultaneously denying a defenseless and besieged population that right. I smile at the irony of it all as another explosion roars in the background.

Al-Jazeera, July 20, 2014, http://bit.ly/1n1YKZR

2

Destitute by Design:
Making Gaza Unlivable

Israel's war on Palestinian industry, economy, and civil society has been long-standing and unrelenting, and nowhere is this policy more visible than in the Gaza Strip, where an elaborate and draconian siege and blockade designed to strangle the productive sectors—the bedrock of self-sufficiency and prosperity—ensures that Gaza remains destitute. A partial list of damages includes 18,000 housing units totally destroyed or severely damaged (leaving about 108,000 Palestinians homeless); the destruction of Gaza's only power plant (which also put the sewage and water treatment plants out of commission); 22 schools destroyed and 118 schools damaged; and at least 24 medical facilities damaged, with some hospitals taking repeated direct hits. Enormous swaths of agricultural land (17,000 hectares, about 42,00 acres) as well as much of its agricultural infrastructure, including greenhouses, irrigation systems, animal farms, fodder stocks, and fishing boats, were severely damaged. Fishing, once an important and vital sector of the coastal enclave, has been restricted to so narrow an area that only the youngest of fish are available to catch, threatening future populations and the livelihoods of the fishermen themselves. Exports are all but prohibited. Imports are determined by the whims of the Israelis controlling access points in and out of the Strip and change on a regular basis, and have included bans on items such as construction material, water filters, and books. The Palestinian Authority estimates that repairing the damages will cost close to $5 billion.[1] This devastation comes on the heels of two previous attacks from which Gaza, gripped by siege, had not yet recovered. These periodic bombing episodes (euphemistically referred to as "wars") ensure that Gaza remain a laboratory in which 1.8 million residents struggle to survive.

The objective was clearly expressed by former Israeli minister of interior Eli Yishai: to "send Gaza back to the Middle Ages."[2] By destroying and damaging Gaza's infrastructure, Israel's strategy seems to have been to extinguish all hopes of self-sufficiency—in other words, to make Gaza unlivable.

"The Tank Shells Fell Like Rain":
Survivors of the Attack on UNRWA School
Report Scenes of Carnage and Destruction
Sharif Abdel Kouddous

Hussein Shinbari is the only member of his family that survived the attack on a United Nations school in Beit Hanoun on Thursday. He is covered in blood. His undershirt, his pants and his hands are all stained a deep red.

After Israel launched its ground invasion into Gaza last week, the Shinbari family left their home in the northeastern town close to the Israeli border and sought shelter at the nearby school. "They told us it was safe," Hussein says, sitting on the ground by the morgue of the Kamal Adwan Hospital in Beit Lahiya.

More than 1,500 displaced Palestinians were staying at the school. The conflict has caused unprecedented massive displacement in Gaza, forcing over 140,000 people to seek shelter in more than eighty UN shelters.

On Thursday afternoon, the people in the Beit Hanoun school were told they were being transferred to another area, away from the shelling and clashes on the streets outside. According to multiple survivors, they were instructed to gather their scant belongings and assemble in the schoolyard to await buses that would take them to another shelter.

At around 2:30 p.m. a barrage of artillery shells crashed into the school, according to witnesses. At least sixteen people were killed and more than 200 wounded, many of them women and children. Hussein lost his mother; his stepmother; his 16-year-old brother, Abed Rabo; his 12-year-old sister, Maria; and his 9-year-old brother, Ali.

"I was the only one who walked out," Hussein says. He helped carry his dying family members to the ambulances that eventually arrived. "I'm not asking Hamas or Fatah for anything," he says. "I only have God left."

The Israeli military says Hamas was firing rockets from Beit Hanoun and that it had told the Palestinian refugee agency, UNRWA, and the Red Cross to evacuate the school. Yet UNRWA spokesman Chris Gunness says the UN had asked the Israeli military for a lull in the fighting to allow for an evacuation but did not hear back. Gunness says precise coordinates of the shelter had been formally given to the Israeli army. The attack marked the fourth time a UN facility has been hit by Israel since the conflict began on July 8.

"These people had no place to go. They are very poor, so they sought the protection of the United Nations," says Dr. Bassam al-Masry, the head of the orthopedic department at the Kamal Adwan Hospital, whose house is adjacent to the school in Beit Hanoun. "Today they were shelled. Why?"

The hospital is filled with heart-wrenching scenes. Men and women being carried in on stretchers. People rushing through the halls with wounded children in their arms. It is unbearably hot and humid. In one corner, six women gather in a knot of grief, sobbing and holding each other. One of them collapses in shock.

Inside the morgue a baby is brought onto the wooden examination table. She is about one year old. She looks unharmed, except when her head is turned to reveal that a small chunk of her neck is missing. The other bodies lie in the refrigerated morgue drawers cocooned in bloodied white shrouds. Only their faces are uncovered.

"We thought the school was safer than our house," says 32-year-old Monther Hamdan. He is lying on a cot with a wounded leg and grasps his father's hand as he speaks. All thirteen members of his family were injured in the attack. They arrived at the school three days ago. "The tank shells fell like rain."

The attack on the UN school came on one of the bloodiest days of the conflict. Approximately 120 Palestinians were killed yesterday, bringing the death toll in Gaza to nearly 800, the vast majority of them civilians, including at least 190 children, according to the Health Ministry. Over a two-day period, a child was killed every hour in Gaza. More than 5,100 have been wounded.

The level of violence has escalated significantly since Israel's ground invasion last week. Calls for a cease-fire seem to have had the opposite effect. A three-kilometer buffer zone has been declared by Israeli military, equivalent to 44 percent of the Gaza Strip. Israeli forces have pushed in from the border backed by tanks and a continued assault from the air. Thirty-two Israeli soldiers and three civilians have been killed.

In southern Gaza, the Israeli military dropped leaflets warning residents to evacuate areas east of Khan Yunis. "The Israeli Defense Forces are not targeting any of you," it says. "If you follow directions, the IDF will not hurt any of you, the civilian population."

Testimonies by the residents of the town of Khuza'a, one of the Palestinian residential areas closest to Israel, belie that claim. They describe a nightmarish ordeal trying to escape the Israeli invasion. Multiple witnesses say they were prevented from getting out by Israeli tanks and

An UNRWA school in Rimal offers shelter to families from Bayt Lahiya (who are originally from Majdal and became refugees in 1948). Euro-Mid Observer for Human Rights reports that 141 government schools, 76 UNRWA schools, and 6 universities were damaged during the assault.[3]
Photo by Ezz Al Zanoon.

troops, that Israeli forces fired on ambulances and that the dead and wounded were left behind in the streets.

"There was no mercy," says Wael Abu Irgala, a 24-year-old resident of Khuza'a. "We saw things you couldn't imagine."

Wael says the Israeli military began indiscriminately shelling Khuza'a on Tuesday at around sunset. By 1 a.m., Israeli troops began knocking on doors and shouting out taunts to the residents inside, calling for the men of the houses to come and face them, says Wael's aunt Asmaa. The next morning Wael and Asmaa and hundreds of the town's residents tried to evacuate, but it would be another twenty-four hellish hours before they made it out.

Town residents gathered on Wednesday morning and held up white flags as they walked. Two handicapped girls were being pushed in wheelchairs. Without warning, an Israeli tank stationed on the main road opened fire, shooting bullets into the crowd. The residents fled in panic. The man pushing one of the wheelchairs was shot, leaving the handicapped girl alone on the street.

"There were wounded on the ground and we couldn't save them," Wael says. "They would shoot anything that moved."

Many people were injured in the attack and a number sought refuge at the house of a local doctor, Kamal Gedeih. He tended to the injured with very basic first aid supplies, including Wael's other aunt, who was shot in the stomach.

Multiple calls were made to local hospitals, human rights organizations and the Red Cross, pleading for help in escaping the conflict, but no one came.

In the afternoon, an airstrike hit the yard of Gedieh's house where the doctor's brother was filling up water bottles for the people inside. It took him ten minutes to die. Another fifteen minutes later, a shell smashed into the side of the building. Gedieh himself was injured along with several others.

Wael and Asmaa decided to leave the doctor's house and took their wounded relative, who was shot in the stomach, and other family members with them. They ended up finding a basement where dozens of other residents were seeking shelter. They spent the night there. There was no water, food or electricity. Several people collapsed from exhaustion.

The shelling and bombardment continued throughout the night. On Thursday morning, they decided to try and make their way out again. They walked in a group with their hands in the air. Some carried white flags.

"We didn't expect to get out alive," says Asmaa. "We walked for five kilometers waiting for death." She says Israeli troops on tanks and deployed in the streets were blocking all the main roads. They gestured which direction for them to go. The relative with the stomach wound had to be half-carried the entire way.

In the assault, the town had been demolished. "We found a burning land, we didn't know the streets or the houses of our own neighborhood," Asmaa says. "It looked like a different world, empty of people."

They finally made it out to Nasser hospital in Khan Yunis late Thursday morning.

The scene at the hospital is one of chaos and overcrowding. People fill the corridors. The wounded are ferried back and forth. One man follows two corpses being carried into the morgue. He is holding a bright blue plastic bag. In it is all that remains of one of his relatives.

"This was the worst night in this hospital," says Dr. Jamal al-Hams, the director general of the hospital. He says at least twenty-one people are dead and 150 injured. "The fridges are full and there's nowhere to put the bodies."

Multiple medical workers and witnesses say the Israeli military did not allow ambulances to enter Khuzaʻa during the brutal assault.

"There are many wounded still inside. They are calling us and we can't get to them," says Dr. Wissam Nabhan at the European Hospital in eastern Khan Yunis. Nabhan says he took four ambulance trips on Thursday morning to try to evacuate people, and every time he came under fire from the Israeli military.

"This was a massacre of the people of Khuzaʻa."

The Nation, July 25, 2014, http://bit.ly/1adr5cW

Poems of Mass Destruction at Gaza University
Refaat Alareer

During the current conflict, the Islamic University of Gaza (IUG), where I teach world literature and creative writing in the English department, has been hit by many Israeli missiles. The administration building has been seriously damaged. Two departments have been completely destroyed: the personnel department and the English department offices. IUG was established in 1978 and served tens of thousands of Palestinians. Now more than 20,000 students study at IUG which has 10 faculties and more than 70 fields of study, ranging from medicine and engineering to languages, education, and psychology.

IUG Students and Israeli Occupation

When I started teaching at the IUG, I met young students most of whom have never been outside Gaza and have suffered greatly under Israeli occupation. This suffering became even worse when Israel tightened its siege in 2006. Many of them could not go to the West Bank for family visits, or to Jerusalem for a simple religious ritual, or to the U.S. or the UK for grants and visits. Even books were not, along with thousands of other commodities, normally allowed in. The consequences of putting this young generation in the dark, the world must know, has far worse ramifications than we would ever expect.

At the beginning my students must have found it difficult to study Yehuda Amichai (because he is an Israeli Jew!) or to accept my "progressive" views about Shylock or Fagin. For many, Fagin was the source of evil;

the embodiment of the devil that destroys society by murdering, at least metaphorically, its future, the little ones, by turning them into thieves and murderers.

Challenging Questions

Only later were they able to open their eyes a little bit and see that Fagin was a mere product of a society that hates those who are different, those with a darker skin or a different race. They came to realize Fagin was even better than the church itself. They saw Fagin offering a shelter for the homeless and making the likes of Oliver feel happy and hopeful for a little bit. Fagin, the Jew, was no longer a Jew. He was a human being, just like anyone of us. Fagin's refusal to wake Oliver up to send him to break into some house and his comment "Not now. Tomorrow. Tomorrow" were no longer seen as ironic, but as evidence of a man with a heart. The most challenging question I asked was, "What would you do if you were Fagin?", a question that invited my students to reconsider issues of race and religion, and transcend them into much higher concepts of humanity and shared interests.

But Shakespeare's classes of *The Merchant of Venice* were trickier. To many of my students Shylock was beyond repair. Even Shylock's daughter hated him! However, with the open-mindedness, dialogue, and respect to all cultures and religions IUG promotes, I worked very closely with my students to overcome all prejudices when judging people, or at least when analyzing literary texts.

Shylock, therefore, was also transcended from a mere simplistic idea of a Jew who wants a pound of flesh just to satisfy some cannibalistic primitive desires of revenge into a totally different *human being*. Shylock was just like us Palestinians exposed constantly not only to Israeli aggression and destruction and racism, but to its war machine of misinformation and defamation. Shylock had to endure many religious and spiritual walls erected by an apartheid-like society. Shylock was in a position where he had to choose between total submission and humiliation by living as a subhuman, or resist oppression by the means available to him. He chose to resist, just like Palestinians nowadays.

Shylock's "Hath not a Jew eyes?" speech was no longer a pathetic attempt to justify murder, but rather an internalization of long years of pain and injustices. I was not at all surprised when one of my students found the similarities between us and Shylock so striking that she altered the speech to:

In Khan Yunis, a girl salvages her books from the rubble of her relatives' home, which was destroyed by Israeli strikes on the first day of the assault. Photo by Eman Mohammed.

Hath not a Palestinian eyes? Hath not a Palestinian hands, organs, dimensions, senses, affections, passions; fed with the same food, hurt with the same weapons, subject to the same diseases, heal'd by the same means, warm'd and cool'd by the same winter and summer as a Christian or a Jew is? If you prick us, do we not bleed? If you tickle us, do we not laugh? If you poison us, do we not die? And if you wrong us, shall we not revenge?

Perhaps the most emotional moment in my six-year teaching career at IUG's English department was when I asked my students which of the characters they identify with more, Othello, with his Arab origins, or Shylock the Jew. Most students felt they were closer to Shylock and more sympathetic to him than to Othello. Only then did I realize that I managed to help my students grow and shatter the prejudices they had to grow up with because of the occupation and the siege. Sadly, the exam papers which I stored in my office have been set ablaze in a way that echoes how Shylock was stripped off his money and possessions. I always wanted to make use of the answers and compile them into a book.

A Merry Sport

But now! Now with all the death and obliteration Israel has been bringing on the heads of Palestinians in Gaza will I be able to repeat that experience? Will I be able to speak about the humanity of Fagin and similarity between us and Shylock, and still look my students in the eye? How are they going to react after what they have seen from the Zionists who are using Judaism as their excuse and discourse to kill us?

From the pictures I saw, the personnel department and the English department are totally destroyed. My office, along with those of my colleagues, is gone. My office, where I met hundreds of students for office hours and further discussions, is gone. The wonderful small department library is gone. I am not sure whether the whole five-story building has to be demolished or whether it can be renovated.

Soon after the attack, an IDF spokesman on Twitter declared they destroyed a "weapons development center!" at the Islamic University. However, a few hours later Israel magnified the reason why it bombed IUG—Israel's defense minister in a press release said, "IUG was developing chemicals, to be used against us." When I tweeted them back, challenging them to produce any shred of evidence, of course I got no reply. We just have to take it for granted that Israel never ever lies. We are even supposed to ignore the glaring inconsistency between the two statements above. To us, the lie, if not very tragic, would be hilarious.

I know my students will not stop joking about me developing PMDs, or Poems of Mass Destruction, or TMDs, Theories of Mass Destruction. Some might even start rereading certain texts in search for any chemical traces, or ask to be taught chemical poetry alongside with allegorical and narrative poetry. I assume [that] *short range stories* and *long range stories* might replace normal terms like short stories and novels. And I might be asked if my exams will have questions capable of carrying chemical warheads!

But why would Israel bomb a university? Some say Israel attacked IUG just to punish its 20,000 students or to push Palestinians to despair. That is true, but to me IUG's only danger to the Israeli occupation and its apartheid regime is that it is the most important place in Gaza to develop students' minds as indestructible weapons. Knowledge is Israel's worst enemy. Awareness is Israel's most hated and feared foe. That's why Israel bombs a university; it wants to kill openness and determination to refuse living under injustice and racism. But again, why does Israel bomb a school? Or a hospital? Or a mosque? Or a 20-story building? It could be, as Shylock put it, "a merry sport"!

Palestinian Wounds and Israeli Impunity

The wounds Israel planted in the hearts of Palestinians are not irreparable. We have no choice but to recover and stand up again, and continue the struggle. Submitting to the occupation is a betrayal to humanity and to all struggles around the world.

And I know it will be a very tough task for me to engage my students in the kind of discussions where we Palestinians fight injustice side by side with many fellow Christians and Jews from all over the world. I believe I know where to start, however. I will start from Ilise and Dan, my Jewish friends I met on our *Gaza Writes Back* book tour in the United States. They have been in constant contact with me to make sure I am okay and that my family is okay. They have been my ray of hope in the face of darkness and oppression. I will tell my students about Jewish Voice for Peace (JVP) whose tremendous work, especially for the boycott, divestment and sanctions campaign, is making a big difference in the Palestinian struggle. I will teach my students that Judaism is hijacked by Israel. I will teach them what Ali Abunimah teaches us: "Despite Zionists' relentless efforts to implicate them, Jews are not collectively guilty of Israel's genocidal crimes against Palestinians. To stand against anti-Semitism means to utterly refuse Zionism's claim that its atrocities are done in the name of Jews everywhere."

And I know they will ask if enough is being done, if these friends still can do more to prevent Israel from committing more horrifying crimes against us. That I will leave to Ilise and Dan to answer, to pro-Palestinians working hard to promote BDS and to JVP's work to bring those Israeli war criminals to court and to end their impunity.

Middle East Eye, August 4, 2014, http://bit.ly/1APUCly

Israel Destroys al-Wafa Hospital as Staff Evacuates All Patients
Allison Deger

The Israeli military has destroyed al-Wafa rehabilitation hospital in the Gaza Strip, after first targeting the facility with five missiles on July 11, 2014. The Israeli military began striking the building around 8:00 p.m. this evening and within two hours all hospital staff and patients had evacuated the only rehabilitation center in the Gaza Strip. As they departed, what remained intact from the medical center burned to the ground.

Al-Wafa is the Gaza Strip's only rehabilitation hospital. Even though Israeli authorities said they did not believe weapons were inside of the facility, Al-Wafa Rehabilitation Hospital was heavily shelled Thursday evening causing an emergency evacuation of all staff and patients. Al-Wafa Rehabilitation Hospital treats long-term injuries and physical disabilities. All of the patients have some degree of paralysis, require around the clock care and many are on oxygen support and feeding tubes.

"We've seen a lot of launches of rockets that came from exactly near the hospital, 100 meters near," said a spokesperson for the Israeli Defense Forces (IDF), continuing, "Obviously the target was not the hospital."

The IDF News Desk also confirmed that the military understood there were no weapons inside of al-Wafa hospital. When asked how far a humanitarian site needs to be to ensure there is not direct fire, the IDF said, "It's not a matter of science, the IDF is very precise and they usually target what they intend to target."

Still the hospital was an army target.

The night of the shelling, Basman Alashi, the hospital director, asked me to inquire with the IDF why they fired on the hospital. When I told him they said it was fired on because it was within 100 meters of a rocket site, but they knew the hospital itself was clean of munitions, he said, "My authority, my control is within my premises, it is my hospital. I cannot control what people do 100 meters from me." He reiterated, "My control is my hospital, my staff my patients. I have nothing to do with what happens 100 meters from the hospital," adding, "A hospital should not be involved in any conflict according to Geneva law."

While under fire from the Israeli military on Thursday, Basman Alashi communicated with the army via a delegate from the International Committee for the Red Cross (ICRC). The military said that they were not only going to shell the facility, but that it would be fired upon so heavily

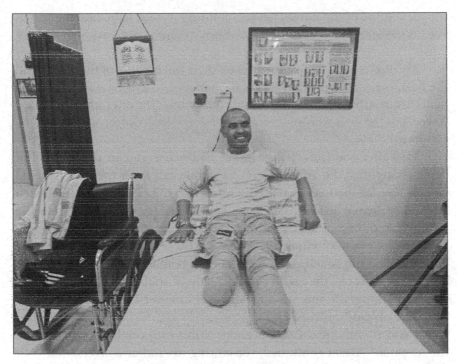

Mahmoud Naouq, 32 years old and married, lost both legs when a tank shell struck his Deir al-Balah home on July 21; unable to travel to Germany for treatment as planned because of the closure of Gaza's border crossings, he received physiotherapy and prosthetic legs at Gaza's Artificial Limbs and Polio Centre. The number of amputees caused by Israel's summer assault is estimated to be about 3,000.[4]
Photo by Mohammed Asad.

that they recommended all people in the hospital evacuate. The ICRC attempted to coordinate the evacuation, relaying messages from the IDF in two phone calls made to al-Wafa's hospital director during the shelling.

"It's already destroyed," said Basman Alashi, director of al-Wafa, continuing, "I don't know how much is left of it, but we have evacuated all of our patients. We lost power, there was a fire in the building."

Alashi spoke to me via telephone from his house in Gaza, unable to cross the Israeli shelling to reach the hospital. "I left the hospital at seven and within two hours they had bombed the hospital." Shells hit every floor of the building, and a fire spread throughout.

After the Israeli army began striking the hospital, Alashi and al-Wafa's 25 nurses made desperate arrangements to relocate the last 17 patients. Many of those in al-Wafa's care are paralyzed and are connected to oxygen

support. Some of the nurses left the building to seek help, braving Israeli
fire on the streets in order to track down an ambulance with an oxygen
tank.

"My nurses were unable to stand on their feet because of the smoke and
the heat," said Alashi. Al-Wafa's staff managed to evacuate all of the patients to a nearby medical clinic inside of a hotel. "The ones who could stay,
stayed, but the ones who lost consciousness and lost control, we moved," he
continued.

Only after the facility was under heavy fire and in the process of
being abandoned did Alashi receive a phone call from the International
Committee for the Red Cross (ICRC) relaying a message from the Israeli
army. A women who identified herself as a delegate of the ICRC said, "the
Israelis asked 'how much time do you need to evacuate,'" said Alashi, answering "two hours." However, within an hour when the woman called
back and said the Israeli army "will halt the bombings, and not bomb the
hospital any more," the facility was already in rubble. Alashi responded,
"Are you joking, are you making a mockery of me? I told her it's too late
they have already destroyed it."

"I said that the Red Cross is cooperating with the Israelis to destroy
the hospital," Alashi continued, recounting his earlier conversation with
the representative from the ICRC. "I'm going to take you, the Red Cross
and the Israelis to the International Criminal Court," he announced before hanging up the telephone.

When I spoke to Alashi his voice was dry and sunken compared to
when we talked a few days ago after the facility was first hit by Israeli fire
on July 11. Five missiles had knocked the hospital taking out exterior walls
and causing significant damage to the fourth floor. After the assault, patients who could be cared for at home were discharged and the remaining
were relocated to the first floor.

Alashi had to rush to get off of the telephone with me; he was on his
way to finally check on his patients now in the safer Sahaba clinic. He
concluded that Israel's destruction of the hospital would only hurt their
military goals. A devastated Alashi said:

> The Israelis and the Red Cross have destroyed the only rehab clin-
> ic in the West Bank and Gaza. They are not solving the issues; they
> are creating more suicide bombers. You cannot solve issues like
> this at all. They are the ones creating suicide bombings, not us.

Mondoweiss, July 17, 2014, http://bit.ly/1y75Nbn

Water Disaster Hits Every Single Person in Gaza
Ali Abunimah

Video and the infographic referenced in the article are available via the website link on page 84.

Right now, none of the 1.8 million Palestinians living in the occupied and besieged Gaza Strip has access to a safe and secure supply of water. The water situation was already severe before Israel's bombardment began on July 7. But now water experts are calling it a disaster. Ninety percent of wells, wastewater treatment plants and desalination plants cannot operate due to power cuts and lack of fuel.

In the video interview, Monther Shublak, director of Gaza's Coastal Municipalities Water Utility, says that much of the infrastructure has been damaged by Israeli bombing. This includes Gaza's central sewage pumping station, which was recently upgraded with German taxpayer funding The wastewater treatment facility in Gaza was hit twice, he says, and could cause an environmental disaster in Gaza City. Three wells and "a long list of water carriers and wastewater carriers" were damaged or destroyed all over the Gaza Strip, he says. The Beach Well, which provides seawater to the only functioning desalination plant, was also destroyed.

Water Workers Killed

Trying to maintain the flow of water to people has been incredibly dangerous. Seven water technicians were killed while on duty at the height of the Israeli attack when almost half of Gaza's territory was declared a no-go zone.

One of the workers, technician Zeyad Al-Shawi, died on July 14 from critical injuries he suffered during an Israeli airstrike on July 12 as he opened valves to supply water to people in Rafah, southern Gaza, the Coastal Municipalities Water Utility reported.

Due to the risks, workers could not access areas to carry out repairs or to operate pumps and open and close valves to direct water to different neighborhoods. Repairs are also hampered because Israel's eight-year-long siege prevents the importation of needed materials.

Water experts estimate the damage to be at least $20 million. "The money of taxpayers or UN agencies is again and again wasted...during these endless wars," Shublak says, referring to the constant cycle of donor-funded infrastructure being destroyed by Israel and then repaired with international aid.

Living Without Water

In the video called *Water Deprived*, Fatma, a 45-year-old mother of nine from the heavily bombed Shuja'iya neighborhood speaks about the difficulty of living with the unsanitary and health-threatening conditions caused by the water crisis.

She and her family were displaced to a school run by UNRWA, the UN agency for Palestine refugees. Three thousand people took shelter in that school alone and Fatma and her family are living in a classroom with 41 people.

"Contamination of water and lack of hygiene in the bathrooms can cause health problems," she says. "We have so many children experiencing diarrhea and fever and they have to be treated now. We don't want to risk the health of our children."

A quarter of Gaza's population was displaced at the height of Israel's attack. As of yesterday, 370,000 people remain in temporary shelter, according to the UN. Up to 100,000 people will need to be permanently re-housed because their homes were destroyed or severely damaged.

Gaza Water Disaster

The infographic below, produced by EWASH (the Emergency Water and Sanitation-Hygiene Group), highlights some of the facts about the Gaza water disaster. It summarizes key facts about the critical damage to the water, sanitation and hygiene sector during the Israeli assault on Gaza, between 8 July and 5 August.

EWASH (ewash.org) is a coordinating body made up various stakeholders in the water, sanitation and hygiene sector in the occupied Palestinian territories. These include national and international nongovernmental organizations, UN agencies, academic and research institutions, the Palestinian Water Authority, the West Bank Water Department and the Coastal Municipalities Water Utility in Gaza.

The Electronic Intifada, August 13, 2014, http://bit.ly/1sDNkio.

Child lying in the rubble of his home in the Shija'ia district, where damaged water pipes create impassable pools, August 27.
Photo by Mohammed Asad.

Farming in Gaza near the Buffer Zone
Rina Andolini

The farmers are rarely talked about. They blend into the background of the lands beyond the destroyed buildings of the towns. The reality is they are facing a battle themselves.

Many farmers have had their homes and farm land attacked. Farm land attacked, I repeat. I mean, who would ever have thought that land could be an enemy that needed to be struck by a missile?

Well, the attacks from the air have stopped, for now, although the buzz of the drones rarely hum a tune of silence, sometimes accompanied by the whooshing high speed winds that the F-16s bring with them.

The farmers' situation is clear cut and simple; they have land and are in fear of tending to it. What is to fear when all you want to do is plow, and sow seeds, and nurture your land to provide food, shelter, and clothing to your family? How is it okay for a person to work in fear of being shot at, for doing nothing other than farm on their land?

The fence in the buffer zone is the cutoff point, so we should be able to go right up to it without fear of being shot at, or even worse, shelled, as the Israeli army rolls around in their tanks pretty much round the clock.

Yesterday, November 8, the farmers went to their land to start plowing away at the soil to get it ready for sowing. They use a tractor. What happened when they went? The Israeli military shot in their direction. Luckily, nobody was hurt, but a tire was shot at and destroyed. These farmers struggle to even pay for contingencies such as these; work hazards caused by Israeli attacks, and why should they even have to? But they do.

So, they called several international activists here in Gaza, and said, "Please come with us to our land, we need to go there with the tractor and do our work but they keep shooting at us."

Of course, we agreed to go and help, and even this morning, they rang two times, to make sure we were coming. They would not start their work without our presence.

This is their situation, they cannot work without fear of being shot at. It is as simple as this. Where in the world do you hear of such crimes against humanity occurring and resulting in no punishment to the aggressor?

It happens here in Gaza, in Palestine, all the time. The Israelis attack, and they continue to get away with it. The world's silence is killing and destroying these people.

I met with a farmer, Rami Salim Kudeih. He is 33 years of age, with a wife and five children, the youngest child being one month old, and the oldest, nine years of age.

I asked what he wanted to grow on this land and he said, "wheat and lentils."

"This is the season for it. The season may leave us and we will not have done any work because we are in constant fear of attacks from Israel. They have killed people here before on this land that is called Um Khamseen."

"When the Israelis shoot, I feel angry and sad. A woman was killed in a nearby field too, within the last two years. My sister has also been injured whilst working on these fields, she suffered from a head injury but now she is better thanks to God, but sometimes in the cold, the pain comes in her head."

The saddest thing of all, is that when I asked Rami, what he thought the international world could do; the world outside of the open air prison that is Gaza, his reply was indeed heartbreaking. It showed me that he had lost hope, that he is living with the situation as it is, with no sight for improvement.

"They [the Israeli military], shoot often, they shoot in our direction, at the land, and alhamdulillah [praise to God] so far no deaths...but we never know what will happen."

"The only solution is for the internationals to accompany us in the fields so we can do our work."

I was expecting a response where he would ask the world to raise their voices and put pressure on the world leaders to put a stop to these crimes against humanity, but in fact, he gave a response which showed his resignation to the life that they are subjected to in Gaza. The life of living in constant fear of being attacked by Israel.

This is not how they should live, this is not how anyone should live, but the people of Gaza do. When will we do something to let these people live the life they have a right to and deserve?

During our time this morning out on the field, we were between 100–150 meters away from the fence, things were quiet, though we did see two Israeli tanks rolling around close by, and then go into hiding.

The farmers managed to carry out their work in peace and then we left.

The point is though, they should not need to have any internationals present, they should be able to go safely to their land without any worries.

International Solidarity Movement, November 9, 2014,
http://bit.ly/1MshWoY

Farming under Siege:
Working the Land in Gaza
Tom Anderson and Therezia Cooper

Corporate Watch researchers visited the Gaza Strip during November and December 2013 and carried out interviews with farmers in Beit Hanoun, Al-Zaytoun, Khuza'a, Al-Maghazi, and Rafah, as well as with representatives from Union of Agricultural Work Committees (UAWC), Palestine Crops and the Gaza Agricultural Co-operative in Beit Lahiya. This is the first of two articles highlighting what their experiences show: that Palestinians face significant and diverse difficulties when it comes to farming their land and harvesting and exporting their produce under siege, and that Israel enforces what amounts to a de facto boycott of produce from the Gaza Strip.

The Land and the Buffer Zones

"There is a 300 meter "buffer zone" in our area. It is common that
people get shot at directly if they enter it. Within 500 meters people
often get shot at. It is unsafe within 1,500 meters of the fence."
—Saber Al Zaneen from the Beit Hanoun Local Initiative

Since the withdrawal of settlers and the end of a permanent presence of
ground troops from the Gaza Strip in 2005, Israel insists that the area is
no longer under occupation. However, as well as still controlling Gaza's
air space, coastline and exports, Israel effectively occupies the area commonly referred to as the "buffer zone," located all the way down the strip
along the border with Israel. A buffer area has existed in Gaza since the
signing of the Oslo accords in 1993, when 50 meters on the Gaza side of
the border was designated a no-go area for Palestinians. Since then, Israel
has unilaterally expanded this zone on numerous occasions, including to
150 meters during the intifada in 2000 and to changeable and unclear pa-
rameters since 2009.

According to the United Nations Office for the Coordination of
Human Affairs (OCHA) the buffer zone takes up 17% of Gaza's total
land, making up to 35% of available farmland unsafe for Palestinians to
use, with the areas nearest the border fence being the most restricted.
Calling the boundaries of the zone "vague, unpredictable" and "uncertain," OCHA has divided the zone into two danger grades: "no-go" areas
where Palestinians risk their lives if they enter as they are considered free
fire zones by Israel (within 500 meters of the fence) and "high-risk" areas,
where the restricted access still has a severe consequences for farmers and
where property destruction and levelling of the land occurs on a regular
basis (within 500 and up to 1500 meters of the fence). These areas are kept
under heavy surveillance by Israel, through the use of military border pa-
trols and equipment as well as surveillance balloons and drone technology. There are regular incursions by Israeli troops into the buffer zone,
sometimes as often as a few times a week.

In the ceasefire agreement during Operation Pillar of Cloud in 2012,
Israel agreed to ease restrictions on some Palestinian farmland and allow
access up to 100 meters from the fence but this promise appears to have had
limited impact on Palestinians. There has been no official announcement
regarding the easing of the restrictions and as the Israeli human rights
organisation Gisha (part of Legal Center for Freedom Of Movement) has
pointed out, advice from Israeli sources is often contradictory, citing the
no go areas as sometimes 100 meters, sometimes 300 meters with no way

for farmers to be sure. What is clear, however, is that Palestinians keep getting shot at from a greater distance than 300 meters and that anyone going
closer than 500 meters from the border is putting themselves in danger. It
is also clear that with so much of their land being out of bounds, farmers
have no choice but to continue to work, at least partly, in areas which are
unsafe.

Since 2008 over 50 Palestinians have been killed in the buffer zone
and, although things have calmed down slightly since the truce in 2012,
four Palestinian civilians have been killed and over 60 wounded by Israeli
forces in the buffer zone so far this year, with five killed and approximately
60 wounded in 2013 according to Human Rights Watch. Most of these
deaths have occurred when farmers have been trying to reach their land
within, or near to, the buffer zone, or during demonstrations where communities have tried to assert their right so reach their fields. One role of
international solidarity activists in the Gaza Strip is to accompany farmers wanting to access and farm their land. Sa'ad Ziada from UAWC estimates that the number of agricultural workers in Gaza has decreased from
55,000 to 30,000 as a result of the siege, with many of the remaining farmers unable to earn enough to survive from their crops.

As well as threatening life, the buffer zone has had a disastrous impact
on Palestinians' ability to make a living in the Gaza Strip, with not only
fields but also property and water resources heavily affected. The Diakonia
International Humanitarian Law Resource Centre states that since
Israel's supposed disengagement in 2005, "305 water wells, 197 chicken
farms, 6,377 sheep farms, 996 complete houses, 371 partial houses, three
mosques, three schools, and six factories have been destroyed within the
'buffer zone,'" and a total of 24.4 square kilometers of cultivated land has
been leveled.

Destroying Livelihoods in Khuza'a

"We can see the Israelis farming the land, and we cannot farm our land"
—Hassan, farmer from Khuza'a

Khuza'a is a village in the southern Gaza Strip, just east of Khan Younis.
It is located only 500 meters from the border fence with Israel and 70% of
the population are farmers. The town has suffered greatly from the Israeli
Occupation Forces' enforcement of the buffer zone and from repeated air
attacks. During Operation Cast Lead in 2008–2009, the village was targeted with white phosphorous, leaving farmland temporarily contaminated. During Corporate Watch's visit to Khuza'a we talked to farmers

representing several generations: Osama, Ahmed, Mohammed, Jihad, Salam and Hassan.

Hassan is 51 years old and has been a farmer in Khuza'a for over 30 years. He owns three different pieces of land, two dunams next to the border fence, two and a half dunams 400 meters from the fence and four dunams 620 meters from the border. He used to have olive trees on the plot by the border, but the land was leveled during an expansion of the buffer zone in 2000. In 2008 his other two pieces of land were bulldozed, including his greenhouses. In 2009 his house was partially burned by white phosphorous, which also affected the land next to him. "The farmers are the victims here" Hassan told us, "when resistance fighters are targeted on the farmland it destroys everything."

Hassan is now trying to grow tomatoes and olives on the two pieces of land furthest from the fence with the support of Unadikum and other international volunteers, who accompany farmers in in the hope that their presence will make the work less dangerous. However, all the Khuza'a farmers reported that they frequently get shot at even when working on land over 500 meters away from the border. "We have no choice, when the Israelis shoot we have to leave the land," Hassan said.

According to the men we talked to in Khuza'a the economic situation for farmers in the Gaza Strip is the hardest it has ever been—not only are none of them making any money, but the siege is slowly killing their ability to be agriculturally self sufficient. Hassan used to earn approximately $1000 a month from his fields before he lost his first bit of land in 2000. Now he has got debts of $60,000 instead and no way of making money. We were told that farmers generally get seeds to plant from the traders which they then pay for after harvest season, but harvests in the Gaza Strip are highly unpredictable: land anywhere near the buffer zones can become impossible to farm at any point and some years whole crops are destroyed during Israeli attacks.

None of the farmers in Khuza'a are currently able to export the produce they do succeed in growing. There has been a near total ban on exports from the Strip since the tightening of the siege in 2007 with only a minimal amount of agricultural produce being allowed for export through Israeli companies every year. No Gaza produce is allowed to be sold in Israel or the West Bank, which has traditionally been Gaza farmers' biggest market. Salam told us that he used to be able to market his produce for sale in Europe but that it had to be done through Agrexco and Arava, Israeli agricultural export companies, and that the last time he managed to export anything was almost ten years ago.

"I have been farming here for 30 years and all the lands have been destroyed," Hassan said with a shrug. "I used to produce 20 tanks of olive oil from my trees every year, but now I have to buy oil even for myself. Should we have to constantly rebuild everything? What will the future for my sons be? I am always arguing with my sons. They want to go to Algeria to find work, and then I will lose my sons too." All these farmers want is the chance to have a future on their land.

Standing in the middle of the fields of Khuza'a, looking past the barren Palestinian land next to the fence and past the military watch tower, you can clearly see healthy looking green crops on the Israeli side of the border. The Israeli fields are close enough for us to hear the low humming of their fertilizing plane as we leave.

Uprooting Families in Beit Hanoun

Beit Hanoun has been one of the towns hit the hardest by Israel's enforcement of the buffer zone. Located in the far north east of the Gaza Strip, only six kilometers from the Israeli city of Sderot and close to the Beit Hanoun (Erez) border crossing to Israel, the population is exposed to frequent incursions by the Israeli Occupation Forces and it shows. Approaching the buffer zone you walk past a big crater in the ground, the result of a 2012 F16 strike, and house rubble can be seen in the distance. The area is under constant heavy surveillance by Israel and several surveillance "balloons" monitor everything that goes on on the ground. According to Saber Al-Zaneen from the Beit Hanoun Local Initiative Israel bulldozed 9,000 dunums of Beit Hanoun's land between 2001 and 2009 including 70 houses. Most of it was farmland. As a result over 350 people living in the area have been displaced from their land. The Beit Hanoun Local Initiative, set up in 2007, is a grassroots group working with, and supporting, marginalised families and farmers living close to the buffer zone with the aim of helping them remain on their land.

In the past, farmers in the area used to grow olives, lemons and oranges close to the border, but all the trees have now been bulldozed. "Communities now grow potatoes, peppers, tomatoes and watermelons on the outskirts of the buffer zone" Saber told us. "You can not grow anything tall at all, no trees are allowed. If plants get higher than about 80 centimeters they will be leveled." Shortly after we visited the area, the Local Initiative assisted the planting of some new wheat fields nearer the fence, challenging the restrictions in the buffer zone.

On top of the access restrictions and the personal danger involved, farmers working the land face the big challenge of being able to access water for their crops. Approximately 60 water wells in the vicinity of the Beit Hanoun buffer zone were bulldozed or bombed between 2001–2009 and finding enough water to grow healthy produce is now a constant struggle for the community. The area we visited had one small mobile water tank for the fields but locals told us that as it requires either electricity or fuel to run they were not always able to use it. Instead they relied on a makeshift pit dug in the field and lined with tarpaulin in order to collect rain water. Gaza suffers from a severe and drawn out fuel crisis which, during our visit at the end of 2013, resulted in mains electricity only being available around 12 hours a day on a six hour off/six hour on basis at best. As a result fuel for personal use is both expensive and hard to come by (for an expanded explanation of the fuel crisis in Gaza see Corporate Watch's briefing Besieging Health Services in Gaza: A Profitable Business).

House Demolitions in Al-Zaytoun

"We plant our plants here to claim our rights to the land. We are not making a profit, we are working for nothing."
—Ahmad from Al-Zaytoun

We met the farmers Ali, Rafat, Nasser, Ahmad, Jawad and Ishmael outside Ahmad's house next to the Malaka intersection area of eastern Al-Zaytoun just south of Gaza City. There used to be a three-story family home on this plot, but there is now a much smaller house next door. This is the result of continuous targeting of the area by the Israeli Occupation Forces, who have a military base close by. Ahmad, who was born on this land, told us that his family's house had been demolished three times: in 2004, 2005, and during Operation Cast Lead in 2008.

"In 2008 they destroyed everything around here," Ahmed said, "they even destroyed my jars of olive oil. We did not have time to bring hardly any of our things. The Israelis came through a gate in the fence in the buffer zone with 14 tanks and four military bulldozers. They were shooting a lot to make us leave before they arrived. We have had to rebuild our home three times."

As in other buffer zone communities, it is not only property which is frequently targeted by Israel—it is anyone who attempts to farm the land. All the farmers we talked to in Al-Zaytoun had some land within 300 meters of the fence. The last shooting incident had occurred just four days before our visit. When there is instability happening in the area, everyday activities for farmers become even more precarious.

The story of the farmers in Al-Zaytoun is a familiar one: before the tightening of the siege in 2007 they all used to be able to make a decent profit from their land, with some farmers getting close to $30,000 a year but now they make no profit at all. Some of them used to export part of their produce, albeit through Israeli companies, but now none of them are able to export anything and all their goods go to the local Gaza market. "No-one has any money so we hardly make anything," said Ahmed. "Sometimes we have to feed some of the vegetables to the animals."

Mustapha told us that farmers in this area have had some help from Norwegian People's Aid who provided them with an irrigation system for the fields, and they also have a tractor but even with equipment taking care of the land is a challenge under siege. Just like the farmers in Beit Hanoun, they rely on access to electricity for the water pump and petrol for the tractor and those things are often not available. "The water is so salty here that we can only plant very specific plants like aubergines, olive trees, potatoes, cabbage, and spinach. Cucumbers and tomatoes can't be planted," said Mustapha. The salty water is the result of the Gaza aquifer having been contaminated by sea and sewage water, partly through a decline in ground water levels and partly as a result of infrastructure damage during Israeli air attacks in 2009. According to the UN 90% of the water from the aquifer, Gaza's only water resource, is not safe to drink.

After the ousting of the Muslim Brotherhood in Egypt in the middle of 2013, life for Gaza's farmers has become even harder. The men in Al-Zaytoun said that they used to be able to be able to buy cheap fertilizers which had come through the tunnels from Egypt at the local market. However, since the tunnels were destroyed this is no longer possible. Products are now both harder to get hold of and more expensive as they have to come through Israel which means that there are no cheap choices and that tax will be added.

Despite all the problems they face the people of Al-Zaytoun continue to work their land, they have no other option. As we walked around their fields they showed us how they have started to re-cultivate land nearer and nearer the fence, moving the area of cultivation forward by around ten meters per week. In Gaza simply farming the land has turned into an act of resistance.

Uprooting History in Al-Maghazi

"It is not the uprooting of the trees themselves that is the worst, it is the
uprooting of our history."
— Abu Mousab from Al-Maghazi

For Palestinians, the buffer zones do not only create financial hardship
and humanitarian crises, they also sever people's connection with their
history. In Al-Maghazi, a primarily agricultural community in the central Gaza Strip, we met Abu Mousab, a farmer who also holds down a
job as an iron welder in order to make a living. Al-Maghazi is a refugee
camp established in 1949 and according to Mohammed Rasi al-Betany
from the Al-Maghazi refugee council, approximately 95% of the population are refugees. However, Abu Mousab's family have lived on the same
piece of land for generations. When we visited, his father, who is in his
late 90s and who used to work for the British Mandate before the creation
of Israel, was asleep in the room next door.

Staying steadfast on the farmland has not been easy for Abu Mousab
and his family. Their land is located approximately 300 meters from the
border fence and, despite the fact that conditions have become a little bit
safer since 2012, working the land is dangerous. "We have to play a kind of
cat and mouse game with the soldiers," Abu Mousab said. "When the soldiers go away we turn on the water and quickly irrigate our plants, but as
soon as they start shooting we have to leave." Only a week before our visit
Abu Mousab's nephew Medhat had been shot at with live ammunition
warning shots when he was trying to weed some crops on the part of the
family's farmland nearest the fence. Some years the family have been able
to access their land so infrequently that the crops have failed, leaving them
with no income from their land. During good years when they do manage
to harvest their barley, wheat, almonds, citrus fruits, olives and apricots
they sell their produce to the local market in the Gaza Strip.

However, many people do not feel able to risk their life to work on the
land. One of them is Mousa Abu Jamal, another farmer from Al-Maghazi.
He used to have ten dunums of farmland planted with olive trees within
the buffer zone, all of which have been uprooted by Israel. When he tried
to go back to re-cultivate his land in the middle of 2012 he was shot at. He
has not been back since.

"I was always told by my father that he who has been raised on his
farmland must stick with his farmland until he dies and that is what we
are doing" Abu Mousab said. His family are so determined not to give up

their heritage that during the bombardment of the Gaza Strip in 2012 they made a decision not to leave the area for relative safety further away from the border. "Ten years ago the Israelis came with Caterpillar bulldozers and destroyed olive trees and several 200-year-old sycamore trees on my land. Those were trees my grandfather used to sit under," Abu Mousab said. "They had to use two of their bulldozers to uproot just one tree, they were so rooted in our history."

Boycott, Divestment, and Sanctions

Israel's siege of Gaza is slowly strangling life in the Strip. It affects farmers' access to land, crops, water and electricity. It also limits people in Gaza's ability to buy food grown in Gaza and makes people more reliant on imports of Israeli goods. The situation for exporters is even worse: only a tiny amount of agricultural produce gets exported each year, all of which has to go through Israeli companies. The ban on Gaza produce being sold in Israel and the West Bank amounts to a *de facto* boycott of Gaza's export industry by Israel.

What Can the Solidarity Movement Do?

During Corporate Watch's visit to the Gaza Strip the people we interviewed made their hopes very clear: they want boycott, divestment and sanctions of Israel, but they also want opportunities to trade and make a living. This presents a challenge to the BDS movement. As the tiny amount of Palestinian produce that is being exported from the Gaza Strip is currently exported through Israeli companies it means that any boycott of, for example Arava, will boycott Palestinian produce too. When asked about this implications of this, farmers were still supportive of a boycott, as they hoped the pressure would be more beneficial to them in the long term than the minuscule benefits the current export levels achieve. "What we need is people to stand with us against the occupation," said Mustapha from Al-Zaytoun. "By supporting BDS you support the farmers, both directly and indirectly and this is a good thing for people here in Gaza."

Farmers all over the Gaza Strip were particularly keen on getting the right to label their produce as Palestinian, ideally with its own country code, even if they have to export through Israel. Country of origin labels for Gaza goods is something the solidarity movement could lobby for.

There was strong support amongst farmers for increased action against Israeli arms manufacturers, as they are often on the receiving end of their weapons.

Mohsen Aby Ramadan, from the Palestinian Non-Governmental Organizations Network, suggested that one good way forward could be to engage farming unions across the world and get them to endorse the BDS call in solidarity with Palestinian farmers—an avenue that has not as yet been properly explored.

Corporate Watch, July 4, 2014, http://bit.ly/1m9dTYQ

Gaza Olive Harvest Hit Hard by War
Rami Almeghari

Yousef al-Serhy and his family were cheerful on Friday evening as they waited in a van in front of the large olive oil extraction facility on Salah al-Din road, south of Gaza City. The children sat on top of the large sacks of olives that would soon be pressed.

"We're waiting our turn, we have two tons of olives grown on our farm," al-Serhy, a father of four who is in his thirties, told the *Electronic Intifada*. "Growing olives has been our main occupation for decades, as my grandfather owned a piece of land in Johr al-Deek," an area east of Gaza City, he explained.

Al-Serhy said that the family's groves in that area were badly damaged in Israel's summer invasion of Gaza, a repeat of what happened during Israel's attack in 2008–2009. But fortunately, the family still owns a piece of land in the Sheikh Ijleen area west of Gaza City. "Only God's care protected the olive trees on that land," al-Serhy said.

"During the war we had difficulty accessing the olive trees. It was only during the times of ceasefire that we managed to get over there and irrigate them," he added, referring to several brief "humanitarian truces" that gave Gaza residents brief respites during the 51 days of bombardment.

Rafat al-Muqayyad, an olive farmer from the Mughraqa area south of Gaza City, told the *Electronic Intifada* that his entire family has worked in olive production since before the 1948 ethnic cleansing of Palestine in their village of Niliya, which now lies inside present-day Israel.

In Gaza, the family managed to continue this tradition, but they have not escaped the impact of the summer assault.

"My olives groves are right next to my brother's," al-Muqayyad said. "While my land was left intact, thank God, my brother's was severely damaged by Israeli army tanks and shelling. I expect to produce about two hundred liters of oil this year," he added.

Machinery Damaged

Though Israel's bombardment was utterly devastating, killing more than 2,100 people and leaving many areas in ruins, for some farmers the harvest has been a bright spot.

Nasser Odeh, owner of the olive oil extraction facility, told the *Electronic Intifada* that his plant has been welcoming hundreds of olive farmers since the beginning of October and he didn't expect demand to let up until mid-December.

No aspect of life has been untouched by the war, however.

"My facility is considered to be one of the biggest and most advanced in the Gaza Strip," Odeh said. "I use Italian-made machines and equipment, but unfortunately, many of my spare parts stored in the facility were damaged by an Israeli strike. We managed to save whatever spare parts we could from under the rubble," Odeh explained as he shifted sacks of olives.

Promises to lift the siege of Gaza, made at the time of the August ceasefire, have not materialized, which means that for plant owners like Odeh, bringing in parts and supplies to rebuild or repair remains virtually impossible. And while the trees may be producing, Gaza's economic situation remains challenging for farmers and consumers alike.

Abdallah Shahin, a farmer from the Maghazi refugee camp in the central Gaza Strip, owns a large olive grove.

"Nowadays we find difficulties marketing our products," he told the *Electronic Intifada*. He cited high unemployment, only further exacerbated by the war, and the fact that tens of thousands of government employees have gone without salaries for months.

Imported olive oil, including a variety known as K18 that comes from Israel, can sell for much less than local oil, which goes for as much as $140 for twenty liters.

Shahin showed the *Electronic Intifada* some of his olives trees, which were partially damaged by Israeli shells, as he and his family were forced to flee to another area until the August 26 ceasefire brought an end to the bombardment.

Sharp Drop

While many individual farmers have managed to bring in good crops, the Palestinian ministry of agriculture in Gaza estimates that the production of olives and olive oil there has dropped about 20 to 25 percent overall compared to 2012.

This is because large areas of farmland along Gaza's eastern boundary were hit hard during the Israeli assault, during which many farmers could not reach their land to tend to and irrigate the trees.

"Therefore, the weight of olives was less, compared to previous years," Hussam Abu Saada, an official with the agriculture ministry, told the *Electronic Intifada*.

Abu Saada said that the Gaza ministry of agriculture will have to facilitate the import of oil from the West Bank in order to meet local demand.

"I own about six acres of olive trees in northern Gaza and my land is located about three kilometers away from the boundary with Israel," Hussein Hammouda, a farmer in his fifties, told the *Electronic Intifada*. "I could not even irrigate my olives trees during the war, and as a result the olives look smaller in size compared to previous years."

Palestinians in Gaza, as in other parts of the country, remain committed to growing olives as a fundamental part of their economy and culture. But even the trees that survive, like the people who care for them, suffer the lasting traumas of war.

The Electronic Intifada, November 4, 2014, http://bit.ly/1IhiU9X

Farmers Forced to Stop Growing Strawberries in Gaza
Rami Almeghari

With its soft sandy soil, plentiful sunshine and an adequate supply of water, northern Gaza has the right conditions for growing strawberries.

To be more precise, it would have the right conditions if farmers were allowed to work in safety—and without restrictive export policies imposed by Israel.

Last summer, Hidaya and Moayad Warshagha had to mostly stay away their small farm in the Beit Lahiya area during a vital time for their crop. Because Israel bombed Gaza for more than six weeks in July and August, tending to their strawberries would have put the couple's lives in danger.

When they managed to reach their farm during a supposed three-day ceasefire, "the area looked like a red hell," Hidaya said. Because the Israeli military was not respecting the ceasefire, "we had to abandon our crop," she added. "All of the strawberries were destroyed." The couple lost $6,000 as a result. The horrific events of last summer were part of a series of problems that have beset the couple.

Gaza farmers used to export strawberries to the occupied West Bank, present-day Israel and Europe. But the siege which Israel imposed on Gaza in 2007 has prevented them from doing so.

The amount of Gaza's land devoted to growing strawberries has reportedly fallen from 2,300 dunums in 2007 to just 600 dunums this year. A dunum is the equivalent of 1,000 square meters.

No Compensation

Moath Abu Ayash employs seven workers on his 4.5 acre holding, also in Beit Lahiya. He can only sell strawberries to the local market, which is "never lucrative," he said.

Like many others in Gaza, his income has plummeted because of the siege. During the first year of the siege, he received some compensation from the Palestinian Authority's agriculture ministry in Ramallah. He has not received any assistance since then. "I cannot afford any more losses," he said.

Many farmers have opted to grow tomatoes and peppers rather than strawberries in recent years, according to Ahmad al-Shafi, the director of an agricultural cooperative in Beit Lahiya. Tomatoes and peppers are less costly to produce.

For the first three years of the siege, exporting strawberries was impossible. As part of a supposed easing of the blockade in 2010, Israel allowed a limited amount of the fruit to leave Gaza.

Restricted Exports

The following year, however, Israel announced that it was closing down Karni, a commercial crossing. Karni had been established in the 1990s as the main terminal for allowing exports from Gaza to pass through Israel.

Its closure has forced exporters to rely on the smaller and poorly equipped Karem Abu Salem crossing (known in Hebrew as Kerem Shalom). During the month of January, Israel only allowed five truckloads of food and agricultural goods to cross Karem Abu Salem, according to data compiled by the UN monitoring group OCHA.

A total of 136 truckloads of agricultural goods were exported in 2014. The level of exports was especially low in June, when just two truckloads were allowed out. There were no agricultural exports at all in July and August, when Gaza was under attack.

The farmers of Beit Lahiya had hoped to export 250 tons of strawberries to the Netherlands, as well as several other countries in Western
Europe and Russia this current season.

"So far we have only managed to export 70 tons of strawberries," said
al-Shafi. "This is not enough."

The Electronic Intifada, February 3, 2015, http://bit.ly/1zyS1eD

Destroyed Factories in Gaza:
An Attempt to Rise Again
Palestine Information Center

With high spirit, Jamal Abu al-Omarin is racing against time to recover
his pickle factory, which was destroyed by Israel during its last war on
Gaza in summer 2014. The destruction reflects the bitter reality that faces
the industrial and the economic sectors in Palestine because of the endless
Israeli crimes.

Complete Destruction

Abu al-Omarin told the Palestinian Information Center (PIC): "Israel has
destroyed parts of the factory using bulldozers, and the other parts were
destroyed by rockets and missiles."

He added: "It was a double loss; they destroyed the factory and about
150 tons of pickles, and we lost the pickle season." He continued: "In spite
of the loss, which is estimated to be more than 400,000 dollars, we are trying to resume the work with the least capabilities we have, so as to meet
the demands of our clients."

Al-Telbani...Heavy Losses

For his part, Muhammad al-Telbani, the director of al-Awda Factories Co.,
talked about the huge loss he suffered as a result of the repeated Israeli artillery shelling on his factory.

He said that his loss is estimated to be more than 25 million dollars.
He clarified that all production lines and main sections were "totally destroyed" along with warehouses full of ready-to-distribute products. The
implications of such destruction were not limited to the factories' owners, as about 450 workers were discharged after all main production lines
stopped.

Wa'el al-Wadeya, whose factory was destroyed by the Israeli occupation forces (IOF), stressed that his losses are about 7 million dollars. He noted that his destroyed factory contained scores of different production lines like potato chips, juices, sweets and biscuits.

Cumulative Effects

According to the General Union of Palestinian Industries, the IOF destroyed 450 economic and industrial establishments completely, and 600 partially, causing an estimated loss of a billion dollars.

Ali al-Hayek, the chairman of the union, pointed out that factories that belong to different important sectors such as food, construction, chemicals, and plastic industries were destroyed.

He underlined that such targeting destroyed what was left of the Palestinian economy after the last two wars and the 8-year siege. He also stressed the importance of compensating the private sector as soon as possible; since these factories were reconstructed with the help of loans.

Owners of the affected factories and establishments are demanding that the Palestinian government and international institutions to officially support them in order to reconstruct these factories and fulfill their developmental role.

Palestine Information Center, November 16, 2014,
http://bit.ly/1yvfs6l

Gaza Fishermen "in God's Hands"
Patrick O. Strickland and Ezz Al Zanoon

Editors' note: Here we reprint only the essay part of this photoessay; the stunning photographs were omitted for space considerations, but can be found at the link provided at the end of this essay.

Hundreds of mourners gathered outside of al-Shifa hospital to protest the killing of Tawfiq Abu Reyaleh, a 34-year-old fisherman shot by the Israeli navy just hours before.

Along with his shipmates on the overnight shift, the late father of four was struck by a bullet when Israeli forces opened fire on their boat on March 7, as they sailed within the six-nautical mile limit that Israel has imposed on Gaza's sea vessels, according to the fishermen. Abu Reyaleh was survived by his wife and four children, who live in northern Gaza.

"We just want to be like fishermen everywhere," his mourning cousin, Emad al-Sayeed Abu Reyala, told the *Electronic Intifada*. "We are not asking for so much; just a basic right. Our rights are not protected—not by the world, not by the Arab countries. Our lives are in God's hands."

"My cousin wasn't the first fisherman to be shot by the Israelis and he won't be the last. There isn't a fisherman in Gaza who hasn't been shot at," Emad said, adding that his son was injured when Israeli naval forces shot him in December. "If there the world has a conscience, it will stop these crimes," he said.

Since a ceasefire ended Israel's 51 days of intensive bombing in late August, Palestinian fishermen in Gaza say they have only been allowed to access an area within six nautical miles off the coast. Yet, according to the 1993 Oslo accords, fishermen should be allowed to sail up to twenty nautical miles offshore. Those who go near that boundary line are likely to be arrested or shot at by Israeli naval forces.

Israel has long tightened restrictions on Palestinian fishermen.

"Over the years, the Israeli military gradually reduced this range, severely damaging the livelihood of thousands of families and the availability of this basic and inexpensive food in the markets, which had served as a significant nutritional source," according to B'Tselem, an Israeli human rights group.

Abdelmuti Ibrahim al-Habil has fished up and down the Gaza Strip's coast for more than a quarter century. "I started working as a fisherman with my father when I was just fifteen years old," he told the *Electronic Intifada*.

His five sons, all in their twenties, work as fishermen with him. As he stands on the shore near Gaza City's port, they work on the boat's stalled motor behind him. After several minutes, the motor finally fires up and they clap and laugh.

"They've been working on fixing the boat for six weeks," al-Habil said, adding that the boat was nearly destroyed when Israeli naval forces sunk it with gunfire on January 26.

Like all Palestinian fishermen in Gaza, al-Habil has long suffered Israeli restrictions and attacks. But he never imagined that Israeli forces would go as far as to sink the boat.

"They arrested my [five] kids," he said, recalling that they were taken to Ashdod, a port city in the south of present-day Israel. "For two days, we had no idea where they were. We didn't know if they died when the boat went under."

After Israeli intelligence and military officers interrogated them for forty-eight hours, al-Habil's sons were dropped off at the Erez crossing between Gaza and Israel.

According to the United Nations monitoring group OCHA, Israeli forces fired live ammunition at Palestinian fishermen at least seventeen times between January 27 and February 9.

In the first half of 2014, before the summer war in Gaza, Israeli naval forces fired at Palestinian fishermen in the six mile nautical zone at least 177 times, "nearly as much as in all of 2013," according to the humanitarian charity Oxfam.

Hajj Rajab, 81, has fished since he was a teenager.

"My father taught me to fish. I taught my children and grandchildren how to finish. I've worked here many years," he told the *Electronic Intifada*. "It used to be good work. Not anymore."

Rajab explained that Israeli shelling targeted dozens of fishermen's storage areas, including his own, last summer.

"They destroyed everything," he said. "They destroyed us...the fishermen." Nonetheless, he continues to go out to sea each day. "There aren't any other choices for fishermen. Most of us have done this our whole lives."

The economic impact of Israel's restrictions has been disastrous for the fishermen.

"Unfortunately, as you see now, they only allow us to reach up to six miles, and sometimes it's only three," Mahmoud al-Hissi, a twenty-year-old father, told the *Electronic Intifada*.

"After six miles, there are rocks and reef on the ocean floor—that's where the real fish are," al-Hissi said. "We could go out and fish for the morning and make money, instead of heading out for 24-hour shifts and barely breaking even."

The fishermen work for a portion of the catch, which they sell in the market after returning to shore, al-Hissi explained. "I sometimes work for 24 hours and then only profit 75 shekels [approximately $19]," he said. "But recently it's been less because there just aren't any fish."

Ahmad al-Hissi, Mahmoud's cousin, explained that fishing has become a dangerous profession in recent years.

"If we stay about a kilometer from the six mile marker, we're fine," he told the *Electronic Intifada*. "But if we get any closer, they'll [the Israeli navy] make problems for us."

Shukri, Ahmad and Mahmoud's shipmate, said that they would be able to make a decent living if they weren't restricted to such a small and overfished space.

"If we could just get out to about nine nautical miles, we'd be rich men," he said.

The Electronic Intifada, March 31, 2015, http://bit.ly/19Hg1na.

Gaza's Economy Shattered by Israeli Siege
Rosa Schiano

A recent report by the Chamber of Commerce, Industry and Agriculture in Gaza says the Israeli authorities have closed Karem Abu Salem (Kerem Shalom) checkpoint, the Gaza Strip's only commercial crossing, for 150 days, 41 percent of working days, during 2013. The report points out that the continued closure of the commercial crossing constitutes a violation of the ceasefire agreements reached in November 2012 after the Israeli "Operation Pillar of Defense" military offensive. Normally Israel keeps the commercial crossing open 22 days per month, says the report, closing it on Fridays and Saturdays. The crossing was closed also during the Jewish holidays for "security reasons." According to the report, in 2013, 55,833 truckloads of goods entered Gaza, 1,578 fewer than in 2012. Israel allowed the export of 187 truckloads of goods from the Gaza Strip to European markets, compared to 234 truckloads, mostly agricultural products, in 2012.

The report also describes the impact of the Egyptian closure of the tunnels since July 2013. This closure caused huge economic losses over the past six months as a direct result of the interruption of economic activities and a fall in production, resulting in a decline of 60 percent of gross domestic product. Unemployment exceeded 39 percent at the end of 2013.

The Palestinian Centre for Human Rights' report on the Gaza Strip's crossings from November 1-30, 2013, documents the impact of the on-going Israeli siege imposed on Palestinians, affecting their economy and social condition. While Israel claims to have eased the blockade, the Gaza Strip has a lack of services, fuel and building materials. According to PCHR's statistics, the materials Israel has allowed to enter do not meet the needs of Gaza Strip's population. In November, Israel closed Karem Abu Salem crossing for ten days, 30.3 percent of the total period. Most imports are consumable. The entry of various raw materials continues to be prohibited, with the exception of very limited types imported under complicated procedures.

Israel has continued to impose a near-total ban on exports to markets in the West Bank, Israel and other countries, excluding limited amounts of agricultural products. Exceptionally, during the month of November, Israel allowed the exportation of 20 truckloads carrying agricultural products, including mints, garlic, basil, strawberries and flowers.

Here we come to a crucial point. Israel allows minimum exports of Palestinian products only to European and non-European markets, not to the West Bank. Why does Israel not allow Palestinians from Gaza to market their products in the West Bank, within Palestine?

It appears that on the one hand, this practice is part of the collective punishment of the blockade, which aims to not allow any economic growth in the Gaza Strip. On the other hand, Israel wants to protect its own market and sell its product in the occupied territories.

"We face many difficulties, mainly due to the closure of the crossing," a farmer in Beit Lahiya, in the northern Gaza Strip, said. "Generally exports take place twice a week. Sometimes we had to freeze strawberries, due to the closure. There are no exports to the West Bank. They are not allowed." The use of the term "export" to refer to the marketing of Gaza products in the West Bank, as if speaking about two different countries, shows the division caused by the barriers of the occupation and its practices that have separated a population. "There is no international law in Gaza," the farmer said. The farmers have to face not only the expenses of transportation, but also the costs of labor and the packaging. According to another farmer in Beit Lahiya, a 2.5 kilogram crate for strawberries costs 12 shekels, about 3 euros. They receive 25 shekels, or 5.25 euros, then earn 13 [shekels] in profit.

"In 1967, Beit Lahiya has begun to grow strawberries," Abu Sami, a farmer in Beit Lahiya, said. "Here, before the arrival of the Palestinian Authority, we marketed our products as Israeli products through the Israeli company Agrexco. As Israeli products, not Palestinian products. Subsequently, the European countries called on Israel to allow the Palestinians to market their products as Palestinian and without taxes. Here we export many kinds of agricultural products such as beans, green zucchini, strawberries, and many kinds of vegetables. We focus on the cash crop and flowers. After the siege, since 2006–2007, Israel closed the crossings and we could not export anymore. The European Union has called on

Israel to allow the Palestinians to export their crops as Palestinian crops, but we should sell our products through Israeli companies." He showed the cardboard box used to export strawberries, on which was printed the brand name of the Palestinian cooperative and the logo of the Israeli company Arava Export Growers.

"The Paris Agreement has tied the Palestinian economy to the Israeli economy," Abu Sami continued. "Most Palestinian products go to Europe, and some to Russia. We asked to sell our products in the West Bank, but the Israeli authorities have refused. They told us, 'this is a political decision.'"

Israeli companies also receive 6 percent from the exports of Palestinian products. "The farmers here have lost a lot," Abu Sami said. "Before 2005, we were planting approximately 2,500 dunums. Now it's only 700. We started planting herbs in Khan Yunis and Rafah, green pepper, cherry tomato. At this time, the cost of strawberries in Europe is too low. We stopped the exports." There will be meetings in the coming days, and the farmers will decide what to over the next few weeks. The cost of material is high. Farmers cannot earn anything from the exports allowed to Europe. The more profitable market in the West Bank is closed to them.

The Paris Protocol, an agreement on economic relations between Israel and the Palestine Liberation Organization, was signed on April 29, 1994, as part of the Oslo Agreements. It has made the Palestinian economy a prisoner of Israel, in both the productive sector and the trade of goods. Imports and exports are under complete control of Israel, which determines quantity, documents, customs, taxes, and time.

Due to the ban on exports, the economic growth of the Gaza Strip is even more difficult. The economic growth could be possible not only with the resumption of exports to foreign markets, but especially through economic and trade exchanges with the West Bank.

International Solidarity Movement, January 15, 2014,
http://bit.ly/1GI7mhC

The Great Game in the Holy Land: How Gazan Natural Gas Became the Epicenter of an International Power Struggle
Michael Schwartz

Guess what? Almost all the current wars, uprisings, and other conflicts in the Middle East are connected by a single thread, which is also a threat: these conflicts are part of an increasingly frenzied competition to find, extract, and market fossil fuels whose future consumption is guaranteed to lead to a set of cataclysmic environmental crises.

Amid the many fossil-fueled conflicts in the region, one of them, packed with threats, large and small, has been largely overlooked, and Israel is at its epicenter. Its origins can be traced back to the early 1990s when Israeli and Palestinian leaders began sparring over rumored natural gas deposits in the Mediterranean Sea off the coast of Gaza. In the ensuing decades, it has grown into a many-fronted conflict involving several armies and three navies. In the process, it has already inflicted mind-boggling misery on tens of thousands of Palestinians, and it threatens to add future layers of misery to the lives of people in Syria, Lebanon, and Cyprus. Eventually, it might even immiserate Israelis.

Resource wars are, of course, nothing new. Virtually the entire history of Western colonialism and post-World War II globalization has been animated by the effort to find and market the raw materials needed to build or maintain industrial capitalism. This includes Israel's expansion into, and appropriation of, Palestinian lands. But fossil fuels only moved to center stage in the Israeli-Palestinian relationship in the 1990s, and that initially circumscribed conflict only spread to include Syria, Lebanon, Cyprus, Turkey, and Russia after 2010.

The Poisonous History of Gazan Natural Gas

Back in 1993, when Israel and the Palestinian Authority (PA) signed the Oslo Accords that were supposed to end the Israeli occupation of Gaza and the West Bank and create a sovereign state, nobody was thinking much about Gaza's coastline. As a result, Israel agreed that the newly created PA would fully control its territorial waters, even though the Israeli navy was still patrolling the area. Rumored natural gas deposits there mattered little to anyone, because prices were then so low and supplies so plentiful. No wonder that the Palestinians took their time recruiting British Gas (BG)— a major player in the global natural gas sweepstakes—to find out what was actually there. Only in 2000 did the two parties even sign a modest contract to develop those by-then confirmed fields.

BG promised to finance and manage their development, bear all the costs, and operate the resulting facilities in exchange for 90 percent of the revenues, an exploitative but typical "profit-sharing" agreement. With an already functioning natural gas industry, Egypt agreed to be the on-shore hub and transit point for the gas. The Palestinians were to receive 10 percent of the revenues (estimated at about a billion dollars in total) and were guaranteed access to enough gas to meet their needs.

Had this process moved a little faster, the contract might have been implemented as written. In 2000, however, with a rapidly expanding economy, meager fossil fuels, and terrible relations with its oil-rich neighbors, Israel found itself facing a chronic energy shortage. Instead of attempting to answer its problem with an aggressive but feasible effort to develop renewable sources of energy, Prime Minister Ehud Barak initiated the era of Eastern Mediterranean fossil fuel conflicts. He brought Israel's naval control of Gazan coastal waters to bear and nixed the deal with BG. Instead, he demanded that Israel, not Egypt, receive the Gaza gas and that it also control all the revenues destined for the Palestinians—to prevent the money from being used to "fund terror."

With this, the Oslo Accords were officially doomed. By declaring Palestinian control over gas revenues unacceptable, the Israeli government committed itself to not accepting even the most limited kind of Palestinian budgetary autonomy, let alone full sovereignty. Since no Palestinian government or organization would agree to this, a future filled with armed conflict was assured.

The Israeli veto led to the intervention of British Prime Minister Tony Blair, who sought to broker an agreement that would satisfy both the Israeli government and the Palestinian Authority. The result: a 2007 proposal that would have delivered the gas to Israel, not Egypt, at below-market prices, with the same 10 percent cut of the revenues eventually reaching the PA. However, those funds were first to be delivered to the Federal Reserve Bank in New York for future distribution, which was meant to guarantee that they would not be used for attacks on Israel.

This arrangement still did not satisfy the Israelis, who pointed to the recent victory of the militant Hamas party in Gaza elections as a deal-breaker. Though Hamas had agreed to let the Federal Reserve supervise all spending, the Israeli government, now led by Ehud Olmert, insisted that no "royalties be paid to the Palestinians." Instead, the Israelis would deliver the equivalent of those funds "in goods and services."

This offer the Palestinian government refused. Soon after, Olmert imposed a draconian blockade on Gaza, which Israel's defense minister termed a form of "'economic warfare' that would generate a political crisis, leading to a popular uprising against Hamas." With Egyptian cooperation, Israel then seized control of all commerce in and out of Gaza, severely limiting even food imports and eliminating its fishing industry. As Olmert advisor Dov Weisglass summed up this agenda, the Israeli government was putting the Palestinians "on a diet" (which, according to the Red Cross, soon produced "chronic malnutrition," especially among Gazan children).

When the Palestinians still refused to accept Israel's terms, the Olmert government decided to unilaterally extract the gas, something that, they believed, could only occur once Hamas had been displaced or disarmed. As former Israel Defense Forces commander and current Foreign Minister Moshe Ya'alon explained, "Hamas ... has confirmed its capability to bomb Israel's strategic gas and electricity installations ... It is clear that, without an overall military operation to uproot Hamas control of Gaza, no drilling work can take place without the consent of the radical Islamic movement."

Following this logic, Operation Cast Lead was launched in the winter of 2008. According to Deputy Defense Minister Matan Vilnai, it was intended to subject Gaza to a "shoah" (the Hebrew word for holocaust or disaster). Yoav Galant, the commanding general of the Operation, said that it was designed to "send Gaza decades into the past." As Israeli parliamentarian Tzachi Hanegbi explained, the specific military goal was "to topple the Hamas terror regime and take over all the areas from which rockets are fired on Israel."

Operation Cast Lead did indeed "send Gaza decades into the past." Amnesty International reported that the 22-day offensive killed 1,400 Palestinians, "including some 300 children and hundreds of other unarmed civilians, and large areas of Gaza had been razed to the ground, leaving many thousands homeless and the already dire economy in ruins." The only problem: Operation Cast Lead did not achieve its goal of "transferring the sovereignty of the gas fields to Israel."

More Sources of Gas Equal More Resource Wars

In 2009, the newly elected government of Prime Minister Benjamin Netanyahu inherited the stalemate around Gaza's gas deposits and an Israeli energy crisis that only grew more severe when the Arab Spring in Egypt interrupted and then obliterated 40 percent of the country's gas supplies. Rising energy prices soon contributed to the largest protests involving Jewish Israelis in decades.

As it happened, however, the Netanyahu regime also inherited a potentially permanent solution to the problem. An immense field of recoverable natural gas was discovered in the Levantine Basin, a mainly offshore formation under the eastern Mediterranean. Israeli officials immediately asserted that "most" of the newly confirmed gas reserves lay "within Israeli territory." In doing so, they ignored contrary claims by Lebanon, Syria, Cyprus, and the Palestinians.

In some other world, this immense gas field might have been effectively exploited by the five claimants jointly, and a production plan might even have been put in place to ameliorate the environmental impact of releasing a future 130 trillion cubic feet of gas into the planet's atmosphere. However, as Pierre Terzian, editor of the oil industry journal *Petrostrategies*, observed, "All the elements of danger are there... This is a region where resorting to violent action is not something unusual."

In the three years that followed the discovery, Terzian's warning seemed ever more prescient. Lebanon became the first hot spot. In early 2011, the Israeli government announced the unilateral development of two fields, about 10 percent of that Levantine Basin gas, which lay in disputed offshore waters near the Israeli-Lebanese border. Lebanese Energy Minister Gebran Bassil immediately threatened a military confrontation, asserting that his country would "not allow Israel or any company working for Israeli interests to take any amount of our gas that is falling in our zone." Hezbollah, the most aggressive political faction in Lebanon, promised rocket attacks if "a single meter" of natural gas was extracted from the disputed fields.

Israel's Resource Minister accepted the challenge, asserting that "[t]hese areas are within the economic waters of Israel... We will not hesitate to use our force and strength to protect not only the rule of law but the international maritime law."

Oil industry journalist Terzian offered this analysis of the realities of the confrontation:

> In practical terms...nobody is going to invest with Lebanon in disputed waters. There are no Lebanese companies there capable of carrying out the drilling, and there is no military force that could protect them. But on the other side, things are different. You have Israeli companies that have the ability to operate in offshore areas, and they could take the risk under the protection of the Israeli military.

Sure enough, Israel continued its exploration and drilling in the two disputed fields, deploying drones to guard the facilities. Meanwhile, the Netanyahu government invested major resources in preparing for possible future military confrontations in the area. For one thing, with lavish U.S. funding, it developed the "Iron Dome" anti-missile defense system designed in part to intercept Hezbollah and Hamas rockets aimed at Israeli energy facilities. It also expanded the Israeli navy, focusing on its ability to deter or repel threats to offshore energy facilities. Finally, starting in 2011 it launched airstrikes in Syria designed, according to U.S. officials, "to prevent any transfer of advanced...antiaircraft, surface-to-surface and shore-to-ship missiles" to Hezbollah.

Nonetheless, Hezbollah continued to stockpile rockets capable of demolishing Israeli facilities. And in 2013, Lebanon made a move of its own. It began negotiating with Russia. The goal was to get that country's gas firms to develop Lebanese offshore claims, while the formidable Russian navy would lend a hand with the "long-running territorial dispute with Israel."

By the beginning of 2015, a state of mutual deterrence appeared to be setting in. Although Israel had succeeded in bringing online the smaller of the two fields it set out to develop, drilling in the larger one was indefinitely stalled "in light of the security situation." U.S. contractor Noble Energy, hired by the Israelis, was unwilling to invest the necessary $6 billion dollars in facilities that would be vulnerable to Hezbollah attack, and potentially in the gun sights of the Russian navy. On the Lebanese side, despite an increased Russian naval presence in the region, no work had begun.

Meanwhile, in Syria, where violence was rife and the country in a state of armed collapse, another kind of stalemate went into effect. The regime of Bashar al-Assad, facing a ferocious threat from various groups of jihadists, survived in part by negotiating massive military support from Russia in exchange for a 25-year contract to develop Syria's claims to that Levantine gas field. Included in the deal was a major expansion of the Russian naval base at the port city of Tartus, ensuring a far larger Russian naval presence in the Levantine Basin.

While the presence of the Russians apparently deterred the Israelis from attempting to develop any Syrian-claimed gas deposits, there was no Russian presence in Syria proper. So Israel contracted with the U.S.-based Genie Energy Corporation to locate and develop oil fields in the Golan Heights, Syrian territory occupied by the Israelis since 1967. Facing a potential violation of international law, the Netanyahu government invoked, as the basis for its acts, an Israeli court ruling that the exploitation of natural resources in occupied territories was legal. At the same time, to prepare for the inevitable battle with whichever faction or factions emerged triumphant from the Syrian civil war, it began shoring up the Israeli military presence in the Golan Heights.

And then there was Cyprus, the only Levantine claimant not at war with Israel. Greek Cypriots had long been in chronic conflict with Turkish Cypriots, so it was hardly surprising that the Levantine natural gas discovery triggered three years of deadlocked negotiations on the island over what to do. In 2014, the Greek Cypriots signed an exploration contract with Noble Energy, Israel's chief contractor. The Turkish Cypriots trumped this move by signing a contract with Turkey to explore all Cypriot claims "as far as Egyptian waters." Emulating Israel and Russia, the Turkish government promptly moved three navy vessels into the area to physically block any intervention by other claimants.

As a result, four years of maneuvering around the newly discovered Levantine Basin deposits have produced little energy, but brought new and powerful claimants into the mix, launched a significant military build-up in the region, and heightened tensions immeasurably.

Gaza Again—and Again

Remember the Iron Dome system, developed in part to stop Hezbollah rockets aimed at Israel's northern gas fields? Over time, it was put in place near the border with Gaza to stop Hamas rockets, and was tested during Operation Returning Echo, the fourth Israeli military attempt to bring Hamas to heel and eliminate any Palestinian "capability to bomb Israel's strategic gas and electricity installations."

Launched in March 2012, it replicated on a reduced scale the devastation of Operation Cast Lead, while the Iron Dome achieved a 90 percent "kill rate" against Hamas rockets. Even this, however, while a useful adjunct to the vast shelter system built to protect Israeli civilians, was not enough to ensure the protection of the country's exposed oil facilities. Even one direct hit there could damage or demolish such fragile and flammable structures.

The failure of Operation Returning Echo to settle anything triggered another round of negotiations, which once again stalled over the Palestinian rejection of Israel's demand to control all fuel and revenues destined for Gaza and the West Bank. The new Palestinian Unity government then followed the lead of the Lebanese, Syrians, and Turkish Cypriots, and in late 2013 signed an "exploration concession" with Gazprom, the huge Russian natural gas company. As with Lebanon and Syria, the Russian Navy loomed as a potential deterrent to Israeli interference.

Meanwhile, in 2013, a new round of energy blackouts caused "chaos" across Israel, triggering a draconian 47 percent increase in electricity prices. In response, the Netanyahu government considered a proposal to begin extracting domestic shale oil, but the potential contamination of water resources caused a backlash movement that frustrated this effort. In a country filled with start-up high-tech firms, the exploitation of renewable energy sources was still not being given serious attention. Instead, the government once again turned to Gaza.

With Gazprom's move to develop the Palestinian-claimed gas deposits on the horizon, the Israelis launched their fifth military effort to force Palestinian acquiescence, Operation Protective Edge. It had two major hydrocarbon-related goals: to deter Palestinian-Russian plans and to finally eliminate the Gazan rocket systems. The first goal was apparently met when Gazprom postponed (perhaps permanently) its development deal. The second, however, failed when the two-pronged land and air attack—despite unprecedented devastation in Gaza—failed to destroy Hamas's rocket stockpiles or its tunnel-based assembly system; nor did the Iron Dome achieve the sort of near-perfect interception rate needed to protect proposed energy installations.

There Is No Denouement

After 25 years and five failed Israeli military efforts, Gaza's natural gas is still underwater and, after four years, the same can be said for almost all of the Levantine gas. But things are not the same. In energy terms, Israel is ever more desperate, even as it has been building up its military, including its navy, in significant ways. The other claimants have, in turn, found larger and more powerful partners to help reinforce their economic and military claims. All of this undoubtedly means that the first quarter-century of crisis over eastern Mediterranean natural gas has been nothing but prelude. Ahead lies the possibility of bigger gas wars with the devastation they are likely to bring.

TomDispatch, February 26, 2015, http://bit.ly/1P5VHNg

The Ancient Mosques of Gaza in Ruins: How Israel's War Endangered Palestine's Cultural Heritage
Ahmad Nafi

In the aftermath of Operation Protective Edge, Israel's 51-day military assault, the Palestinians in Gaza are faced with the huge task of reconstruction. Most of the shattered civilian infrastructure can be replaced, but Palestine's cultural heritage in Gaza, built over a thousand years and more, has been damaged irrevocably. Many of Gaza's most ancient sites have been left in ruins by Israel's attack on the territory. Houses of worship, tombs, charity offices, and cemeteries have all been damaged by the shelling, but Gaza's historic mosques have been the worst affected. Many of these sites date back to the time of the first Islamic caliphs, the Ottoman Empire, and the Mamluk Sultanate.

Protective Edge damaged 203 mosques, of which 73 were destroyed completely. Two churches were also damaged, according to the Palestinian Ministry of Endowments and Religious Affairs. The targeting of mosques by the Israel Defence Forces (IDF) in the latest offensive was three times more than in the 2008–2009 attack, the ministry's report said.

The destruction of Gaza's ancient mosques has brought the total losses incurred by the religious affairs ministry to an estimated $50 million, said Dr. Hassan Al-Saifi, its undersecretary in the Gaza Strip.

"There are a number of ancient mosques that hold memories of the Islamic and Arab history in Gaza," said Al-Saifi, "and of course, the people are incredibly saddened over the loss of this heritage." The losses are likely to deny future generations their history as well as the material and economic benefits that might be acquired from these sites.

The most significant of those mosques which were destroyed was the 7th century Al-Omari Mosque in Jabaliya, Gaza's oldest and largest. Named after the second caliph Umar bin Al-Khattab, it dates back to 649 AD, making it 1,365 years old. It accommodated 2,000 worshippers for the congregational prayers. The portico and minaret were built 500 years ago during the Mamluk period; it was destroyed by Israel on August 2, 2014 and its hallmark minaret and courtyard stands in ruins.

The Great Omari Mosque tells the story of Gaza's civilization and cultural history as it is believed to stand on the site of a former Philistine temple and a later 5th Century Byzantine church. It has acted as an important landmark ever since it was built.

Close by, Gaza's second oldest mosque was also reduced to ruins. Al-Sham'ah Mosque was destroyed on July 23 in Hayy Al-Najjarin in Al-Zaytun Quarter in Gaza's Old City. It was built 700 years ago, in 1315, by the Mamluk Governor.

Another historic site was razed to the ground on the following day. The Mahkamah Mosque was a fine example of Mamluk architecture located off the main Baghdad Street in the Shuja'iya neighborhood. It featured a Mamluk minaret and florally decorated arch at its entrance and was built in 1455 on the orders of Sayf Al-Din Birdibak Al-Ashrafi, a member of the sultan's staff. Shuja'iya neighborhood experienced some of the most intense shelling of the war in July that resulted in thousands of residents being forced to flee their homes.

The large Omar Ibn Abd al-Aziz Mosque in the Strip's northern city of Beit Hanoun is a modern building but is a central mosque that serves a large segment of the town. It was destroyed by shelling on August 25. Other destroyed mosques of cultural significance include the centuries-old Al-Montar Mosque and tomb, hit on July 11.

Gaza's only 3 churches also fell victim to the conflict. The Orthodox Church of St. Porphyrius is the oldest church in Gaza, dating to the 1150s, in Al-Zaytun Quarter of the Old City. The church's cemetery was damaged when the area was shelled in July in another attack on Gaza's rich religious heritage. Gaza Baptist Church received major damage from the shelling of a police station nearby and Gaza's Latin Church had damage to peripheral buildings owned by the parish.

These sites have historical importance and provided irreplaceable material evidence of Palestinian culture and history. Al-Saifi believes that by destroying mosques, "the occupation was erasing the historical proof and evidence of our presence in Palestine."

The devastation of hundreds of years of Gaza's Islamic history would be expected to have done harm to Gaza's identity, but Al-Saifi insists that Israel could not erase the Palestinian memory and the peoples' right to exist. "I believe that the Israelis will not succeed in this because to us, mosques are not merely stones, but hold great and holy value to all of the Muslim generations."

The damage to these irreplaceable landmarks has led Israel to claim that it targeted mosques and civilian buildings used for military purposes, such as the stockpiling of weapons and as meeting points for the fighters of the Qassam Brigades. The IDF alleged that Hamas "cruelly abused mosques by using them for terror activities" in a statement to the Associated Press.

Hamas has denied the accusation and many in Gaza feel that the al-legation is an attack on their way of life. "Every citizen in Gaza is proud of these fighters," Dr. Al-Saifi said, "and mosques are completely open places; they do not contain any shelters or secret rooms, they are open houses of worship." He went on to say that Israel knowingly targets civilian sites. "There is no doubt that the Israeli intelligence agencies have their eyes and ears in Gaza, and they are certain that these are fabrications."

The damage done to these sites has undermined the territory's social infrastructure. For the residents of Gaza, many of the targeted mosques provided social, educational and health facilities.

The Palestinians are of the opinion that Israel does not distinguish between military and civilian targets in their aggression against Gaza. Their suspicions appear to be validated by UN OCHA figures released in a recent report. They suggest that at least 80 percent of those killed were civilians. These figures indicate that Israel has found little difficulty in treating civilian infrastructure as legitimate military targets considering that it has targeted churches and other buildings not accused of being used by Qassam fighters.

Many have noted Israel's disproportionate use of force in areas that it associates with enemy fighters. It is an army that is used to inflicting widespread devastation on the civilian population, which is supposed to serve as a deterrent.

For Al-Saifi, this strategy is abhorrent: "Honestly, the targeting of mosques on such an unprecedented large-scale reflects the barbaric and brutal nature of the Israeli occupation, and the army's frustration and sense of failure, as it reached an impasse. It resorted to targeting civilians and places of worship, which have been guaranteed protection and immu-nity under all international conventions."

The pursuit of collective punishment is an international war crime and it appears that these violations by Israel have been observed clearly by in-ternational institutions. The retiring UN High Commissioner for Human Rights, Navi Pillay, condemned the operations in Gaza. In a statement to Britain's *Guardian* newspaper she said, "There seems to be a strong pos-sibility that international law has been violated."

In a similar incident, despite being given the coordinates of UNRWA schools they were bombed under the pretext of the presence of missiles. "Even though the Arab and foreign UNRWA spokesperson stressed and confirmed that the occupation's claims were fabricated," complained Al-Saifi. The UN has condemned the bombing of these schools and notified

*Israeli shelling damaged the ancient al-Sousi mosque in Shati refugee camp
in the northern Gaza Strip, but the center of the main structure continued
to be used by residents for prayer. According to Euro-Mid Observer for
Human Rights, Israeli shelling during the 51-day attack completely destroyed
62 mosques and 10 Muslim cemeteries; 109 mosques were partially destroyed,
together with one church and one Christian cemetery.[5]
Photo by Mohammed Asad.*

the IDF of their locations repeatedly. It was alleged by Israel that mosques
and UNRWA schools all facilitated the activities of the Palestinian resistance groups.

Because of this, Al-Saifi has questioned Israel over its accusations of
"terror" activities in historic mosques; he believes that the world has seen
through Israel's empty justifications of war crimes. "All of the international community organizations and international observers know that
these are lies."

Indeed, the targeting of religious and cultural sites as civilian sites
constitutes a violation of international humanitarian law; it is covered by
Article 4 of the Hague Convention of 1954 for the Protection of Cultural
Property. Under this convention, all feasible precautions must be taken
to avoid damage of cultural property in cases of war. It is also designated
a criminal act under Article 8 of the ICC Statute which stipulates that

"intentionally directing attacks against buildings dedicated to religion...
[and] historic monuments...constitutes a war crime."

In recent months, the destruction of historic monuments and houses
of worship has usually been associated with radical groups like Islamic
State (ISIS) rather than state actors like Israel. In July, ISIS destroyed the
mosque of Prophet Younis (Jonah) in Mosul and several Shiite Mosques
in Iraq. ISIS's presence has warranted considerable responses from the international community. Yet Israel's attack on Gaza's heritage of the same
nature has created little response.

The international community and Israel itself will be reluctant to label
the assault on Gaza an act of terror. Domestically, it is believed that Israel's
agenda of eliminating the people of the Gaza Strip in the name of "security" stands above criticism from anyone and everyone. "Israel wanted to
give itself an excuse" to commit acts of brutality, claims Al-Saifi.

In Palestine, there has been considerable pressure to get the international community to hold Israel to account for its actions. "The Palestinian
Authority," insists Al-Saifi, "must go to the ICC in The Hague...in order for
us to witness the occupation being prosecuted, just as the criminals in
Yugoslavia and Bosnia were prosecuted."

Middle East Monitor, September 10, 2014, http://bit.ly/1CWWo5g

3

Elsewhere in Palestine...

As Gaza bled, Palestinians throughout the country felt its agony. This chapter explores not only the Palestinian response to Israel's brutal offensive but also the events that unfolded in the weeks prior to and during the offensive. Racist rampages by Israeli settlers and vigilantes made the streets unsafe for Palestinians; from Jerusalem in particular, eyewitnesses reported several attempted kidnappings of Palestinian children by vengeful Israelis on the loose, finding support for their lawlessness in the wildly irresponsible statements of public officials and rabbis. Palestinian citizens in Israel, whose presence has long been a thorn in the side of the government, found their own status as precarious as ever. The Gaza Strip remained sealed, the Rafah and Erez crossings closed. Viewed as a whole, the events of the summer of 2014 are simply the most recent expression of Israel's systematic campaign of suppression and control of the Palestinian nation.

Administrative Detainees on Hunger Strike Issue Their Will as They Stand "at the Edge of Death"

Shahd Abusalama

Our Palestinian detainees have been battling the Israel Prison Service (IPS) with their empty stomachs since April 24, embarking on the longest-known mass hunger strike in the history of the Palestinian prisoners movement. Hunger is the only remaining weapon they can use against the IPS and its well-armed Israeli occupation soldiers.

They launched this hunger strike to call for an end to their detention with no charge or trial based on secret "evidence" submitted to a military court that is kept from the detainees and their lawyers—an unjust policy that Israel calls administrative detention. One hundred and twenty administrative detainees launched this mass hunger strike, which grew to involve nearly three hundred prisoners, according to the rights group Addameer.

Our dignified prisoners are striking in protest of Israel's violation of an agreement reached with the IPS after the 28-day mass hunger strike that ended on May 14, 2012. According to that deal, the use of administrative detention—the key issue behind the hunger strike—would be restricted and administrative detention orders would not be renewed without fresh evidence being brought before a military judge. However, Israel did not abide by the agreement and has continued its practice of arbitrary administrative detention.

Strikers Hospitalized

Administrative detainee Ayman Tbeisheh from Dura village near Hebron in the occupied West Bank has exceeded one hundred days of refusing food in protest of his administrative detention orders which have been continuously renewed since his last arrest in May 2013, according to al-Quds al-Arabi newspaper. Tbeisheh has spent a total of eleven years in Israeli jails, including nearly five years under administrative detention.

According to Addameer, Tbeisheh first began to refuse food on May 22, 2013, immediately after his four-month administrative detention order was confirmed in a military court. He suspended his strike after 105 days, when he thought he reached a deal with the IPS. But this was soon broken as his order was again renewed, despite his deteriorated health.

Ayman Tbeisheh told Palestinian lawyer Ibrahim Al-Araj, who managed to visit him during his previous hunger strike, "I will continue this open hunger strike until I put an end to the ghost of administrative detention that keeps chasing me."

Soon after he regained some of his physical strength, he re-launched his hunger strike on February 24, 2014. Tbeisheh has since been placed in Assaf Harofe Medical Center where he lies shackled to a hospital bed that may become his deathbed at any moment.

Ayman's condition is no different than the rest of administrative detainees whose hunger for freedom and dignity drove them to launch the mass hunger strike that has been continuing for 51 days. Eighty hunger strikers have been hospitalized as a result of their ongoing hunger strike, but they persevere in this battle for dignity.

Despite their weak bodies that are drained of energy, their hands and feet are shacked to their hospital beds. They are threatened with force-feeding on a daily basis, an inhumane and dangerous practice that Israel's parliament, the Knesset, is close to setting into law.

Death Penalty

My father, who spent a total of fifteen years in Israeli jails, calls force-feeding "a death penalty." He participated in the Nafha prison mass hunger strike in 1980 which lasted for 33 days. He was subjected to force-feeding and thankfully survived. But his comrades Rasem Halawa from Jabaliya refugee camp and Ali al-Jaafary from Dheisheh camp were victims of this murderous practice that aimed to break their hunger strike, and were killed after being subjected to force-feeding.

The Israel Prison Service escalates its oppression of the hunger strikers as their health constantly deteriorates. They put them in windowless isolation cells, keep their hands and legs shackled for tens of hours, deny them family and lawyer visits, and they even deny them access to salt, which is necessary for their survival.

The strikers are committed to "hunger until either victory or martyrdom," the same as Khader Adnan, Hana al-Shalabi, Mahmoud Sarsak, Samer Issawi, and other ex-detainees who freed themselves after heroic battles of hunger strike against the IPS.

Prisoners' Letter

Below is my translation of a letter our administrative detainees managed to smuggle on June 8 to call upon humanity and people of conscience for popular and international support of their battle for justice.

The ex-detainee Allam Kaaby read it during a press conference in front of the sit-in tent erected in front of the International Committee of the Red Cross in Gaza in solidarity with our Palestinian prisoners' open-ended mass hunger strike.

Despite the chains and the prisons' bars and walls, this is a will from those who are standing at the edge of death to the guards of our homeland, Palestine.

After leaving the isolation cells which are no longer able to tolerate our pains, illnesses and corroded bodies, from our hospital beds to which we are shackled by chains and guard dogs, from amidst the jailers who keep watching our heart monitors that may announce our death any moment, from the edge of death, we send our call which could be the last for some of us. It might be the time to announce our will before we embrace our people as dignified martyrs. Our call is our voice, our scream, our will. We are the administrative detainees who are heading towards immortality, towards embracing the sun of dignity which might mark at the same time, the end of the battle for dignity. We raise our voice, hoping that it will reach our revolutionary people.

First, we call upon you to intensify your support of the hunger strikers who are not yet martyred; the fighters who fight our fascist enemy with their bodies deserve from you a stand of loyalty that prevents the continuation of our bloodshed which will never stop until the achievement of our just demands.

Second, the pains of hunger damaged some of our organs but some organs must be still intact. As death is waiting for us, we declare that nothing will stand in the way of our sacrifices, even death. Therefore, we donate our functioning organs to the fighters, poor and oppressed people who are in need. We are waiting a visit from the International Committee of The Red Cross to endorse these donations.

Third, we call on you to stay faithful to our blood and the blood of all martyrs who sacrificed their souls over the course of our Palestinian struggle. Faithfulness is not just through words, but through revolutionary practice that knows no hesitance nor weakness.

Fourth, hold on to our historical and legitimate rights and never give up an inch of Palestine, from the river to the sea. The right to return is the bridge to our historic rights. These rights cannot be restored without resistance, which is the only language that our enemy understands.

Fifth, don't fail prisoners who remain alive after us, as those who sacrifice their freedom as a price for their people's freedom deserve freedom rather than death.

To our dignified people in Palestine and diaspora, to the free people and freedom fighters worldwide, we will let our screams be heard despite the darkness of Israeli jails, which are graves for the living. To people of dead conscience worldwide, our Palestinian people will continue the struggle until victory. We bid farewell with smiling faces.

Reading their words, which embrace pain and disappointment, must make us all ashamed as we watch them die slowly. Changing our profile pictures to a picture that shows solidarity with their battle for dignity cannot do them much help. We have to move beyond superficial solidarity to serious actions that will bring meaningful change to them. Act before we count more martyrs among Palestinian heroes behind Israeli bars. Their death would be our shame.

The Electronic Intifada, June 11, 2014, http://bit.ly/1FcABaq

Merciless Israeli Mobs Are Hunting Palestinians
Rania Khalek

All eyes are on Gaza, where the death toll from Israel's merciless bombing campaign has topped 1,000.

But back in Jerusalem, where sixteen-year-old Muhammad Abu Khudair was burned alive by Jewish vigilantes in a "revenge killing" incited by Israeli politicians early this month, right-wing lynch mobs continue to roam the streets in search of Arabs to attack.

Their most recent victims are twenty-year-old Palestinians Amir Shwiki and Samer Mahfouz from the Beit Hanina neighborhood in occupied East Jerusalem. The pair were severely beaten into unconsciousness on Friday night by Israeli youths armed with iron bars and baseball bats.

Mahfouz told the Israeli newspaper *Haaretz* that he and Shwiki were on their way to the light rail when they were stopped by "a man [coming]

from the direction of Neve Yaakov," an illegal Jewish-only Israeli settlement in occupied East Jerusalem.

"He said give me a cigarette. I told him I don't have any, and he heard [from my accent] I'm Arab and went away, coming back with his friends, maybe twelve people. They had sticks and iron bars and they hit us over the head," Mahfouz recounted.

Haaretz added, "According to the victims, police officers that arrived at the scene did not call an ambulance, and they were instead evacuated by passersby to receive medical treatment at a Beit Khanina [sic] clinic. They were later rushed to Hadassah University Hospital, Ein Karem in serious condition."

Though investigators believe the beating to be racially motivated, no one has been arrested.

Police Complicity

Israeli police have a pattern of ignoring hate crimes against Palestinians, as was the case immediately following the reported kidnapping of Muhammad Abu Khudair. Police did not immediately respond when his family called to report that he had been kidnapped and they actively thwarted efforts to locate those who murdered him by spreading false rumors that Abu Khudair was murdered by his family in an "honor killing" over his sexuality.

Police also neglected to respond when Abu Khudair's murderers tried to kidnap ten-year-old Mousa Zalum from the same East Jerusalem neighborhood two days earlier.

When police aren't busy ignoring Jewish vigilante violence against Palestinians, they are actively participating in it.

On Thursday night last week, police teamed up with a Jewish mob assaulting two Palestinian men while they were delivering bread to grocery markets on Jaffa Street in West Jerusalem from their van.

The men—identified by Ma'an News Agency as twenty-year-old Amir Mazin Abu Eisha and Laith Ubeidat (age not specified)—were encircled and beaten with empty bottles by a mob of some twenty to thirty Israelis, according to their attorney, Khaldun Nijim.

Rather than assist the men as they were being attacked, Nijim told *Ma'an*, "The Israeli police stopped them in their van and pointed guns at them."

Nijim added, "After they drove away a few meters, the police shot at them. They then stopped and were assaulted again."

After barring an ambulance from transferring Abu Eisha, who sustained head and ear injuries, to the hospital for medical treatment, police detained the two Palestinian men at the Russian Compound police station close to the scene and charged them with "having a knife and obstructing the work of police," according to Nijim.

Abu Eisha and Ubeidat were eventually released on bail but are currently under ten days of house arrest. Meanwhile, several of the mob participants filed complaints against their victims, accusing the men of trying to assault them with a knife.

Racist Activism on the Rise

The same Ma'an article notes that in Jerusalem, "Jaffa street has been covered with flyers warning Arabs not to 'touch' Jewish women in recent weeks, as part of a right-wing Jewish campaign to prevent mixing among Jews and Arabs."

The fliers were probably designed and distributed by Lehava, a fanatical anti-miscegenation group whose sister organization, Hemla, receives state funding to "rescue" Jewish women from romantic relationships with Arab men.

Leanne Gale, an anti-racist activist living in Jerusalem, recently reported on her blog that Lehava has been holding nightly gatherings in West Jerusalem's Zion Square and littering all of Jerusalem with stickers and fliers in Arabic that state, among other things, "Do not even think about a Jewish woman."

Other catchphrases adorned on Lehava T-shirts and stickers include "Jews love Jews" and "The women of Israel for the nation of Israel," according to Gale.

Fascist Mobs from Haifa to Tel Aviv

Violent mobs of anti-Arab fascists aren't isolated to Jerusalem.

Last week in Haifa, the Arab deputy mayor and his son were brutally beaten by a mob of Jewish supremacists chanting "death to Arabs" and "death to leftists" in response to a rally against the Gaza onslaught. Police did nothing to stop the assault.

Similar fascist demonstrators have surfaced in supposedly liberal Tel Aviv as well, verbally and physically attacking Palestinians and leftists protesting the war on Gaza.

Israeli blogger Elizabeth Tsurkov, who has been regularly attending and live-tweeting the racist attacks against anti-war demonstrators in recent weeks, heard a new racist chant mocking the more than two hundred children slaughtered by Israel's merciless bombing campaign in Gaza: "Tomorrow there's no school in Gaza, they don't have any children left." [*Eds.: The original article includes a screen capture of the chant.*]

Incitement from the Top

While calls for extermination have been rampant both in the streets of Israel and on Israeli social media for months, the "death to Arabs" sentiment is not isolated to vigilantes.

Take for example Israeli lawmaker Ayelet Shaked, a rising star in the far-rightwing Jewish Home party, who recently called for genocide by slaughtering Palestinian mothers to prevent them from giving birth to "little snakes."

Fast forward several weeks, and the United Nations is reporting an alarming rise in miscarriages and premature births in Gaza, where newborn infants are dying due to electricity blackouts that shut down their incubators.

Another Israeli public official inciting violence is Dov Lior, Chief Rabbi of the illegal West Bank settlement Kiryat Arba, who issued a religious edict declaring that it is permissible under Jewish religious law for the Israeli army to "punish the enemy population with whatever measures it deems proper," even if that means "exterminat[ing] the enemy."

Since then, portions of Gaza have been reduced to rubble in apocalypse-like scenes that look indistinguishable from the flattened cities of Syria.

With all eyes glued to Israel's destruction of the besieged Gaza Strip, little attention is being paid to the heightened levels of racism in Israeli society as demands for "death to Arabs" echo across the country with devastating consequences for Palestinians from Shuja'iya to Qalandiya to Jerusalem to Haifa.

The Electronic Intifada, July 27, 2014, http://bit.ly/1rNlpdO

As Israel Bombs Gaza,
It Kills Palestinians in the West Bank Too
Maureen Clare Murphy

Two Palestinians were unlawfully killed by Israeli soldiers at during a protest in the occupied West Bank village of Beit Ommar on July 25, an investigation by Human Rights Watch has found.

A third man killed at the protest "also appeared to have been killed unlawfully," the rights group states.

Human Rights Watch's status of the third man seems to be different because witnesses say he was throwing stones when he was fired on, though the New York-based group concedes "he was 35 meters away when he was shot and could not have posed an imminent deadly threat to Israeli forces."

This qualifier is dubious at best, given that Palestinians defending themselves with rocks hardly justifies lethal use of force by the invading and occupying Israeli military.

Human Rights Watch again uses cautious language when it states: "Some offenses by Israeli forces in the West Bank as part of their occupation could be subject to prosecution as war crimes."

This tip-toeing language is jarring when compared to the violent reality in the Israeli-occupied West Bank this summer.

Collective Punishment

During the month of June, Israel launched its largest military assault on the occupied West Bank in more than a decade, invading refugee camps, villages and cities across the territory. Six Palestinians were killed by Israeli forces during the military operation, all of them civilians. Hundreds were arrested, universities were raided and soldiers stole Palestinian property worth $3.5 million.

The pretext for the assault was the disappearance of three Israeli youths who were hitchhiking between settlement colonies in the West Bank on June 12. It was later revealed that the Israeli police, intelligence officials and the prime minister knew within hours of the kidnapping that the teens had been killed.

Following the campaign of collective punishment and the discovery of the teens' bodies on June 30, the Israeli government, starting with Prime Minister Benjamin Netanyahu at the top, fanned calls for retribution and revenge for the teens' deaths.

On July 2, sixteen-year-old Muhammad Abu Khudair was abducted near his home in the Shufat neighborhood of eastern occupied Jerusalem. His body was found hours later in a Jerusalem forest; a preliminary autopsy indicated that the boy was burned alive.

Three Jewish Israelis confessed to the brutal crime and reenacted it for investigators.

Meanwhile, mobs of Israeli youths continue to roam the streets of Jerusalem looking for Palestinians to attack. Two twenty-year-old Palestinians were recently beaten unconscious by youths wielding iron bars and baseball bats.

Palestinians in Jerusalem live in fear of being the next victims in an increasingly violent environment.

Killings Across the West Bank

Elsewhere in the occupied West Bank, at least seventeen Palestinians have been killed by Israeli forces and civilians since the beginning of the military's slaughter in the Gaza Strip on July 7.

Palestinian rights group Al-Haq has investigated and summarized the circumstances of each killing, painting a picture of an army bound by no restraints on the use of force.

The victims include:

- Mahmud Hatem Shawamra (27) of the al-Ram neighborhood of Jerusalem, shot dead by three live bullets after throwing a Molotov cocktail at an army jeep on July 21.
- Mahmud Saleh Hamamra (33) of Husan village near Bethlehem, shot in front of his wife and small child outside his shop by invading soldiers who had situated themselves next to his store on July 21.
- Muhammad Qasem Hamamra (20), also of Husan village, shot in the head by a live bullet from a distance of one meter, after clashes erupted following Mahmud Hamamra's funeral on July 22. An eyewitness told Al-Haq that Israeli soldiers fired bullets into the air for no apparent reason during the funeral procession. During confrontations with protesters following the funeral, no gunshots were heard. "As Muhammad was killed by live fire, it is assumed that the Israeli soldiers used a sound suppresser when firing the bullets," Al-Haq states.
- Muhammad Zeyad Araj (17), shot with live fire in the head, thigh and arm during the #48KMarch mass protest which set out from al-Amari refugee camp in Ramallah and marched on

to Qalandiya checkpoint on July 24. "That night, there were more than 142 people wounded with live bullets," states Al-Haq.

- Eid Rabbah Fudeilat (28), shot by eleven live bullets in the legs, shoulder and in the back in al-Arroub refugee camp in Hebron on July 25. In the time preceding Eid's shooting, his brothers had called him to ask him to intervene with soldiers who were firing on demonstrators; the fire was preventing them from reaching their home. Eid approached the soldiers and got into an argument with one. "A soldier pushed Eid, who responded by punching the soldier several times. He then ran away to where his brothers and nephew were. When Eid had run about 10 meters away from the soldiers, they opened fire in his direction. Eid fell forward onto his face approximately 40 meters away from his house," according to Al-Haq.

- Basem Sati Abul Rub (19), shot in the center of his chest with a live bullet while throwing stones at soldiers near al-Jalameh checkpoint north of Jenin city on July 25. Al-Haq states: "According to Al-Haq's field researcher, there were 27 people at the hospital that had been injured at the protest. Most were injured in the lower parts of the body and had been hit with live bullets. According to witnesses, the sound of live bullets during the protest was rare. However, due to the number of injuries caused by live bullets, it is suspected that the Israeli forces used a sound suppressor when firing bullets."

- Khaled Azmi Odeh (20), shot with a live bullet by a motorist driving an Israeli-plated civilian car near Huwwara checkpoint outside the city of Nablus on July 25.

- Tayyeb Saleh Shihada (21) was wearing a mask and throwing stones at Israeli soldiers at Huwwara checkpoint on July 25 when he was shot with a live bullet in the head.

- Nasri Taqatqa (14) was shot with a live bullet in the chest during confrontations between Palestinian youths and Israeli soldiers in Beit Fajjar village near Bethlehem on July 26.

- Alaa Jihad Ezghir (21) was declared dead on July 29 after he was injured on July 23 when he was shot in the stomach while throwing stones at soldiers at the entrance of Ithna village near Hebron.

- Oday Nafez Jabr (19), shot and left to bleed for ten minutes on August 1 after attempting to run away from an Israeli soldier who had pointed a gun in his direction during a Gaza

solidarity protest in Saffa village near Ramallah. "The demonstrators had yelled at the soldiers that someone was injured
but the Israeli forces continued firing tear gas and live bullets," according to Al-Haq.

- Tamer Faraj Samur (22) was shot with a live bullet in the stomach after a peaceful demonstration escalated into confrontations near Gishori factories outside of Tulkarem on August 2.

The three men from Beit Ommar whose killings were investigated by
Human Rights Watch are also among the seventeen victims. After Friday
prayers on July 25, hundreds of Beit Ommar residents marched to an
Israeli military watchtower at the village's entrance to protest the assault
on Gaza. Israeli forces pushed them back by firing teargas and rubber-
coated steel bullets.

Hashem Abu Maria was attempting to cross the street after the protest had dispersed when he was shot, witnesses told Human Rights Watch.
Abu Maria, married with three children, was a human rights defender
working with Defence for Children International Palestine.

Sultan al-Zaaqiq and Abd al-Hamid Breigheth were shot by Israeli
forces about twenty minutes later, according to Human Rights Watch's investigation. Al-Zaaqiq was reportedly throwing stones at the soldiers from
approximately 35 meters away when he was shot by live fire; Breigheth was
shot in the leg and abdomen when he ran to assist al-Zaaqiq.

"In the course of half an hour in Beit Ommar, Israeli forces left three
families without a father," stated Sarah Leah Whitson, Human Rights
Watch's Middle East and North Africa director.

Evading Justice

Human Rights Watch notes that the Israeli military has a poor record
of bringing soldiers to justice for the use of live ammunition against
Palestinian protesters who pose no threat. At least 46 Palestinians were
killed in such circumstances from 2005 to early 2013, according to the
Israeli human rights group B'Tselem, as mentioned in the Human Rights
Watch report.

"Since September 2000, Israeli forces have killed more than 3,000
Palestinians who did not participate in hostilities in the West Bank and
Gaza, according to B'Tselem's data," Human Rights Watch adds.

"But the military justice system has convicted only six Israeli soldiers
for unlawfully killing Palestinians, with seven-and-a-half months as the
longest jail sentence, according to Yesh Din, another rights group."

Even when the willful killing of Palestinian children is caught on video, Israeli soldiers are able to evade justice. Security cameras owned by a local shopkeeper recorded the shootings of Palestinian boys Nadim Nuwara, 17, and Muhammad Abu al-Thahir, 16, at a demonstration near the Ofer military prison in the occupied West Bank village of Beitunia on May 15.

The footage released by Defence for Children International Palestine showed the boys walking slowly in a calm scene when they were shot, posing no threat. The Israeli military ordered the owner of the security cameras who captured the footage to dismantle his cameras and confiscated recording devices owned by other shopkeepers in the area.

The Electronic Intifada, August 6, 2014, http://bit.ly/1v8SIMl

The Constant Presence of Death in the Lives of Palestinian Children
Nadera Shalhoub-Kevorkian

At a gathering at the Abu Khudair house in Jerusalem after Muhammad Abu Khudair was burned alive, a mother narrated a conversation she had with her daughter:

> Lama: "If I die, will they burn me like they burned Muhammad Abu Khudair? What will happen to us? If I die like all the children in Gaza, how could I play or sing?"
>
> Her mother: "But, you must keep on singing, nothing in this house is like you playing and singing. You are my little girl."
>
> Lama: "No Mama, I won't sing, because my voice is afraid to be happy, I can't even draw, because my hands do not want to draw the sun and the flowers. Mama, did they bomb the sun? Can they?"
>
> Her mother: "No, no one can take the sun or the moon from us."
>
> Lama: "I know, the children are dying in Gaza, and all the colors died in Gaza.... Mama, if I die, will you ever have a home? ...Don't worry, I will draw you a home, and children, they will sing and bring all the colors back to us...but, why do they fear children and kill them Mama?"

Lama's voice is one of the many young voices that present serious questions, not only to her parents in Palestine, but to the world, about our failed morality. Scenes of displaced, injured and dead Palestinian children affected by the attack on Gaza are shared in the international media, yet their ordeals and suffering in the continuous attack on their society remain insufficiently examined and under-discussed. These are things that have occurred every day since the 1948 Nakba ("catastrophe") in which their parents and grandparents were forced off their lands and into exile in places like Gaza and the West Bank, Jordan, Lebanon, Syria and elsewhere. Today, the innocent children in Gaza pose questions that seem innocent, like those quoted above, but these inquiries must actually be interpreted as political questions that should challenge world leaders.

Numerous publicized reports and documents published by international and local Israeli and Palestinian human rights and children's rights organizations teach us that politically motivated abuses against children are additional tools of Israel's colonial dispossession of the Palestinian people. According to an update from Defence for Children International-Palestine, citing statistics from the United Nations, over 400 Palestinian children have been killed since Israel began its military offensive on Gaza. Over one three-day period of the conflict, a Palestinian child was murdered every hour, according to a report by the United Nations Office for the Coordination of Humanitarian Affairs (OCHA).

Lama's questions, like many other Palestinian children's questions, are matters of urgent concern in Palestine today. How can one reply to Lama's question: "Why do they fear us Mama?" How can we explain that the conquest, the fear, and the continued dispossession of Palestinian life and land are the result of the settlers' ideology and of the policies that have resulted from their own constant feeling of being threatened simply by the presence of the indigenous Palestinian population?

Childhood experience in Palestine is characterized by constant anxiety, the loss of homes, fear for safety even in children's bedrooms, and worry over the meaningful objects they possess, such as toys. Palestinian children's experiences are preconditioned by the larger socio-political context, that of living under the structural machinery of settler colonialism.

Israel is aware of the power that each Palestinian child possesses by virtue of their mere existence, and therefore, they need to keep children under constant threat of disappearing. For the colonizer, life passes not only through the capacity to kill the "other" in order to live, but also through the capacity to control the death of the "other" even after they are dead. Within the Israeli context, Palestinian children are viewed as security threats and therefore thrust outside the accepted and established human rights framework—one that sanctions the high civilian death toll that has been experienced in Gaza over the last few weeks—and into a discriminatory structure of power. In hearing Lama's questions, one realizes how ever-present death is in her life.

Evicting the natives and targeting them at such an early stage in life serves to further the demonization, criminalization, incarceration, and killing of Palestinians, denying them the right to resist their own oppression. How else can we explain the statement by Nobel Peace Prize Laureate Elie Wiesel condemning the use of children as "human shields" in an ad so offensive in its comparison of Palestinian culture to "barbarism" that the *London Times* refused to run it? In this instance, even a Nobel Laureate and Holocaust survivor joined the settler colonial machinery of violence and uprooting to legitimate the regime and its expansion through continuous colonial appropriation.

During the attack on Gaza, the dead bodies of children became contested politicized objects. While some reporters and anonymous Twitter commenters highlighted the horror of the murder of innocent young civilians, the Israeli state sanctioned these actions, transforming children into approved tools to further the eliminatory regime of dispossession in Palestine. Yet despite the death and the hardship these particular Palestinians face, Lama's narrative and the story of other children like her show that Palestinian children have already created their own kind of resistance. Even in the rubble, subjected to vicious shelling and an uncertain atmosphere of uprooting and loss, children find a way to draw their home, whether or not they actually still have a physical house, and speak out against the Israeli oppression by refusing to stop singing. These children find new ways to live, to play, to bring back the sun and create life.

Children's dead and living bodies bear great significance and meaning, revealing the relationship between living, death and living death within Israel's colonial regime of death. The all-too-ample evidence of Israel's arbitrary power over the lives and bodies of Palestinian children and their abused and stolen childhoods challenges the securitized claim that "Israel has the right to self-defense." The senseless deaths of Palestinian children, and the hardships and discrimination they experience in life even when they are permitted to live, show that the claim that Israel is simply "protecting itself" is racialized, immoral, and unethical. The very claim collectively disciplines and punishes the entire Palestinian community and inscribes deadly terror on children's lives and deaths. Palestinian children's space—their homes, their playgrounds, their schools and even their drawings—become specific spaces of power where Israeli forces can exhibit their control.

In the context of a past history and continuing infliction of displacement, dispossession and violence, the attacks against Palestinians in Gaza should be considered an act of genocide. Israel targets and kills Palestinian children, not just because they pose a threat as "future terrorists," but because they are the builders of the next generation. This feeds into the larger eliminatory strategy and therefore requires immediate political intervention—not just in the form of a ceasefire or truce, but by ensuring that these crimes against humanity and, in particular, against the Palestinian population, can no longer be committed by Israel or supported by the international community.

Mondoweiss, August 22, 2014, http://bit.ly/1q6E56R

Palestinian Civil Society in Israel Demands Urgent Action on Gaza
The Arab Association for Human Rights

We, the undersigned organizations, express extreme concern at the rapidly deteriorating situation within the Gaza Strip and urge the international community to take immediate action to halt the deadly aggression being waged against Palestinian civilians in Gaza. We also urge the UN to initiate a fact-finding mission to investigate alleged war crimes and crimes against humanity.

Since Israel launched its military offensive dubbed "Operation Protective Edge" on July 8, 2014, over 175 Palestinians have been killed in Gaza, 80 percent of whom the UN humanitarian office (OCHA) reports to be civilians, and over 1,280 have been injured.

The victims have included entire families, women, children and the elderly. Israel has launched over 1,500 air strikes in the past seven days, deliberately targeting homes and other civilian facilities and has fired dozens of shells at Palestinian communities located near the border between the Gaza Strip and Israel and along the coast; approximately 900 houses have so far been destroyed.

In a further escalation of events, Israel has bombed a number of houses without any prior warning whilst civilians have been inside, dramatically raising the death toll and the number of casualties. Targets bombed by the military where civilians have been present have included a café, an emergency medical building, a facility for the disabled, three ambulances and a clearly marked media car. Schools, mosques, an ambulance center, nongovernmental organization offices, fishing boats and a hospital have also been struck.

We, the undersigned organizations, strongly condemn Israel's unlawful targeting of civilians, civilian areas, and civilian property, which is illegal under international law and amounts to collective punishment.

We call for an immediate end to hostilities against the Palestinian civilian population of Gaza, and for thorough, independent and genuine investigations to be launched into all violations of international human rights and humanitarian law. We emphasize that this indiscriminate violence persists amidst the context of the continued closure of Gaza, which restricts freedom of movement and access to basic humanitarian resources. Furthermore, the Netanyahu government has failed to present any viable or equitable solution to the situation.

The Palestinian Arab community in Israel has mobilized in protest at the increase in violence towards Palestinians by both the state and individuals, within the West Bank, Gaza and Israel. As well as the recent assault on Gaza, this has also included the brutal murder of 16-year-old Muhammad Abu Khudair, nationalistic attacks on Arab individuals by Jewish extremists on ethnic grounds, and demonstrations which have met with no police interference calling for "death to Arabs."

However, Palestinian protesters have been met with excessive use of force by security services and mass arrests and detention, including that of minors. Almost 400 Palestinians have so far been arrested in the continuing protests, and scores of people remain in detention.

We strongly oppose the culture of racism and incitement towards Palestinians in Israel and the occupied Palestinian territories, which has been exacerbated by recent statements by the Israeli political leadership who have sought to inflame ethnic tensions and mobilize support for violence towards Palestinians.

Provocative statements made by Prime Minister Benjamin Netanyahu and other leading politicians have sought to inflame tensions and promote an "us versus them" mentality. Furthermore, social media campaigns which have included contributions from Israeli military personnel, have widely promoted indiscriminate violence towards Palestinians.

We call on the international community to monitor closely the recent escalation of attacks on civilians in the Gaza Strip, and to raise concerns of alleged war crimes and crimes against humanity based on the Rome Statute.

We also urge the UN to initiate a fact-finding mission to investigate these events. We further encourage you to keep in contact with the undersigned Palestinian civil society organizations in Israel for information, assistance, materials or advice on the above.

[Signed]
Arab Association for Human Rights
Adalah
Mada al-Carmel—Arab Center for Applied Social Research
Women Against Violence
Kayan Feminist Organization
Mossawa Center—The Advocacy Center for Arab Citizens in Israel
Association for Arab Youth—Baladna
I'lam Media Center for Arab Palestinians in Israel
The Galilee Society—The Arab National Society for
Health Research & Services
Arab Cultural Association
Hirakuna—Forum for Social Solidarity, Voluntarism
    and Young Leadership
AlZahraa Organization for the Advancement of Women
AlQaws for Sexual & Gender Diversity in Palestinian Society

The Arab Association for Human Rights website, July 14, 2014,
http://bit.ly/1lhtspt

Israel Arrests Activist for Hosting Skype Chat with Resistance Icon Leila Khaled
Patrick O. Strickland

Israel, reputedly the only democracy in the Middle East, is willing to arrest its own citizens for communicating on the Internet.

That was the experience of Samih Jabarin when he recently arranged for Leila Khaled, the Palestinian resistance icon, to address the al-Warsheh cultural center in Haifa—a city in present-day Israel—via Skype.

As soon as Khaled had completed her opening remarks and invited questions from members of the audience, three Israeli secret police officers entered the center unnoticed and quietly escorted Jabarin, its owner, from the building. He was released after interrogation later that night (July 11), but al-Warsheh was closed by police two days later.

Shabak, Israel's secret service (also known as the Shin Bet), had previously tried to pressure Jabarin into canceling the event.

"The Shabak called me that Friday morning [July 11] and demanded that I come to their Haifa offices for interrogation," he told the *Electronic Intifada*. "I refused because it was dangerous—how could I be sure it wasn't some extremist from Im Tirtzu or another right-wing Zionist group?

"'Okay,' they told me, 'we will have to arrest you tonight,' which they did."

Intimidation

Interrogators "tried to intimidate me by mentioning my one-and-a-half-year-old daughter's name several times, just to show me that they know about my family," he said. He was also warned that he would be punished for arranging a conversation with Khaled, who one of his interrogators called "that scum terrorist."

Although Jabarin has not been charged with any offense, he was threatened with prosecution on numerous different charges. In the past, Palestinian citizens of Israel who visit Arab countries or make contact with Palestinians abroad have faced a draconian charge known as "contact with a foreign agent."

Jabarin said, "We decided to talk to Leila Khaled as a way to break the division" between Palestinians in Israel and those elsewhere. "Her history is important to us and it's part of our history. We aren't content watching videos of her talks online or reading her writing. She's part of our people and we will speak to her if we want," he added.

Best known for her roles in two plane hijackings in 1969 and 1970, Khaled is a member of the Popular Front for the Liberation of Palestine. During her Skype presentation, she told dozens of local Palestinian activists that "you are living under Israeli occupation as well," like Palestinians in the West Bank and Gaza.

"Racist Laws"

"You live under the Zionist occupation and its racist laws every day," Khaled added.

Comprising approximately twenty percent of Israel's total population, an estimated 1.7 million Palestinians carry Israeli citizenship and reside in cities, towns and villages across present-day Israel. According to

Adalah, a group which advocates for the rights of Palestinians in Israel, they face more than fifty discriminatory laws that stifle their political expression and severely limit their access to state resources, including land.

Jabarin is one of a few hundred Palestinian citizens of Israel to have been arrested since early July. The wave of arrests was the largest targeting the community since October 2000, when Israeli police shot dead thirteen Palestinians in Israel during demonstrations that month.

This month's protests were held in response to the brutal murder of sixteen-year-old Muhammad Abu Khudair in occupied East Jerusalem. Approximately thirty children were among 128 Palestinian citizens of Israel to be imprisoned for longer than a week.

The arrests have continued as Palestinians in Israel stage almost daily protests against Israel's ongoing military assault against the Gaza Strip. On July 18, Israeli police officers attacked a Haifa demonstration in solidarity with Gaza, arresting at least 29 people.

Jabarin said that the closure of al-Warsheh is part of a broader crackdown on Palestinian citizens of Israel. "The government is scared of anything that stresses Palestinian identity inside" present-day Israel, he said.

Two well-known figures—the British member of parliament George Galloway and the Pakistani-British author Tariq Ali—had been scheduled to speak via Skype to an audience at al-Warsheh on July 18. But their talk has been postponed due to the closure.

"Physical Separation"

Ilan Pappe, an Israeli historian and author of more than a dozen books, said that Israel's strategy of dividing Palestinians politically, culturally and geographically dates back to the state's establishment in the wake of the ethnic cleansing of Palestine in 1948. An estimated 156,000 Palestinians became citizens of the newly declared state, many of them internally displaced from their property.

Since Israel occupied the West Bank, including East Jerusalem, and the Gaza Strip during the 1967 War, Palestinians in Israel "are ruled differently than those in the West Bank, than those in Jerusalem and those Gaza," Pappe told the *Electronic Intifada*.

Israel today "uses a policy of ghettoizing Gaza in order not to have to deal with a Palestinian community inside Israel and the West Bank together with a Palestinian community inside Gaza," he said. "There is a real physical separation."

Yet Pappe argues that widespread access the Internet and the rise of social media have proven a challenge to Israel's policy of fragmenting Palestinians. "The Internet has in many ways undone the geographical and political borders that separate Palestinians," he said.

Samih Jabarin vows to keep on organizing educational and cultural activities, availing of the opportunities afforded by modern technology. "We will open al-Warsheh again even if it means going to prison," Jabarin said. "We know our comrades will continue it. Even if we have to reopen in a different place or under a different name, we are going to keep doing this as long as there's an occupation."

The Electronic Intifada, July 26, 2014, http://bit.ly/1bM7XTR

Arrabeh's Eid in Gaza's Shadow
Hatim Kanaaneh

The video referring to Rafeef Ziadeh's recitation of her poem, "We Teach Life, Sir" is available at http://bit.ly/1nL4lzc.

Shortly after an unremarkable Galilee summer's sunset the "Allahu akbar" cries of half a dozen muezzins confirmed the sighting of the new moon and the commencement of celebrating Eid Al-Fitr ending the fasting month of Ramadan. I perked my ears attentively straining to pick up any special announcement marking the 22nd day of the ongoing massacre in Gaza. I didn't have to wait for long. When the young man leading the prayers in the mosque closest to the household hosting our breaking of the fast reached the end of the fifth and last formal prayer of the day he waxed inventive in asking for God's favors on our collective behalf. He started with the usual requests of forgiveness of our transgressions and shortcomings in performing our duties toward Him and for mercy on all of us and on all of our parents "for tending me in childhood." He then progressed to ask for God's punishment of our oppressors specifying two by name, the Zionist enemies and their Egyptian collaborators. He needn't be more specific. He must have assumed, correctly I should add, that all his flock knew what sins General Sisi had committed: banning the Moslem Brotherhood and sealing the Rafah border with Gaza. Still, the young imam saved the harshest of curses for the Zionist infidels: "Please God, dry up all of their women's uteruses!" he pleaded. I broke out laughing at the anatomically

specific ill wish. My communist host objected. He didn't quite agree to
the cursing of General Sisi but he would like to allow the drying up of the
Zionist uteruses.

"How is that different from 'Death to Arabs?'" he wanted to know.

"But the young man is an employee of the Ministry of Religious
Affairs," I argued. "He collects a monthly salary from the Zionists' trea-
sury, for God's sake!"

"So do members of the police force protecting fascist gangs attacking
Arab civilians for no reason except their race. It is Israel's version of democracy and balancing of the forces of evil."

❧

The cacophony of loudspeakers exploding one after the other from seven
different directions ended the dawn's bucolic peace waking me from a fit-
ful sleep. For a moment I almost understood the attitude of a colleague, a
Polish immigrant physician as I recall, who informed me in my Ministry
of Health days that she had encouraged officials of the Jewish city of Upper
Nazareth where she lived to run their collected sewage refuse openly down
the valley to the Arab village of Reineh because of the latter's disturbing
of the Jewish resident's sleep with their dawn time calls for prayer. My two
children at markedly divergent time zones around the globe were text-
messaging us throughout the night. Israel's deadly incursion into Gaza
and the ensuing air travel confusion in and out of Israel's own airport had
thrown a monkey wrench in our family's scheduled annual summer get-
together in Arrabeh. But my outrage quickly dissipated.

I decided to take advantage of the morning's cool weather to pick
some dew-washed figs and cactus fruits from my orchard. But first I had
to check the Internet: The death toll had exceeded the magic figure of
one thousand. Somehow, that wasn't as sad as my friend Ramzy Baroud's
pained status on Facebook decrying his family's fate. They were on the run
again, refugees from their shelter as refugees in Gaza. I wanted to advise
patience, forgiveness and magnanimity. Then I wondered how magnani-
mous I would have felt if I and my family had been driven out of our home
in Arrabeh to have a Polish or a Brooklyn immigrant family live on my
father's land, collect its olive crop and enjoy its figs and cactus fruit, and
then to have them now send their son in an American jet fighter bomber
to chase me further away from 'their homeland?'

As I picked my daily supply of summer fruit, the sudden silence
that descended on the empty village streets after the end of the morning
prayers in the mosques had a deadly quality. There were no children with
toy guns out celebrating on the streets, no flares and no fireworks. I went

for a stroll on the newly paved desolate street in our neighborhood risking the likelihood of a village rumor about my sanity. The neighbors had lined the entire sidewalk with a thousand candles in memory of Gaza's martyred children. The butcher sat on a chair and twirled his moustache. A lone skinned lamb hung by the door. Usually on a day like this he would have two or three of his children helping him out. He offered me the standard sip of black coffee:

"No family gatherings to celebrate the Eid today," he said more in apology than in anger or dismay. "Men coming back from the mosque look like a snake had spewed its poison in their faces."

I agreed. I realized that none of the neighborhood's children, including the dozens of grandnephews, had come dressed in their new clothes to knock at our door for the usual Eid treats and monitary gifts.

The first and only holiday visit I made on this sad Eid morning was to an octogenarian former patient of mine. He is terminally ill and needed help with an injection. After the usual but subdued formalities of exchanging Eid greetings I asked for his opinion regarding what was going on in Gaza.

"I am dying anyway. I wish someone would take me back there and give me my old English rifle," he responded, tears rolling down his leathery cheeks.

As a young man he had enlisted in the British Mandate border police and served in Gaza training young recruits in marksmanship. Desperation, at the personal and national level, fueled his wish for martyrdom, he explained.

As I returned I checked my email again. Someone had posted a moving poem in English beautifully recited by its animated Palestinian author, Rafeef Ziadeh, declaring her body "a TVed massacre." I couldn't hold my tears of sadness and pride in her concluding line: "We Palestinians wake up every morning to teach the rest of the world life, Sir!"

I watched the video. Twice. The second time I cried more. Then I saw it a third time, then a fourth, a dozen times. And I cried more each time than the last. At first, as I sat with a pair of tweezers to pick the few tiny thorns from my hands I pondered the adaptive defense mechanism of the cactus. Then I switched to more distressing thoughts: Even if they hadn't taken over my home and though they had left me some of my land, those foreigners had stolen my culture, I realized. They had claimed my cactus fruit, the Sabra, as the simile for their children who were born on my land.

Let us join hands, Ramzy! We all are in this together.

A Doctor in Galilee [blog], July 30, 2014, http://bit.ly/1GldJS1

Why Palestinian Citizens of Israel Are No Longer Safe

Ron Gerlitz

About a month ago I wrote here that the fabric of relations between Palestinian and Jewish citizens of Israel was worsening, and that this was not just an escalation but a frightening new era of Jewish-Arab relations in Israel. In retrospect, we were just at the start of the deterioration and had no idea what was in store for us.

Since the onset of the war in Gaza, the scale of the assaults on Palestinian citizens of Israel has increased dramatically, as have their intensity. Today we find ourselves in a new and appalling chapter of relations between Arab and Jewish citizens of Israel. The lengthy article in last Friday's *Haaretz* weekend magazine (Hebrew) was a comprehensive and systematic account of the campaign of physical and verbal violence directed at Palestinian citizens, the campaign by the right wing to have Arab workers fired and the profound fear that prevails among them.

Why Is This Happening?

There are many explanations. I would like to offer another, less widely-known explanation for this outbreak of racism. In recent years we have witnessed two contradictory trends in relations between Jews and Arabs in Israel: groups that push toward equality and those that work in the opposite direction; groups that work for the creation of a shared society and better relations between Jews and Arabs, and those that work for segregation and worse relations. I have argued in the past that both trends are present in the public, media, bureaucracy and the political arena.

Despite systematic discrimination by the government and profound racism (which of course is nothing new), Arab society in Israel, in cooperation with various factors in Jewish society, including in several government ministries, has been able to effect a significant improvement in its socioeconomic status, to somewhat reduce the inequality, to challenge state institutions and to enjoy substantial and authentic political representation in the Knesset. As Arab society has become stronger in recent years, we have witnessed the first signs of its integration into the centers of power, economy and society in Israel.

We are not talking about some submissive and fawning integration. A generation that did not grow up under military rule has had the courage to bolster its Palestinian national identity, and its bond with the Palestinians in the occupied Palestinian territories and the Arab world. Many prominent representatives of Palestinian communities in Israel, especially in the Knesset and civil society organizations, sharply assert the rights of Israel's Palestinian citizens, both as individuals and as a collective. They demand equal individual and national rights, and an abolition of the special privileges enjoyed exclusively by Jews.

What's most relevant in understanding the events of the past month is that Arabs' increasing strength is not hidden and has not developed only in concealed regions far removed from Jewish life. On the contrary; it has been open and visible and has created further points of daily contact between Jews and Arabs, in diverse arenas.

Note the new Israeli reality of recent years. When I was a child in the 1970s, the only Arabs encountered by Jews who didn't visit Arab localities were manual laborers. The situation is totally different today. A Jewish citizen who goes into a drugstore will almost always encounter an Arab pharmacist; should he/she need to go to the emergency room they may very well be treated by an Arab doctor. Ten years ago, I managed an algorithm development team in a startup company. At the time, an Arab employee of a high-tech firm was an exceptional phenomenon. Today we are in the midst of a revolution in which many Arab citizens hold jobs in the high-tech sector, the jewel in the crown of the Israeli economy. As Odeh Bisharat wrote in *Haaretz*, "Whoever, back in the 1950s, destined the Arabs to serve as hewers of wood and drawers of water, is now getting them as leaders in high-tech."

Jewish university students have Arab lecturers, and sometimes even an Arab department chair or college president. There has already been an Arab minister and an Arab director-general of a government ministry. Perhaps symbolic of the new reality is that not only the common man is exposed to the rising power of Israel's Palestinian citizens. The chief judge of the panel that convicted the former president of the state, Moshe Katsav, and sentenced him to a long prison term was a Palestinian citizen.

A Counter-Reaction

As long as Israel's Palestinian citizens were powerless and excluded, they did not threaten Jewish hegemony. Today, though, Jews are no longer always at the top of every ladder in Israel. This situation undermines the world order of the radical nationalist right, which is terrified by the loss of absolute Jewish hegemony, and is stirred to take countervailing action. In contrast to those on the left and among Palestinian citizens themselves

who belittle the economic and social integration of Arabs, it may well be
that it is those on the right who have accurately identified the latent potential and consequently see it as a real threat. They are gearing up for a battle
to halt what they view as a dangerous process and endeavoring to reduce
the rights enjoyed by Arabs.

This a reaction to the fact that Arabs are a much greater presence in
our lives than those who would preserve the Jewish hegemony can stomach. The lawsuits against the state, the stronger representation in higher
education and the job market, the presence of Arabic language in public
spaces (quite simply because there are now more Arabs in shopping malls,
universities, workplaces, and so on)—all of these factors amplify the sense
of threat, and spawn a desire to make Arab citizens disappear, or at least to
push them as far down the socio-economic ladder as possible.

In recent years this reaction has been fueled by right-wing politicians.
Avigdor Lieberman, supported by his cohorts in other parties in the current and past government coalitions, has sponsored an unprecedented
wave of legislation targeting Palestinian citizens. With the support of the
prime minister, the electoral threshold was raised—a brutal step with the
potential to banish Palestinian citizens from the political system. And
then, of course, there is the ultimate solution: Lieberman's proposal to
strip hundreds of thousands of Israeli-Arabs of their citizenship by transferring their home districts to a future Palestinian state. Right-wing leaders have sent clear and unmistakable message to Palestinian citizens of
Israel: If you don't shut up you'll come to a bitter end.

But despite the great damage caused by these politicians' assault on
Arab citizens, Arab society has not surrendered to the evil wind blowing
from the Knesset. They have been joined by Jewish advocates for equality
who continue to employ effective strategies to promote equality and full
integration into Israeli society and the economy.

So What Has Happened in These Last Two Months?

The new phenomenon of the last two months is that the populist, nationalist, radical right has been stirred to action. What its representatives in the
Knesset proved unable to achieve, it is now trying to do on its own. Under
the cover of its political leaders' silence or with their encouragement, it has
unleashed an assault on Palestinian citizens in order to force them to bow
their heads, quite literally. It is simply unable to countenance Palestinian
citizens' increased power, especially not their greater visibility in public
spaces.

If Arabs were employed only in cleaning and agriculture, and submissively shuttled home to their towns and villages every evening, Knesset members on the right—now joined by the rightists in street—would not make an effort to expel them from the labor force, political arena and public spaces. Note that most of the incidents of the past months occurred in places that are shared by Jews and Arabs—the mixed towns and the integrated commercial centers and employment zones in Jewish towns. Hair-raising nightly marches that feature cries of "Death to the Arabs!" took place in Upper Nazareth. Arabs were attacked not in their own localities, but on shared public buses and in the streets of mixed cities.

Of course, the strongest reaction was to the strongest trend: Arabs integration into the labor market. For the first time, we are witnessing an unprecedented and systematic attempt by members of the radical right to encourage the dismissal of Arab workers. The more senior an Arab's position, the stronger the demand that he be axed. I doubt that the right-wing hooligan gangs would be motivated to invest significant energy in demanding the firing of an Arab cleaner. But when it comes to encouraging the dismissal of Arab physicians and pharmacists, professionals in the service of local authorities, shift managers, salespersons and service providers, right-wing gangs will work with all their might.

They simply find it impossible to endure a Palestinian citizen in a senior position, one who inverts the only power relation that the racists want to see between Jews and Arabs: Jews at the top and Palestinians at the bottom. For a racist, it is unacceptable that a Jew might have to depend on an Arab (as a physician, pharmacist or service rep). Here another factor enters and explains why this outburst happened precisely now. That same racist was willing to 'endure' the situation as long as the Israeli-Arab kept his mouth shut and did not speak out against the government or against that most sacred institution of all: the army.

And now we have to speak the truth, even if it is unpleasant for so many Jewish readers. In all of the violent conflicts of Israel against the Palestinians or the Arab world, a majority of the country's Arab citizens, quite naturally, identified with the members of their own Palestinian people and not with IDF soldiers who were fighting against it. Although some Jews knew or intuited this, on some level or another Palestinian citizens' identification with those the IDF was firing at was not an overt presence in shared spaces. Arab workers were careful not to express their views when in the company of Jewish colleagues.

What Changed the Rules?

But today, in July 2014, the appalling number of Palestinians killed in Gaza (more than 1,800, including 400 children) and the existence of social networks have totally altered the picture. For the first time since the deep penetration of social networks, the IDF is killing many Palestinians and the pictures of dead children show up on Palestinian citizens' smartphone screens almost immediately. It is inhuman to expect them to support those who are conducting the killing of their people.

Social media has also made it possible that almost every citizen's opinion of the war, be they Jewish or Palestinian, is exposed for all to see. What Palestinian citizens could once keep within the confines of family and friends has now become known to all. The situation was not symmetrical in the past. Arabs always knew what their Jewish colleagues or customers were thinking, because they heard them saying that it was necessary "to crush the intifada," "to route out Hezbollah," "to flatten Gaza so as to teach Hamas a lesson," etc. They listened, and for the most part kept silent. But during the last month of violence in Gaza, when the atrocities crowded their Facebook pages, along with denunciations of the IDF and its soldiers, they "liked" posts and perhaps even shared them and added a few words of their own. What used to be hidden is now exposed to the world. What the right wing views as Palestinian citizens' disloyalty to the state, the IDF and its soldiers – and, worst of all, hope for the enemy's victory – is now public knowledge.

And it is precisely here that the anti-Arab radical right lost it once and for all. The Kahanist hooligans in the street may have remained mute and helpless in the face of growing Arab economic power; but it cannot abide both their increased strength and their hostility to the IDF and the national narrative; all the more so when soldiers are dying. So it goes on the war path. It calls on the government to go all the way and kill Palestinians in Gaza in order to crush Hamas, while it goes to war itself against the Palestinians at home—the Palestinian citizens on our streets.

The same social network that made it possible to learn that one's Palestinian colleague or pharmacist was not praying for an IDF victory (to put it mildly) enabled the radical right to organize quickly and effectively against Palestinian citizens and to demand their banishment from shared public space. In the best case, the demand targets those who were found not to be falling in line with the national narrative; very soon, however, as happens with every racist movement, the pressure grows into a call to throw them all out (such as the demand that the Rami Levy supermarket chain fire all its Arab workers).

The Knesset and the Street Join Forces for a Common Cause

It is important for me to note that I am focusing on Jewish society's responsibility for the deterioration in relations; however Arab society, too, bears some responsibility, although much less. Rocks were thrown at Jewish vehicles in the last month in a few places. It is important to mention that some of the statements against the state by Arab political leaders, although legitimate, critically impair the ability of those of us in a Jewish society who wish to promote equality and to recruit support for our efforts.

In a democratic state, one is permitted to argue that the basic ideology of the majority group—Zionism, in the Israeli case—is colonialist and racist. Personally, I object to these arguments, but they are certainly permissible. But it is not reasonable to expect that such charges will spur the Jewish majority to join the struggle for the rights of the Arab minority. The dismissals of Arab workers during the war were unacceptable; but Arab employees' displays of joy at the death of soldiers, when they work with Jewish colleagues, is atrocious behavior, and certainly does not promote shared life between Jews and Arabs.

The summer of 2014 has demonstrated that the internal national conflict between Jewish and Palestinian citizens of Israel, which to date has been a non-violent conflict overshadowed by the occupation and the violent Israeli-Palestinian national conflict, has not been able to maintain the status quo, as bad as it was. Israel launched a military operation and the IDF bombed and shelled Palestinian citizens' own people—in many cases their relatives—and ignored their familial, emotional, personal and national bonds with the Palestinians of Gaza. The fabric of relations within Israel proved unable to absorb this, and almost collapsed.

Thus three different factors came together this summer: the increased strength of Arab society and the greater presence of Palestinian citizens in shared spaces; the war in Gaza, which left the Arab and Jewish sectors totally polarized; and social media networks, which made all this visible.

And precisely at a time when these three factors were operating, the dangerous link-up between the radical right in the government and the even more radical right on the streets emerged and provided momentum for the escalation. In the past month right-wing politicians, including government ministers, have made unprecedented statements against Palestinian citizens of Israel. They have exploited their identification with the Palestinians under bombardment in Gaza to incite against them and to depict them as supporters of terrorism. The High Arab Follow-Up Committee's decision to call for a general strike in solidarity with the victims in Gaza was a legitimate and non-violent response. But in response the Israeli foreign minister proposed a boycott of Arab businesses that took part in the strike to cause a severe blow to the Arab economy.

And here Lieberman and the Kahanist hooligans on the streets complement one another. While some burst into a neighborhood pharmacy and demand that the Arab woman behind the counter be fired; Lieberman operates on a much grander scale and seeks to expel Arabs from the centers of economic power, or at least to return them to their "natural" role as manual laborers. For years politicians have been trying to expel several Arab parliamentarians from the Knesset; this year, for the first time, they registered a partial success. Meanwhile, their supporters in the street are trying to have the voters who elected these MKs fired from their jobs. The process is not preplanned and coordinated, but it is a combined operation in which both elements—the Kahanists in the street and some politicians of the radical right—are inciting and working in tandem, in different arenas, in pursuit of the same goal. This collaboration makes the situation even worse by making it much harder to curb. The assault against Palestinian citizens is taking place in the Knesset, in the government, on social networks, in the media and, of course, also on the streets.

Where Do We Go from Here?

About a month ago I wrote: "I have not given up hope. I still believe that there can be a better future for the relationship between Arab and Jewish citizens of Israel." I added that history has proven that "ethnic conflicts far more intransigent and violent than this one have been resolved, while conflicts that seemed mild have declined into bloodshed. All options are on the table."

Today the situation is much more ominous. The optimistic scenario is that this period will be seen in retrospect as the extreme right wing's rearguard action, its last hoorah before the failure of its campaign against the establishment of a shared and equal society in Israel. Much more horrendous scenarios are possible, of course: the expulsion of the Arab minority from the Israeli economy and society, or harsher discrimination. It is even possible that the Arab sector may revolt against absorbing the blows and resort to a fierce counter-reaction, which, heaven forbid, would trigger a violent battle between Jews and Arabs in Israel. I do not think this scenario is likely, but it can no longer be dismissed as wholly unthinkable.

The harsh news for all of us who are working to create a shared and equal society is that our past successes—the strengthening of Arab society and the creation of shared spaces—are precisely what encouraged the counter-reaction. Even if, by means of a supreme effort, we are able to prevent deterioration in the coming years and manage to promote Arab participation in the centers of social and economic power in Israel, the radical right will mobilize all its forces to try to halt this process. We will have to continue to build a shared society, but now we will also have to prepare for the reaction. In addition to our investment in building, we will also have to invest in preparing our response to this counterattack.

If we, Jewish and Arab citizens who seek a better and shared future in this land, choose life, we have no alternative: We must prepare ourselves for a difficult and protracted struggle. It is in our hands. No one else will do it for us.

+972 *Magazine*, August 13, 2014, http://bit.ly/1adLoqw

4
Gaza Burns, the World Responds: Analysis and Commentary

Israel's 2014 assault on Gaza elicited a global outpouring of support and solidarity unseen in recent years. People of conscience watched the terror unfold live on their screens and timelines and did what they knew how. In newspapers and on e-zines and in blogs, they deconstructed Israeli actions and doublespeak. Some addressed the "what" of Israel's assault and drew broad parallels to Israeli actions of the past, while providing much needed context, rightly noting that it should be seen as part of a systemic Israeli attempt to pound the Palestinians into subordination. Other analysts attempted to explain the "why": why exterminate 2000 some men, women and children, given Israel's already shaky moral standing in the world? Was Israeli policy borne of desperation, the need to maintain a settler-colonial project begun with violence, or was it simply a sick attempt to keep Gaza in check? Gaza has been in survival mode for over a decade, we are reminded, reeling from a crippling siege aimed at bringing them to their knees with the complicity of neighboring Egypt and American allies in the region, such as Saudi Arabia. Most important, we are reminded that this assault had nothing to do with rockets or tunnels, and everything to do with maintaining control over Palestinian land and lives.

Something Rotten in the Operations Manual
Sharif S. Elmusa

An antecedent of the mass killing and destruction of entire neighborhoods in Gaza—all the while blaming the Palestinians themselves for the carnage and picturing them darkly as terrorists sacrificing their own children—can be found in S. Yizhar's 1949 novella, *Khirbet Khizeh*. Its author, who served as an intelligence officer in the Israeli army at the time, describes the siege and expulsion of the population of this fictional Palestinian village by Jewish irregulars in 1948. The novel's narrator opens with the "operational orders" and instructs the officers in charge that "no violent outbursts or orderly misconduct...would be permitted." He then explains that this order would be unintelligible without first inspecting the "information" section, which warns the recruits against "infiltrators," "terrorist cells," and other such menacing presences.

The "hope" was that they would expel the inhabitants and blow up or burn their dwellings—as happened in real life in about 500 Palestinian villages—"with such courtesy and restraint, born of true culture, and this would be a sign of a wind of change, of decent upbringing, and, perhaps, even of...the great Jewish soul." The implicit question posed here is, Can a malevolent purpose be accomplished with courtesy and refined manners?

Khirbet Khizeh has proven prophetic in foretelling the enduring Israeli "habits" of dealing with the Palestinians. The operation orders have become Israel's overarching Operations Manual of policy and *hasbara*, or propaganda, of the practices of violence and dispossession, of racial exclusion, of rendering the Palestinians a state of exception. The Operations Manual gives guidelines for evading moral responsibility for the malevolence, and projecting it instead on the Palestinians themselves. And it is not the Operations Manual of Israel alone; it also circulates in various editions in the corridors of power and mainstream media in the United States, and to a lesser extent in Europe.

The Operations Manual has been well at work during the Gaza invasion and its aftermath. It instructed officers of the armored brigades, captains of navy ships, and air force pilots to bomb-destroy-target civilians and their houses, schools, shelters, hospitals, and mosques. The "information" section warned of Hamas terrorists and infiltrators, lethal rockets, and sinister tunnels. The "hope," as in the cleansing of Khirbet Khizeh, must no doubt have been that what is now branded "the most moral army

The destruction of the Shija'ia district of Gaza City, July 20. A Ma'an News article
on the devastation described the area as "a moonscape strewn with bodies."
At least 68 people were killed in that district on that day.[1]
Photo by Mohammed Asad

in the world" would leave behind the colossal wreckage of the houses of
the poor, thousands of civilians dead and wounded, among them hundreds of children, lasting traumas in every mind and heart—the hope was
that it would do it once more, with refinement and restraint, the hallmarks
of Israeli culture.

Nonetheless, the magnitude of the carnage in this 2014 round, broadcast in real time around the globe, and with the United Nations Goldstone
Report already charging Israel with war crimes in its 2009 campaign
against Gaza, would be too taxing even for Israel—which has been in-
oculated against accountability by more than 40 U.S. vetoes in the UN

Security Council. After all, the Palestinians were getting pummelled, but they were resisting valiantly with means that lag a hundred years behind Israeli materiel, and those who could reach Israel through the tunnels targeted only the military; there were alternative venues to spread the news of the war; and the United States itself was still trying to wiggle out of its debacles in Afghanistan and Iraq. People in numerous capitals and cities around the globe, including many Jews, took to the streets and to their computer screens to protest, and to demand a halt to the bloody expedition. And several South American governments—whose countries had for long been fertile grounds for U.S. economic and military exploits—recalled their ambassadors from Tel Aviv.

To fend off the gathering tide, the Israeli propaganda machine and its affiliates flipped the pages of the information section of the Operations Manual to the "alibi" clauses. The alibi consisted of simple declarative statements, like missiles and advertisement: "Hamas uses children as human shields," or "Israel has the right to defend itself." More acrobatic formulations came from the Israeli military: "Some bomb shelters shelter people, some shelter bombs," the former shelters are clearly Israel's whereas the second are the tunnels dug by Hamas. Elie Wiesel summoned the sacred for the task. Taking advantage of his status as Noble Peace Laureate and of his parents dying in the Holocaust, he published a full page advertisement on August 4, 2014, in the *New York Times* with a horror movie photograph of a Hamas sniper, and the heading "Jews rejected child sacrifice 3,500 years ago. Now it is Hamas's turn."

It does not take an analytic philosopher to uncover the logic that underlies such assertions: Palestinians do not care about their children and do not value their lives, or that they are so naïve as to believe that the Israelis won't harm their civilians if their fighters hid behind them, or are cowards who are afraid to engage the Israeli military. Repeated by the White House and by the leaders of Britain, France, and Germany and disseminated by dedicated Israeli media militias in cyberspace, these sound bites became devastatingly effective gospel, a frame with which to perceive and interpret what happens on the ground.

When it comes to Palestinians valuing their own or their children's lives, it is first of all axiomatic that both human and nonhuman animals instinctively value the life of their offspring, except perhaps in pathological cases or moments. The instinct is linked to the genetic drive toward self-perpetuation. Humans also acquire it from culture in the broad sense. As children, we watch grown-ups grieve at the loss of their close relations and friends.

I learned the value of the brother from my mother repeating year after year the story of how her brother Ahmad was killed defending our village al-Abbasiyya, near Lod, in 1948. He was one of the rag-tag volunteers, and was shot after his rifle malfunctioned. The village had been occupied by Jewish forces on May 5, 1948, then retaken by the resistance and held for a month, only to be captured for good. My mother and other relatives remembered him as an exceptionally warm and generous man. He was not religious, and did not perform the ritual daily prayers and did not fast in Ramadan. When family members went to retrieve his body from the police station, he smelled so sweet, my mother stressed, because he was a martyr. And at the moment of the story, she wept every time she told it, as if the words and the tears became his reincarnation.

Cultures make sense of death each in its own way. In the United States the official mourning rituals refer to the soldiers killed on the battlefield as "fallen," and remind us that they "did not die in vain." Instead of the imaginary heavenly rewards for the martyrs, the fallen are "laid to rest," if their families so wish, in Arlington National Cemetery. For my mother, and in the Palestinian vernacular in general, "martyr" connoted that the person died nobly, for a purpose, defending Palestine. It did not suggest that people sought to be martyrs, only that they would be considered so if they died in the line of duty.

Israel's allegation that for Palestinians life is cheap has a long pedigree among Western imperialists. The words of General Westmoreland, quoted in the 1974 film *Hearts and Minds* about the Vietnam War, always stuck in my mind. Generalizing, the general opined, "The Oriental doesn't put the same high price on life as does a Westerner. We value life and human dignity. They don't care about life and human dignity." Westmoreland is a worthy heir to the notorious lights of European empires, the likes of the Britons Cecil Rhodes (South Africa) and Lord Cromer (Egypt), and the French Field Marshal Bugeaud (Algeria). This history of dehumanizing the "Orientals" still lurks below the surface in Western culture, despite the anti-colonial struggles and the Civil Rights Movement in the United States that made it impolitic to voice such unalloyed prejudice publicly. The need for "Orientals," for barbarians, as a "kind of solution," persists. Today they are the Arabs and Muslims, and the Israeli information section of the Operations Manual feeds on and into the latent racism.

What is a human shield anyway, this alloy of the human and the technological? True, we are all cyborgs these days, with one prostheses or another; in the "human shield," however, the human is grafted onto the metal, which makes it a strange coinage that works only metaphorically; human flesh is poor armor. Deploying children as shields therefore assumes that the Palestinians believe that the Israeli army is indeed a moral army that would be ever so conscientious in its choice of targets, cognizant of the children's presence and their vulnerability, and fire its missiles and shells with utter refinement as to spare the children, and by extension the fighters.

In fact, more than 60 percent of Gazans are refugees from numerous Khirbet Khizehs. Since 1948, they have been through small and big "wars" waged by Israel, through two uprisings, and two previous major invasions in 2009 and 2012. The Palestinians know only too well the long history of abuse of children and adults by Israeli army and security, which has been documented by first-hand accounts, journalists, and reports by human rights organizations. Here is how Gideon Levy, writing in *Haaretz* on 24 August put it, "We must admit the truth: Palestinian children in Israel are considered like insects. This is a horrific statement, but there is no other way to describe the mood in Israel in the summer of 2014." Did this piece of information come to the attention of Elie Wiesel before he wrote his eloquent advertisement, or did he prefer the bliss of denial?

Still, why did the Israeli army finish off the life of more than 2,100 people, more than three quarters of them civilians, when its casualties were less than 80? Why kill 500 children and introduce to the vocabulary of war the "unknown child," unknown because the members of his or her family were all gone? Why wipe out entire families? Why did one soldier publicize on the Internet that he knocked out 13 children? Why did the navy willfully gun down kids playing on the seashore? Why did the air force destroy the sole electric power station and the greenhouses that farmers used to plant flowers for export to Europe? Why did Israel feel it must inflict this immeasurable misery on Gaza? Why did it do all this despite steady protests and appeals from so many people and from the United Nations and the Red Cross and numerous world bodies? What did the Operations Manual tell the officers to do? What types of "information" did it supply them with? Who are the barbarians?

French Field Marshall Bugeaud once exhorted his men in Algeria during the 1838 expedition to Constantine, "you must show yourselves strong everywhere at once to influence the Arab mind. It is useless to try treating [sic] with the Arabs, unless we are victorious; they would laugh in our faces. The Arabs respect and honour no one but the victorious enemy."

Are these the kinds of thought that went on the mind of Israeli leaders like Moshe Yaalon, the defense minister during the Gaza campaign? In the light of Algeria's history, it is hard to resist laughing in the face of the dead general. And, it would be truly sweet to "laugh our joy" in the faces of a few Israeli generals--for a moment.

In the denouement of *Khirbet Khizeh*, the narrator sums up:

> "We came, we shot, we burned; we blew up, expelled, drove out, and sent into exile." What for? So, as to have "Our very own Khirbet Khizeh," with problems of absorption, a cooperative, a school, political parties, and maybe even a synagogue.

In other words, multiplied a few thousand times, the terrible deeds were committed so that Israel could be established. Could it be that the maintenance of a project begun with violence and disregard for the natives of the land requires like means?

Institutionalised Disregard for Palestinian Life
Mouin Rabbani

One either rejects the killing of non-combatants on principle or takes a more tribal approach to such matters. In the case of Israel and the Palestinians, the global outpouring of grief and condemnation over the killing of three Israeli youths in the occupied West Bank is the moral equivalent of Rolf Harris denouncing Jimmy Savile.

Over the past 14 years, Israel has killed Palestinian children at a rate of more than two a week. There seems to be no Israeli child in harm's way that Barack Obama will not compare to his own daughters, but their Palestinian counterparts are brushed aside with mantras about Israel's right to self-defense. The institutionalized disregard for Palestinian life in the West helps explain not only why Palestinians resort to violence, but also Israel's latest assault on the Gaza Strip.

The current round of escalation is generally dated from the moment three Israeli youths went missing on June 12. Two Palestinian boys were shot dead in Ramallah on May 15, but that—like any number of incidents in the intervening month when Israel exercised its right to colonize and dispossess—is considered insignificant.

Binyamin Netanyahu immediately blamed Hamas for the three Israeli teenagers' disappearance. The White House almost as quickly confirmed Hamas's guilt, which has since been treated as established fact by the media. Yet the culprits remain at large and their institutional affiliation unclear. For its part Hamas, which like other Palestinian organizations never hesitates to claim responsibility for its actions and is prone to exaggerate its activities, has this time denied involvement.

What we do know is that a distress call made by one of the Israeli youths on June 12 included the sound of gunfire, which led the Israeli security establishment to conclude they had been killed. Netanyahu suppressed the information, and used the pretext of a hostage rescue operation to launch an organized military rampage throughout the West Bank. His demagoguery, even by his standards, plumbed new depths of vulgarity. To blame the subsequent burning alive of a 16-year-old Palestinian on a few errant Israeli fanatics (after attempts to portray it as the murder of a gay boy by his own family had failed) is to pretend such barbarism exists independently of the colonial and political contexts that produce it.

If it was known that there were no hostages to be rescued, what was Israel trying to achieve? A key objective was reversing the tentative steps taken by Fatah and Hamas towards national reconciliation. Israel prefers a divided Palestinian polity partially ruled by militant Islamists to a unified one led by the pliant Mahmoud Abbas, who remains committed to negotiations and publicly proclaims security collaboration with Israel to be "sacred." Concerned that a reconciliation at a time of growing Palestinian unrest could lead to another uprising, Israel sought to pre-empt it. In doing so, it rearrested a number of Palestinians released in the 2011 prisoner exchange with Hamas. In the context of the latest collapse of American-sponsored diplomacy, and a growing global consensus that Israel, its appetite for Palestinian land and failure to fulfil its commitments regarding prisoner releases were to blame, Netanyahu leaped at the chance to change the narrative from colonialism and its consequences to terrorism.

Israel's actions have produced major unrest in the West Bank and among the Palestinian community in Israel, as well as a new confrontation with the Gaza Strip. It's all still a long way from a third intifada, however, primarily because the organizational infrastructure that produced and sustained the first two is degraded, no longer exists, or is controlled by leaders who prefer the perks and privileges of office to struggle and sacrifice.

Hamas, too, would rather avoid a large-scale confrontation with Israel. But, in contrast to recent months, it is now meeting violence with violence rather than enforcing calm. It has less to lose than at any point since it took power in Gaza in 2007. Its main objectives in the recent reconciliation agreement—payment of salaries for its civil servants, reopening the Rafah crossing on the Egyptian border, reconstruction in the Gaza Strip, and enhanced regional and international legitimacy—have failed to materialize. The new Palestinian Authority government, though formed with Hamas's endorsement, acts as if Gaza does not exist, and continues to co-operate with Israel against Hamas in the West Bank. The unremitting hostility of Egypt's new rulers to Gaza and Hamas means there isn't a credible mediator, unless Turkey or Qatar steps into the breach.

Taken together, these developments could make for a confrontation between Israel and Hamas longer and more intense than either party bargained for.

London Review of Books (blog), July 9, 2014, http://bit.ly/VK2hl8

International Solidarity with Palestine Grows with Israeli Assault
Beth Staton

Three weeks ago, a coalition of organizations published a heartfelt and urgent call for action. "We Palestinians trapped inside the bloodied and besieged Gaza Strip call on conscientious people all over the world to act," it said. "Protest and intensify the boycotts, divestments and sanctions against Israel until it ends this murderous attack on our people and is held to account."

The plea, from groups including trade unions, women's organizations and press representatives, was issued four days into the Gaza onslaught. It wondered, grimly, if the number killed in the new fighting would reach the 1,400 of Operation Cast Lead in 2008. Now, the death toll stands at 1,865. It isn't likely to remain at that figure for long: the carnage, which razed entire neighborhoods, left Gaza with wounds from which it's difficult to imagine a recovery.

Such a bleak picture suggests the coalition's call went unanswered. And indeed, throughout the weeks of Operation Protective Edge, governments have maintained trade and military aid to Israel, with rarely more than muted censure of civilian casualties.

But the call was recognized in other ways. For the past month, the streets from Sana'a to Washington, D.C., have been flooded with demonstrators demanding an end to the carnage and the Israeli occupation. Online appeals for peace have attracted tens of thousands of signatures. The campaign to boycott Israel—already steadily gaining momentum—has achieved major victories and adopted new tactics.

"Even with public opinion in the United States, recent polls have shown that the only demographic really supporting Israel is old, white Republican men," said Josh Ruebner, Policy Director at the U.S. Campaign to End the Occupation. "There's a clear indication that support for Israel is becoming a more marginalized phenomenon."

In the July air of Kensington, a wealthy West London neighborhood overlooking Hyde Park, that sense of a changing mood was tangible. In a last-minute demonstration just a few days after the operation began, several thousand people, with a powerful showing from the city's many Muslim communities, brought "Free Palestine" chants to the Israeli Embassy, shutting down traffic through the upscale High Street and commandeering a red London bus. Two weeks later, 45,000 demonstrators marched from Downing Street to the embassy. London was just one among scores of global cities whose streets were transformed by fury following atrocities in Gaza.

"Now, international activists are showing their own government how the Palestinians are suffering," said Mousa Abu Maria, an activist with the Palestine Solidarity Project in the West Bank. "They show that people stand with us, behind Gaza, and that we are not alone."

But although mass protests are photogenic, do they achieve anything? It's a pertinent question for activists in Palestine and around the world, and one that's closely tied to deeper conundrums about the role that international campaigning should play in the Palestinian struggle. Mezna Qato and Kareem Rabie argue that global activism can mistakenly focus exclusively on discrete issues—violations of international law or bloody onslaughts such as the current attack on Gaza or the occupation itself—missing the broader fight for Palestinians self-determination. That's amplified by superficial, fleeting involvement, a tendency to victimize and speaking on Palestinians' behalf. By disregarding Palestinian action and "believing the road to liberation lies elsewhere," Palestinian activist Maryam Barghouti explains, "you are not expressing solidarity; you are expressing a white savior mentality." If the Palestinian struggle is against colonialism and for national liberation, when Western activists attempt to shape its terms they just perpetuate the imperialism behind the oppression they are trying to fight.

For the last month, Friends of Al-Aqsa has set its sights firmly on Gaza, in the context of ending the siege and occupation, and from a broader human rights perspective. "I think the central and most important factor for us is to work for justice and for equality, to say that all people should be treated equally before the law," said Ismail Patel, chair of the organization. "Most people can agree on that. We must have some kind of standard globally, and highlight the hypocrisy that takes place by allowing some people to get away with certain things and not others."

Friends of Al-Aqsa has drawn on diverse tactics in its work. It's been instrumental in organizing marches across the United Kingdom—and is increasing its efforts to lobby political representatives and recruit volunteers—with a hope to turn those involved into active advocates who can rally further support in their communities and media. And central to its strategy is the Boycott, Divestment and Sanctions, or BDS, campaign called for by Palestinian civil society in 2005 and perhaps the most clearly defined framework that international Palestine activists are organizing around.

Reiterated in the July 12 call to action and pushed hard since Operation Protective Edge, BDS has been building momentum for years. "We work very closely with the Palestinian BDS National Committee responding to Palestinian civil society campaigns," said Josh Ruebner. "This is what Palestinians are asking for from civil society." And it's crucial that the BDS strategy doesn't just look to end the occupation, but calls on equality for Palestinian citizens of Israel and the right of return. "We agree that any just peace needs to address these components as well," he explained.

The U.S. Campaign to End the Occupation expects an uptick in BDS campus actions in the fall, spurred, in part, by horror at the terrible images and rising death toll in Gaza. And recent weeks have witnessed dramatic developments in the campaign both large and small: Brazil, Chile, Ecuador, El Salvador and Peru recalled their ambassadors from Israel; George Soros, Tesco and John Lewis all distanced themselves from settlement profits; and on August 4, the U.K. National Union of Students voted to endorse BDS.

"We have the beginning of a global movement now," said Patel. "Our role is to translate that into political action. Now opinion needs to shift to such a level that the narrative changes, that people support the Palestinians."

In the West Bank, Abu Maria knows international action has to be carefully coordinated with the goals and strategy of Palestinian civil society. "To make real work with Palestinians directly is very important," he said. "Now the Palestinians have seen how internationals are important to our community, and since 2003 the international solidarity is growing day by day."

"I am from Beit Ommar," he continued. "The Friday before they killed three people, and shot maybe 60 people. Why? Just because they demonstrated for people in Gaza. That's why international solidarity is so important now."

Waging Nonviolence, August 8, 2014, http://bit.ly/1FaQxaB

Gaza Traces
Kim Jensen

A shorter version of this essay will be published in Extraordinary Rendition: American Writers on Palestine *(New York: OR Books, Fall 2015) edited by Ru Freeman.*

We have been asked where we stand, as writers and artists, in relation to the systematic human rights violations against the Palestinian people. In order to approach this question, I want to draw closer to this mesmerizing image of three children on a beach in the Gaza strip that was widely shared on social media during the Israeli assault this past summer. Studying the photograph and the story of its origins may shed light on what it means to bear witness to a human catastrophe.

During the military siege on Gaza in the summer of 2014, many international journalists were staying at Al-Deira Hotel, overlooking the Mediterranean. Reporters and cameramen often watched the children of fishermen playing on the beach in front of the hotel, and sometimes went down to play with them.

At 4 pm on July 16, a day of heavy bombardments, the Israeli navy targeted a ramshackle hut where fishermen stored their nets. No Palestinian resistance fighters were present, as numerous eyewitnesses testified, but a group of children was playing nearby. After the first explosion, the survivors ran for safety. A few seconds later, the Israelis let loose a second attack

The Bakr boys running on the beach, as filmed by a journalist for the
French television network TF1.
Screen capture by Trevor Hogan.

directly aiming at the fleeing children. Four of them—Ismael Muhammad Bakr, Zakaria Ahed Bakr, Ahed Atif Bakr, and Muhammad Ramiz Bakr—were killed. Journalists who witnessed and filmed the incident later reported that it was abundantly clear, even from a distance, that the running figures on the beach were unarmed children.

This haunting photograph was captured and tweeted by the Irish rugby player and Palestine solidarity activist Trevor Hogan. On the evening of the beach massacre, he was sitting in his living room in Dublin watching the news coverage, and happened to notice a fleeting image of running children. Rewinding and fast-forwarding—Trevor finally managed to isolate the frame. He snapped an iPhone picture and posted it online, creating one of the most indelible images from Israel's summer offensive.

I choose to reflect on this image and not the images of the aftermath: the children's bent, dismembered bodies in the sand. The disturbing pictures of their corpses—the unthinkable outcome of modern warfare—are revolting and obscene. To demand an extended gaze upon them is a different project, equally legitimate. It is important for people, especially those of us whose governments perpetrate such war crimes, to see and to know exactly what bombs, mortar shells, and missiles do to living bodies—and to confront our own complicity.

But I want to return to the spirit in which Trevor Hogan created this image. Overwhelmed by feelings of horror, disgust, and helplessness, he worked with a clear intention: to create something that would "allow people who don't wish to view a graphic image of war crimes to connect with the gravity of what had happened while highlighting the split second in time before their lives were taken." His objective was to move people to action.

How to read this photograph without context? At first glance and to the uninitiated, it might read simply as a blurry snapshot of some appealing children in the distance. Upon further study, we might think of it as a representation of childhood itself, wistful, hazy in detail—a frozen moment of transient, ephemeral innocence. Even if we knew of the tragic war surrounding the children, we might believe that this was the boys' last moments of play on the beach.

But this is not an image of joy; it's an image of terror. These children weren't playing; they were fleeing for their lives.

They have now become traces on our screens, traces left behind from the persistent carnage inflicted on the people of Palestine. Like raindrops streaking a windowpane, the image lifts this moment into permanence. It resurrects other stories. In a cascade of associations, it reawakens the memory of Huda Ghaliya who watched her family slaughtered before her eyes on a beach in Beit Lahia. It resuscitates twelve-year old Muhammad al-Durra dying in his father's arms during the Second Intifada, and the powerful requiem that Mahmoud Darwish wrote for him: "Muhammad/ is a poor angel, trapped at close range/by a cold-blooded hunter/in the eye of a camera that captures each movement/of a child becoming one with his shadow."

For me the photograph also conjures the sad, luminous spirit that inhabits the writings of American poet and novelist Fanny Howe who has spoken of her work as an attempt to "describe a preserved radiance—and to show that there is an invisible "elseness" to everything." She writes: "You go on because of it, but it's the thing you can't quite see."

This image from Gaza, something of the magic and sorrow in it, provides a visual corollary of that preserved radiance and that "elseness" that Howe describes. The enigmatic combination of beauty and grief. The glow of the yellow sand, a kind of halo for the fleeing children.

The fact that we have this image at all is a matter of chance and craft. It was chance that Western journalists were on hand to film to the casual, deliberate slaughter of innocent Palestinian civilians that has been ongoing for over sixty years. It was also chance that this committed activist happened to be watching the news and realized he had seen something important.

Chance is at play in the symbolic elements of the composition. The children's clothing—the green, red, and white shirts when combined with the looming shadow on the foreground form the colors of the Palestinian flag—lifting this fleeting moment to the level of mythos and national iconography. Fate is already printed here, maktoob, written, as if martyrdom was already stamped on this moment.

The children's faces are darkened, anonymous—like most of the nameless victims of war and violence. Their facelessness makes them all the more universal. In their impersonal presence they become emblematic of all children—we recognize that these could be any children, could be our children, your children, our neighbor's children.

They hover in shadow in that tenuous space just before they become bodies. The photograph neither memorializes them as the boys that they were with their individual personalities and traits nor does it reduce them to inanimate flesh.

These are some of the elements of chance, but craft is also at work.

Trevor intentionally captured the perfectly matching strides of the children, apprehended midflight like sea birds, the joy of innocence, the tenuous connection to the earth at that instant. The graininess of the photograph is part of its quiet splendor. The children's vertical figures are the only rupture in a study of horizontal lines. They disrupt and animate the composition. Bewildering, fragmented, and anachronistic—the forms come to us as if through a filter of sadness.

"Beauty," Fanny Howe says, "is the presence of something else wanting to be born. It's like a figure that we are rushing for, both to touch and to save. It flies ahead—and we rush after it. We reach for it." This eternally frozen moment embodies that beauty we seek and rush toward. It has the quality of a prayer or a sacred text in that it has the potent ability to reach the deepest recesses of human trauma.

This low-quality, third-hand image that I now call "Gaza Traces" is, in its way, a work of art. It has elements of fiction—the artifice of the frozen moment, which is an impossible, imaginary figment. The artifice manages to save these children, protecting them for eternity from inevitable violence.

Despite the preserved nature of the image, we do see fate arriving. The children are already silhouettes, thin limbed, almost disappearing. The composition already suggests their vulnerability. The shadow before them and the indifference of the ocean behind them seem to want to swallow them.

Once we read "Gaza Traces" this way, and we make the decision to face the gravity of the situation, we are also faced with an inevitable question: Do we have the right to extract a private meaning from the unthinkable grief of others?

As a poet and writer, I find Herbert Marcuse's defense of the revolutionary nature of art helpful in answering this question. Marcuse argues that by virtue of its aesthetic transformation, authentic art estranges the viewer from oppressive social conditions, and indicts the established reality. "Art," he says, "alienates individuals from their functional existence and performance in society—it is committed to an emancipation of sensibility, imagination and reason…" Authentic art does not exploit pain, it helps us to see and feel our way through it and past it.

A critic may argue that this moment of aesthetic transformation cannot help these children in a besieged place that has become nothing more and nothing less than the first concentration camp of the twenty-first century. This is correct. It does not.

But it does help those who are still living to come to greater awareness of the despotism that is around us and in us. As the veils of false consciousness are torn asunder, like bodies rendered, the true nature of social reality is exposed and we have no ethical choice but to strengthen our resolve to be more committed, more receptive, more compassionate, and more engaged.

Despair is chronic; no one can say that this is the world they would have chosen. But art does puncture holes in this pervasive despair and renders things visible that were previously invisible. Art shows us where to look and what to see. We need to see these children. Before and after.

We cannot turn away from the Palestinian people and their need to be free from violence, dispossession, and cultural erasure.

It is nearly impossible to know what our 'responsibilities' are as artists when we face this kind of ongoing human catastrophe. I would say there is no special responsibility that artists have above and beyond the responsibility that all humans have. The thing that distinguishes artists is that we have made it a regular and formal practice to observe, think, frame, reframe, to try to create work that will do justice to our moment. These activities put us in proximity to ethical questions as a matter of course.

But let's be reminded that the fishermen's children were filmed almost by accident and preserved in the public sphere by a young activist who does not identify himself as an artist, but who took the time to see and to act. This shows us the potential of each of us has—to activate our senses and to take a stand on matters of universal concern. There is nothing elite, nor sanctified, nor otherworldly about making art.

Nothing we can do will bring back the children who were killed on the beach on July 16 2014, or the thousands who lost their lives last summer. Nothing will bring back the limbs of the limbless, or repair the skin of those who were permanently disfigured, or close the wounds of those who were left psychologically and emotionally scarred. The personal and collective loss is unfathomable.

The words we write here, the poems we share, the images we capture will not undo the pain and injustice, and we would be naive to think they do. Yet they may help us find solace in community and rediscover joy in a shared liberational vision. These works can give us the strength to keep going—to reach out in solidarity to a people in struggle.

Controversial, Illegal, and Documented: Israeli Military Strategies in Gaza
Sami Kishawi

As Israel rolls deeper into its military offensive against the Gaza Strip, its tactics against the territory's densely packed civilian population are becoming more and more clear. Over the last 17 days, the death toll has risen to at least 797 Palestinians, most of whom were civilians and nearly two hundred of whom were children. Despite near-global condemnation, Israel has not dialed down the brutality. The following is a list of ten documented Israeli military strategies that are responsible for the disturbingly high casualty count.

1. Israel is one of the best equipped militaries in the world and its weapons industry is responsible for many technological advancements in modern warfare. It should come as no surprise, then, that Israel has the capacity to strike its targets with extreme precision. In the past, Israel has assassinated Hamas members so precisely that others riding with them in their cars or walking alongside them have survived. This has not been the *modus operandi* for Israel's last three major offensives against the Gaza Strip, particularly this latest one. Even U.S. Secretary of State John Kerry commented on Israel's military strategy, sarcastically calling it one "hell of a pinpoint operation."

2. Israel contends that it warns Gaza residents of imminent air strikes and shelling campaigns and instructs them to flee. However, the crippling siege and total blockade that Israel has imposed on the territory means that Palestinians have no place to go. This allows Israel to kill two birds with one stone, as the saying goes. It can publicly claim that it works to minimize civilian casualties while at the same time killing Palestinians wantonly and with impunity.

3. One of Israel's methods of warning families in Gaza of an imminent strike is through a "knock on the roof," a missile that does not contain an explosive warhead. The missile is intended to hit the target and to underline the seriousness of the warning. However, the warning missile strikes its target at about the same forceful velocity as the explosive missile that comes next, collapsing walls and roofs over families attempting to flee. Many Palestinians have been killed by the warning missiles that were allegedly employed to save their lives, including a group of children who were feeding ducks on their roof, CNN reports. In another recorded instance, the explosive missile came only 58 seconds after the "knock," which is barely enough time for residents to clear the area.

4. Israel strikes buildings that are very clearly sheltering civilians. Palestinians who are able to heed the warnings and flee are not necessarily any safer. On Monday, July 21, Israel launched an air strike against an eight-story building in downtown Gaza City that Israeli military officials had previously urged Palestinians to seek refuge in. Over a dozen were killed. On Sunday, just one day earlier, an Israeli air strike took the lives of Hassan Al-Hallaq's mother, two children, and wife who happened to be nine months pregnant. Hassan had relocated his family from their apartment outside of Gaza City into the city center, distancing themselves from the border and Israel's buffer zone and expecting his family's chances of survival to jump. But an air strike was still ordered against his parents' home and much of the family was killed.

5. Israel frequently launches air strikes at around sunset when families are most likely to be together, indoors, and breaking their Ramadan fasts.

6. Israel contends that Hamas forcibly puts Palestinian civilians in the line of fire, specifically by keeping them in buildings from which Hamas fighters operate. Although this has never once been supported with conclusive evidence, the Israeli government touts it as the primary reason for the high civilian death toll. But Palestinians rarely have any place to flee, especially when more than a third of the Gaza Strip falls under a military buffer that Israel strikes regularly and without warning. United Nations shelters are at maximum capacity and Israel has no qualms about attacking these buildings either, which is what happened on Thursday, July 24, killing at least 16 and injuring more than 200 in a United Nations school in Beit Hanoun. Palestinians who refuse to leave their homes or surrounding areas do not automatically become legitimate targets. As Mohammed Suliman said under intense shelling in Gaza City, "I look forward to surviving. If I don't, remember that I wasn't Hamas or a militant, nor was I used as a human shield. I was at home."

7. Israel uses flechette shells, banned DIME weapons, and U.S.-manufactured M107 shells in the Gaza Strip. Flechette shells, typically fired from a tank, explode above their targets and release thousands of miniature metal darts that piercingly cover a wide range. DIME weapons, which produce small and compact explosions, are densely packed with tungsten powder which acts like shrapnel but dissolves in human tissue, making it very difficult for physicians and investigators to determine the cause of the injuries. M107 shells explode into nearly two thousand metal fragments that rain on the areas surrounding their immediate targets. Not only has Israel chosen against striking its targets with careful precision, it also employs the use of weapons that cause maximal damage to anyone within the blast radius.

8. Many of the homes that have been targeted belonged to former Hamas fighters who had retired and transitioned back into civilian life—upon encouragement from the international community, no less—as government security guards charged with maintaining order on the streets or guarding important government structures, such as passport offices and ministry buildings. Israel still considers these former fighters as legitimate targets and has repeatedly launched strikes against them and their families. The logic that former Hamas fighters are legitimate targets suggests that former Israeli soldiers could also be legitimate targets. The logic that members of a government security force are legitimate targets suggests that Israeli reservists could also be legitimate targets. Israel disagrees and

instead maintains a double standard that ultimately punishes the people of Gaza.

9. Israel has launched a rather bizarre public relations campaign to justify its offensive against Gaza. Social media accounts linked to the Israeli military frequently upload and circulate cartoons that allegedly explain Israel's motive for the assault. One of the more notable ones was published during the latter period of Israel's intense shelling of the Shuja'iya neighborhood in east Gaza City which killed an estimated 72 Palestinians within the first twenty-four hours. The cartoon, which depicts Hamas fighters placing weapons in tunnels underneath civilian homes, gave Israel the legitimacy it felt it needed to continue striking the neighborhood. At least 17 children were among the victims.

10. Israel frequently launches follow-up strikes against targets it just hit. Commonly referred to as "double tap" strikes, the general purpose of the tactic is to kill other fighters who return to the scene to retrieve the remains of their partners. But the use of this tactic has drawn ire from the international community especially because the victims tend to be rescue workers and other civilians who rush to the scene. In Israel's case, the "double tap" is much more discreet. The follow-up strikes typically hit locations in the close vicinity of the previous strike. On July 16, Israel fired a shell at a Gaza City beach where a group of boys had just been playing football. The boys ran away from the initial blast but a second shell struck them moments later. Witnesses to the tragic scene said that it seemed as though the Israeli military was chasing the boys with shells. Four children were killed and a fifth was critically wounded.

The United Nations Human Rights Council has launched an independent investigation into various allegations of war crimes committed by Israel in the occupied Gaza Strip. The Council agreed to investigate by a vote of 29 countries in favor, 17 abstaining, and one—the United States—voting against the measure.

Sixteen Minutes to Palestine (blog), July 24, 2014,
http://bit.ly/1CsxBFD

Why Gaza Fought Back
Ramzy Baroud

My old family house in the Nuseirat refugee camp in Gaza was recently rebuilt by its new owner, into a beautiful three-story building with large windows adorned by red frames. In Israel's most recent and deadliest war on Gaza, the house sustained significant damage. A large hole caused by Israeli missiles can be seen from afar, in a part of the house where our kitchen once stood.

It seems that the original target was not my house, however, but that of our kindly neighbor, who had spent his entire working-life toiling between manual jobs in Israel, and later in life as a janitor for UN-operated schools in Gaza. The man's whole lifesavings were invested in his house where several families lived. After "warning" rockets blew up part of his house, several missiles pulverized the rest.

My entire neighborhood was also destroyed. I saw photos of the wreckage-filled neighborhood by accident on Facebook. The clearance where we played football as little kids was filled with holes left by missiles and shrapnel. The shop where I used my allowance to buy candy was blown up. Even the graveyard where our dead were meant to "rest in peace" was anything but peaceful. Signs of war and destruction were everywhere.

My last visit there was about two years ago. I caught up with my neighbors on the latest politics and the news of who was dead and who was still alive underneath the shady wall of my old house. One complained about his latest ailments, telling me that his son Mahmoud had been killed as he had been a freedom fighter with a Palestinian resistance movement.

I couldn't fathom the idea that Mahmoud, the child I remembered as running around half-naked with a runny nose, had become a fierce fighter with an automatic rifle ready to take on the Israeli army. But that he was, and he was killed on duty.

Time changes everything. Time has changed Gaza. But the strip was never a passive place of people subsisting on hand-outs or a pervasive sense of victimhood. Being a freedom fighter preceded any rational thinking about life and the many choices it had to offer growing up in a refugee camp, and all the little kids of my generation wanted to join the fedayeen.

But options for Gazans are becoming much more limited than ever before, even for my generation.

Since Israel besieged Gaza with Egypt's help and coordination, life for Gazans has become largely about mere survival. The strip has been turned into a massive ground for an Israeli experiment concerned with population control. Gazans were not allowed to venture out, fish, or farm, and those who got even close to some arbitrary "buffer zone," determined by the Israeli army within Gaza's own borders, were shot and often killed.

With time the population of the strip knew that they were alone. The short stint that brought Mohammed Morsi to power in Egypt offered Gaza some hope and a respite, but it soon ended. The siege, after the overthrow of Morsi, became tighter than ever before.

The Palestinian leadership in Ramallah did very little to help Gaza. To ensure the demise of Hamas, Mahmoud Abbas' Palestinian Authority carried on with its "security coordination" with Israel, as Gaza suffered a Draconian siege. There was no question, that after all the failed attempts at breaking the siege and the growing isolation of Gaza, Gazans had to find their own way out of the blockade.

When Israel began its bombardment campaign of Gaza on July 6, and a day later with the official launch of the so-called Operation Protective Edge, followed by a ground invasion, it may have seemed that Gaza was ready to surrender.

Political analysts have been advising that Hamas has been at its weakest following the downturn of the Arab Spring, the loss of its Egyptian allies, and the dramatic shift of its fortunes in Syria and, naturally Iran. The "Hamas is ready to fold" theory was advanced by the logic surrounding the unity agreement between Hamas and Fatah; and unity was seen largely as a concession by Hamas to Abbas' Fatah movement, which continued to enjoy Western political backing and monetary support.

The killing of three Israeli settlers in the occupied West Bank in late June was the opportunity for Israeli Prime Minister Benjamin Netanyahu to test the misleading theory on Hamas' weakened position. He launched his war that eventually mounted into a genocide, hoping that Hamas and other resistance groups would be forced to disarm or be completely eradicated—as promised by various Israeli officials.

But it didn't. From the very first days of the war it became clear the resistance could not be defeated, at least not as easily as Netanyahu had expected. The more troops he invested in the war on Gaza, the more Israeli army casualties increased. Netanyahu's response was to increase the price of Palestinian resistance by inflicting as much harm on Palestinian civilians as possible: He killed over 1,900, wounded nearly 10,000, a vast majority of whom were civilians, and destroyed numerous schools, mosques, hospitals, and thousands of homes, thus sending hundreds of thousands of people on the run. But where does one run when there is nowhere to go?

Israel's usual cautious political discourse was crumbling before Gaza's steadfastness. Israeli officials and media began to openly call for genocide. Middle East commentator Jeremy Salt explained. "The more extreme of the extreme amongst the Zionists say out loud that the Palestinians have to be wiped out or at the very least driven into Sinai," he wrote, citing Moshe Feiglin, the deputy of the Israeli Knesset, who called for "full military conquest of the Gaza strip and the expulsion of its inhabitants. They would be held in tent encampments along the Sinai border while their final destination was decided. Those who continued to resist would be exterminated."

From Israeli commentator Yochanan Gordon, who flirted with genocide in "when genocide is permissible," to Ayelet Shaked, who advocated the killing of the mothers of those who resist and are killed by Israel. "They should follow their sons. Nothing would be more just. They should go as should the physical houses in which they raised the snakes. Otherwise more little snakes are raised," he wrote on Facebook.

References to genocide and extermination and other devastatingly violent language are no longer "claims" levied by Israeli critics, but a loud and daily self-indictment made by the Israelis themselves.

The Israelis are losing control of their decades-long *hasbara*, a propaganda scheme so carefully knitted and implemented, many the world over were fooled by it. Palestinians, those in Gaza in particular, were never blind to Israel's genocidal intentions. They assembled their resistance with the full knowledge that a fight for their very survival awaited.

Israel's so-called Protective Edge is the final proof of Israel's unabashed face, that of genocide. It carried it out, this time paying little attention to the fact that the whole world was watching. Trending Twitter hashtags which began with #GazaUnderAttack, then #GazaResists, quickly morphed to #GazaHolocaust. The latter was used by many that never thought they would dare make such comparisons.

Gaza managed to keep Israel at bay in a battle of historic proportions. Once its children are buried, it will once again rebuild its defenses for the next battle. For Palestinians in Gaza, this is not about mere resistance strategies, but their very survival.

Counterpunch, August 13, 2014, http://bit.ly/1OUuhK9

Blaming the Victims
Diana Buttu

Israel's crimes—whether the expulsion of Palestinians in 1948, the military occupation and colonization of Palestinian (and other) territory, or periodic massacres—are invariably accompanied by a media discourse designed to explain, justify, and obfuscate the facts. After more than sixty-six years, and despite abundant factual evidence and extensive academic scholarship giving them the lie, tired, old Israeli mantras that demonize Palestinians and deny their existence as a people continue to live on. The massive attack on the Gaza Strip in the summer of 2014 was no exception, with Israel now using both the media and its own discourse to legitimate the Dahiya doctrine—a policy deliberately targeting civilians and civilian infrastructure to induce such suffering among the population that it creates deterrence.

The Dahiya Doctrine

In the summer of 2006, during Israel's so-called Lebanon war, Israeli forces bombed Dahiya, a suburb south of Beirut, leveling much of it to the ground. At the time, Israel's chief of staff, Gen. Dan Halutz, bragged that the army's targeting of infrastructure would "turn back the clock in Lebanon twenty years"[2] and made the argument that inflicting gross damage on civilian areas would send a deterrent message to any armed group that was hostile to Israel. The purported justification for this massive bombing was the presence of Hezbollah partisans, both combatants and noncombatants, in the area. At the time, human rights organizations condemned the Israeli attacks as "serious violations of international law," describing them as "indiscriminate, disproportionate, and otherwise unjustified"[3] but as with other Israeli war crimes, the international community remained largely silent.

The policy of massive bombardment remained unnamed until the then head of the Northern Command, Gen. Gadi Eizenkot, articulated what became known as the Dahiya doctrine in a newspaper interview just months prior to Israel's 2008–2009 attack on the Gaza Strip. "We will apply disproportionate force on [every village] and cause great damage and destruction there. From our standpoint, these are not civilian villages, they are military bases," Eizenkot told *Yedioth Ahronoth*. "This isn't a recommendation. This is a plan. And it has already been approved."[4]

The Dahiya doctrine is in clear violation of the international legal requirements of proportionality and discrimination. But in order to obscure the killing of more than 2,100 Palestinians, the bombing of the Gaza Strip's sole power plant, 62 hospitals and clinics, 220 schools, tens of thousands of homes and countless mosques, the entire population of the Gaza Strip needed to be transformed into enemies—faceless, nameless, irrational beings whose deaths were celebrated by their own or who were deliberately killed to harm Israel's image. Israel's media campaign was a precise reflection of its military campaign, depicting Palestinians as irrational individuals who attacked Israel for no reason and who, ultimately, had only themselves to blame for their own deaths.

Eliding the Occupation, the Siege, and Ongoing Military Attacks

As part of its effort to demonize Palestinians, the Israeli *hasbara* machine singled out Hamas, portraying it as an irrational actor which, for no logical reason, was carrying out a military attack on Israel. In so doing, Israel stripped its narrative of any reference to the political context, portraying itself as an ordinary country facing a crazed enemy. Ignored by Israeli officials and, worse still, by mainstream media, were any references to Israel's eight-year blockade of the Gaza Strip, its persisting military occupation, and its own military actions and cease-fire violations in the lead-up to the massive onslaught. The omissions included a ferocious security sweep through the West Bank, in which hundreds of Palestinians were detained, injured, and even killed, as well as multiple air strikes on the Gaza Strip that killed more than ten Palestinians before a single rocket was fired from the territory.

This media portrayal of Israel as a "normal" entity, devoid of a repugnant colonial history, whether past or present, stands in stark contrast with the candid statements of some of the country's previous military and political figures. In 1956, for example, Israeli army chief of staff Moshe Dayan noted in his oration at the funeral for an Israeli security officer from the kibbutz of Nahal Oz, who had been ambushed by fedayeen from Gaza:

> Let us not today fling accusations at the murderers. What cause have we to complain about their fierce hatred for us? For eight years now, they sit in their refugee camps in Gaza, and before their eyes we turn into our homestead the land and villages in which they and their forefathers have lived. We should demand his blood not from the Arabs of Gaza but from ourselves....[5]

While Dayan also argued that Israel should both heavily arm itself and be prepared for perpetual conflict with Palestinians, he understood that such a permanent conflict was the logical result of Israeli action—and said as much. Dayan's candor contrasts sharply with the opacity of the current Israeli establishment, whose narrative echoes Prime Minister Netanyahu's oft-repeated view that Hamas "is another instance of Islamist extremism, violent extremism that has no resolvable grievance."[6] Not only were Palestinians (and specifically Hamas) now irrational actors, attacking Israel for no good reason, they were further transformed from nationalist, political actors into an unhinged and extreme Islamist threat. At the same press conference where he uttered the words quoted above, Netanyahu added, "Hamas is like ISIS, Hamas is like al-Qaeda, Hamas is like Hizballah, Hamas is like Boko Haram." The Israeli prime minister even tweeted, "RT THIS: Hamas is ISIS. ISIS is Hamas. They're enemies of Peace [sic]. They're enemies of all civilized countries."[7]

These comparisons, particularly with ISIS, were both illogical and incorrect. Hamas has a nationalist agenda while ISIS has an anti-nationalist agenda, and al-Qaeda has denounced Hamas on numerous occasions. But the comparisons were made anyway, to convince a largely ill-informed Western audience that Israel faces the same "global terror" threat as the one being fought by the United States and to elicit support for Israel's brutal actions against Hamas-controlled Gaza. In the face of this irrational, demonic enemy, Israel could then claim it was acting in self-defense and portrayed itself as a victim of barrages of rockets. During another press appearance, Netanyahu noted that, "There's only been one other instance where a democracy has been rocketed and pelleted with these projectiles of death, and that's Britain during World War II...Israel is undergoing a similar bombardment."[8]

Technology, such as the Red Alert smartphone app using data provided by the Israeli army, assisted in spreading this narrative. The app, downloaded more than one million times during the attack on Gaza, sounded a high-pitched alarm each time a rocket was launched, irrespective of whether the rocket landed in the water, on an army base, in a field, or elsewhere. For journalists covering the attack, the Red Alert app proved to be a formidable tool in helping paint a picture of the rocket fire as well as the psychological impact of Israeli sirens.

Israeli statements to the Western media omitted describing not only the crude quality and accuracy of the projectiles used on the Palestinian side, but also the high-tech Iron Dome system in place to stop them.

Interestingly, and well in accordance with past habit, in the English language media, Israel portrayed itself as the underdog, whereas in the Arabic-language media, it presented itself as the strong and almighty nation that was impervious to Hamas's weak and "useless" rockets. As noted by Prof. William Youmans of George Washington University, "Israeli military spokesman Avichay Adraee tweeted in Arabic to his more than 119,000 followers that the rockets are 'weak' and a 'failure' and that the threat is exaggerated by Hamas."[9] In one tweet, Adraee apparently noted, "As usual rockets fired by Hamas exploded in the sky."[10] By Israel's own account, the Iron Dome system achieved an "almost 90 percent success rate." Yet, despite the "weak" rockets that "as usual... exploded in the sky" and a missile defense system operating at a success rate of "almost 90 percent," Israel continued to portray itself as the hapless victim, facing a formidable and irrational enemy that had ordinary Israelis cowering in shelters. This deceitful narrative was quickly revised after the flight cancellations by several foreign carriers and a few brief closures of Ben Gurion Airport when Israel had to decide whether it was a nation under siege, and hence one to and from which air travel was unsafe, or whether it was still a summer vacation destination, safe enough even for the likes of billionaire and former New York mayor Michael Bloomberg, who flew in on El Al, the Israeli national carrier, in a show of solidarity.

Blaming Palestinians for Their Own Deaths

Alongside its portrayal of Hamas as an irrational, demonic actor, Israel needed a means to explain away bombing hospitals, schools, mosques, shelters, medical clinics, and ambulances, as well as entire residential neighborhoods. As with the 2008–9 assault on Gaza, once again the high Palestinian death toll proved to be the Israelis' Achilles' heel: twenty-one hundred Palestinians killed, 70 percent of whom were classified as noncombatants, including over five hundred children. To counter what former U.S. secretary of state Madeleine Albright deemed an "image" problem,[11] Israeli officials adopted a new approach that consisted in blaming Palestinians—specifically Hamas—for their own deaths. Thus, according to that view, Hamas was responsible because they fired rockets from areas that Israel subsequently bombed or because Hamas gave specific orders for civilians to remain in areas that were about to be bombed. In other words, Palestinian civilians were unknowingly serving as Hamas's human shields. Despite the fact that countless journalists and others refuted these allegations and despite the fact that it has since been established that Israel has continued its own practice of using Palestinians as human shields,[12] Israel's vocal allegation was repeated ceaselessly.

Palestinian civilians used by Hamas as human shields was a talking point in the 2008–2009 Operation Cast Lead, but this time around the Israeli media machine took it one step further: as a means of further dehumanizing Palestinians, Israel cynically began focusing (and repeating) claims that Palestinians enjoyed a "culture of martyrdom" and hence did not care whether civilians were killed, provided that they had the effect of harming Israel's image. In a CNN interview on July 27, Netanyahu asserted, that Hamas "want to pile up more and more dead bodies of Palestinian civilians"[13] and on another occasion he echoed the words of the *Washington Post* commentator, Charles Krauthammer,[14] saying, "... they [Hamas] use telegenically-dead Palestinians for their cause. They want—the more dead, the better."[15] The dehumanization did not stop there, however. Soon all Palestinians, not merely Hamas, wanted to see more of their own dead, and no one was innocent. In other words, Palestinians became knowing human shields or, worse still, no longer civilians worthy of protection. In an opinion piece titled "In Gaza, There Is No Such Thing as 'Innocent Civilians,'" Israel's former national security adviser Giora Eiland noted, "...they [Palestinians in Gaza] are to blame for this situation just like Germany's residents were to blame for electing Hitler as their leader and paid a heavy price for that, and rightfully so."[16]

These statements, like those uttered by leaders in other conflicts where mass atrocities have been committed, were made precisely to dehumanize Palestinians and to justify Israel's defiance of international law governing occupation and war. As Thomas Friedman explained in regard to Israel's 2006 attack on Lebanon, the strategy is "to inflict substantial property damage and collateral casualties on Lebanon at large. It was not pretty, but it was logical. Israel basically said that when dealing with a non-state actor, Hezbollah, nested among civilians, the only long-term source of deterrence was to exact enough pain on the civilians—the families and employers of the militants—to restrain Hezbollah in the future."[17] Thus, it became easy for Israel to justify the killing of non-combatants—they were either members of Hamas or human shields of Hamas—and to explain away the wholesale destruction of Palestinian infrastructure in Gaza by arguing that it was used by Hamas or for the benefit of Hamas.

The dehumanization did not simply come from Israel's *hasbara* machine—journalists and even the Palestinian leadership inadvertently aided the endeavor. In the belief that they had to add "balance" to a lopsided war and lopsided civilian casualties, several reporters covered an injured owl in Israel's zoo and recounted the elephants' distress at the sound of the high-pitched sirens. Palestinian children with body parts scattered among the rubble were apparently too commonplace to be journalistically relevant.

After the 2008–2009 and 2012 attacks on Gaza (Operation Cast Lead and Pillar of Defense), it was to be hoped that the Palestinian Authority (PA) would have learned to do more than simply remain silent as Israeli bombs rained down on the population, indiscriminately killing children. Palestinian officials were nowhere to be seen or heard in the first few weeks of the assault, probably fearing that speaking out would entail defending Hamas. But their silence in the face of so much brutality spoke volumes and reinforced Israel's assiduously crafted message that there were really no innocents in Gaza. The official Palestinian silence also demonstrated the persistent absence of a Palestinian media strategy not only addressing Israel's outlandish claims but also putting forth the Palestinian narrative without having to be dragged into responding to such claims. Despite the creation of a number of PA, Palestine Liberation Organization (PLO), and Fatah media organizations, now in place for more than two decades, a unified media strategy remains nonexistent. Instead, as the U.S. mainstream media ratcheted up its aggressive tone—with some talk shows turning into shouting matches or punching contests—individuals attempting to speak out about Palestinian rights, and to highlight Israel's criminal behavior, were subjected to vitriol.

My personal experience with the mainstream media required me to devote significant time and energy to challenging the unquestioned characterizations according to which Palestinians both wanted and deserved to be the victims of Israeli bombs. In the dozens of interviews I gave, virtually every one featured an interviewer asking me questions that cemented rather than challenged Israel's media discourse. Without missing a beat, reporters asked questions about Hamas's charter, Palestinian textbooks, and streets named after "martyrs" as though the charter, the textbooks, and the streets in question were responsible for the dropping of 20,000 tons of bombs on 1.8 million beleaguered individuals and as if every person in Gaza were a combatant. The fallout from the interviews was no less bad, with pro-Israel activists sending me death and rape threats after a media appearance in which I said that oppressed peoples around the world, including Jews in the Warsaw Ghetto, had dug tunnels for their survival.

One can only hope that there will be no more massacres in the Gaza Strip, that the news media will learn to question Israel's outlandish claims, and that the Mahmoud Abbas–led Fatah and PA will realize that Gaza and its residents are not the enemy. Absent such changes, I fear that Palestinians will, once again, have to defend their very right to exist and Israel will further entrench the Dahiya doctrine.

Journal of Palestine Studies 44, no. 1 (Autumn 2014), pp. 91–96.

The Palestinians' Right to Self-Defense
Chris Hedges

If Israel insists, as the Bosnian Serbs did in Sarajevo, on using the weapons of industrial warfare against a helpless civilian population then that population has an inherent right to self-defense under Article 51 of the United Nations Charter. The international community will have to either act to immediately halt Israeli attacks and lift the blockade of Gaza or acknowledge the right of the Palestinians to use weapons to defend themselves.

No nation, including any in the Muslim world, appears willing to intervene to protect the Palestinians. No world body, including the United Nations, appears willing or able to pressure Israel through sanctions to conform to the norms of international law. And the longer we in the world community fail to act, the worse the spiral of violence will become.

Israel does not have the right to drop 1,000-pound iron fragmentation bombs on Gaza. It does not have the right to pound Gaza with heavy artillery and with shells lobbed from gunboats. It does not have the right to send in mechanized ground units or to target hospitals, schools and mosques, along with Gaza's water and electrical systems. It does not have the right to displace over 100,000 people from their homes. The entire occupation, under which Israel has nearly complete control of the sea, the air and the borders of Gaza, is illegal.

Violence, even when employed in self-defense, is a curse. It empowers the ruthless and punishes the innocent. It leaves in its aftermath horrific emotional and physical scars. But, as I learned in Sarajevo during the 1990s Bosnian War, when forces bent on your annihilation attack you relentlessly, and when no one comes to your aid, you must aid yourself. When Sarajevo was being hit with 2,000 shells a day and under heavy sniper fire in the summer of 1995 no one among the suffering Bosnians spoke to me about wanting to mount nonviolent resistance. No one among them saw the UN-imposed arms embargo against the Bosnian government as rational, given the rain of sniper fire and the 90-millimeter tank rounds and 155-millimeter howitzer shells that were exploding day and night in the city. The Bosnians were reduced, like the Palestinians in Gaza, to smuggling in light weapons through clandestine tunnels. Their enemies, the Serbs—like the Israelis in the current conflict—were constantly trying to blow up tunnels. The Bosnian forces in Sarajevo, with their meager weapons, desperately attempted to hold the trench lines that circled the city. And it is much the same in Gaza. It was only repeated NATO airstrikes in the fall of 1995 that prevented the Bosnian-held areas from being overrun by advancing Serbian forces. The Palestinians cannot count on a similar intervention.

The number of dead in Gaza resulting from the Israeli assault has topped 650, and about 80 percent have been civilians. The number of wounded Palestinians is over 4,000 and a substantial fraction of these victims are children. At what point do the numbers of dead and wounded justify self-defense? 5,000? 10,000? 20,000? At what point do Palestinians have the elemental right to protect their families and their homes?

Article 51 does not answer these specific questions, but the International Court of Justice does in the case of Nicaragua v. United States. The court ruled in that case that a state must endure an armed attack before it can resort to self-defense. The definition of an armed attack, in addition to being "action by regular armed forces across an international border," includes sending or sponsoring armed bands, mercenaries or irregulars that commit acts of force against another state. The court held that any state under attack must first request outside assistance before undertaking armed self-defense. According to U.N. Charter Article 51, a state's right to self-defense ends when the Security Council meets the terms of the article by "tak[ing] the measures necessary to maintain international peace and security."

The failure of the international community to respond has left the Palestinians with no choice. The United States, since Israel's establishment in 1948, has vetoed in the UN Security Council more than 40 resolutions that sought to curb Israel's lust for occupation and violence against the Palestinians. And it has ignored the few successful resolutions aimed at safeguarding Palestinian rights, such as Security Council Resolution 465, passed in 1980.

Resolution 465 stated that the "Fourth Geneva Convention relative to the Protection of Civilian Persons in Time of War of 12 August 1949 is applicable to the Arab territories occupied by Israel since 1967, including Jerusalem." The resolution went on to warn Israel that "all measures taken by Israel to change the physical character, demographic composition, institutional structure or status of the Palestinian and other Arab territories occupied since 1967, including Jerusalem, or any part thereof, have no legal validity and that Israel's policy and practices of settling parts of its population and new immigrants in those territories constitute a flagrant violation of the Fourth Geneva Convention relative to the Protection of Civilian Persons in Time of War and also constitute a serious obstruction to achieving a comprehensive, just and lasting peace in the Middle East."

Israel, as an occupying power, is in direct violation of Article III of the Geneva Convention Relative to the Protection of Civilian Persons in Time of War. This convention lays out the minimum standards for the protection of civilians in a conflict that is not international in scope. Article 3(1) states that those who take no active role in hostilities must be treated humanely, without discrimination, regardless of racial, social, religious or economic distinctions. The article prohibits certain acts commonly carried out against noncombatants in regions of armed conflict, including murder, mutilation, cruel treatment and torture. It prohibits the taking of hostages as well as sentences given without adequate due process of law. Article 3(2) mandates care for the sick and wounded.

Israel has not only violated the tenets of Article III but has amply fulfilled the conditions of an aggressor state as defined by Article 51. But for Israel, as for the United States, international law holds little importance. The U.S. ignored the verdict of the international court in Nicaragua v. United States and, along with Israel, does not accept the jurisdiction of the tribunal. It does not matter how many Palestinians are killed or wounded, how many Palestinian homes are demolished, how dire the poverty becomes in Gaza or the West Bank, how many years Gaza is under a blockade or how many settlements go up on Palestinian territory. Israel, with our protection, can act with impunity.

The unanimous U.S. Senate vote in support of the Israeli attacks on Gaza, the media's slavish parroting of Israeli propaganda and the Obama administration's mindless repetition of pro-Israeli clichés have turned us into cheerleaders for Israeli war crimes. We fund and abet these crimes with $3.1 billion a year in military aid to Israel. We are responsible for the slaughter. No one in the establishment, including our most liberal senator, Bernie Sanders, dares defy the Israel lobby. And since we refuse to act to make peace and justice possible we should not wonder why the Palestinians carry out armed resistance.

The Palestinians will reject, as long as possible, any cease-fire that does not include a lifting of the Israeli blockade of Gaza. They have lost hope that foreign governments will save them. They know their fate rests in their own hands. The revolt in Gaza is an act of solidarity with the world outside its walls. It is an attempt to assert in the face of overwhelming odds and barbaric conditions the humanity and agency of the Palestinian people. There is little in life that Palestinians can choose, but they can choose how to die. And many Palestinians, especially young men trapped in overcrowded hovels where they have no work and little dignity, will risk immediate death to defy the slow, humiliating death of occupation.

I cannot blame them.

Truthdig, 23 July 2014, http://bit.ly/1kYAraO

No Exit from Gaza: A New War Crime?
Richard Falk

This is a modified version of a post published online, July 15, 2014, at the recently established very informative website, Middle East Eye. *As the casualty totals continue to mount while the world looks on in stupefied inaction, the attacks go on; at the very least, from a humanitarian perspective, there should be a global outcry demanding that children, mothers, and those sick and disabled be allowed to leave the Gaza Strip until current hostilities end. Yet this is a gap in international humanitarian law, refugee law, and the moral sensibilities of the combatant states.*

As the hideous Israeli assault on Gaza, named Operation Protective Edge, by the IDF enters its second week, overdue international appeals for a ceasefire fall on deaf ears. The short lived July 15th ceasefire arranged by Sisi's Egypt had many accompanying signs of bad faith from its inception, including the failure to allow Hamas to participate in the process, insultingly conveying the proposed terms of the ceasefire through public media. The vague terms depicted, alongside the failure to take any account of Hamas' previously announced conditions, suggest that this initiative was not a serious effort to end the violence, but rather a clever ploy to regain moral credibility for Israel thereby facilitating the continuation and even intensification of its violent military campaign that was never defensive in conception or execution. Rather than being a real effort to end the violence, such a 'ceasefire' seems best understood as a sophisticated form of escalation produced by a descent into the lower depths of Israeli hasbara. Such an Israeli tactic was facilitated by the active complicity of the Egyptian government that shares with Israel an undisguised wish to destroy Hamas. Cairo regards Hamas as an offshoot of the Egyptian Muslim Brotherhood, an organization that has been criminalized and viciously repressed, and has collaborated with Tel Aviv ever since Sisi took over control of the Egyptian government.

Throughout Protective Edge Bibi Netanyahu has been telling the world that no outside pressure will alter Israel's resolve to reach its military and political goals to disable Hamas for the indefinite future. The main official justification for such aggression is to make sure this time that Israelis will never again have to seek shelter from Hamas rockets, an elusive result that Netanyahu acknowledges could require a prolonged military campaign combining ground forces with a continuing air and naval assault. Others claim on Israel's behalf that this attack on Hamas is a just response to its involvement in the kidnapping incident a month ago in which three Israeli settler teenagers were seized by two Palestinians, and soon afterwards brutally executed. Such a rationale would still be a hyperbolic form of collective punishment directed at the entire civilian population of Gaza, even if there had been a Hamas connection to the earlier crime, an involvement alleged from the very first moment, and yet up to now not substantiated by evidence even in the face of Hamas' denial of any involvement. The internationally respected human rights and international law specialist resident in Gaza, Raji Sourani, has written that the scale and ferocity of Protective Edge is an application of what he labels the "Gaza Doctrine," a deliberate reliance on disproportionate force in any encounter in Gaza. The Gaza Doctrine is a renewal of what was originally known as the "Dahiya Doctrine" after the destruction of the Dahiya residential neighborhood in south Beirut, where many of Hezbollah's faithful were living, during the 2006 Lebanon War. The inability of Hamas to mount any sort of defense for the people of Gaza or even to provide protection via shelters and the like, epitomizes the criminal nature of Protective Edge, and more generally, of totally one-sided warfare.

Leaving aside the debate on causes and justifications, the civilian population of Gaza, estimated to be about 1.8 million with women and children comprising 75% of the total, are trapped in an overcrowded war zone with no shelters and no apparent exit from terrifying danger. Even if families are lucky enough to avoid direct physical injury, the experience of screaming jet fighters attacking through the night, targeting, attack, and surveillance drones flying overhead 24 hours a day, sustained naval artillery barrages, not to mention the threats and warnings of an imminent ground invasion, combine to create a nonstop horror show. It has been convincingly confirmed by mental health specialists that these realities result in a trauma-inducing phenomenon on a massive scale with prospects of lasting and irreversible psychological damage, especially to children.

With these elements in mind, the idea of fulfilling the basic objective of international humanitarian law to protect civilians caught in a war zone is being violated by Israel, although not altogether. Israeli officials claim that leaflets dropped on some intended targets, otherwise forbidden, that give residents a few minutes to vacate their homes before their living space is reduced to rubble, exhibits a humane intent and satisfies the requirements of international humanitarian law. Such a self-sanitizing gesture fails to discharge the obligations of an Occupying Power under international humanitarian law.

In a further escalation of the attacks, perhaps the prelude to a ground invasion, residents of northern Gaza are being told to flee the area, and tens of thousands have apparently done so. Hamas apparently urged these same people not to leave their homes dismissing Israeli threats as intimidating propaganda. Cynically interpreted, Hamas appears to be informing Israel that if they go ahead and invade, there will be responsible for causing many Palestinian civilian casualties, and the shock caused by such carnage will help eventually swing the international balance of opinion strongly in their favor.

The entrapment of the Gazan population within closed borders is part of a deliberate Israeli pattern of prolonged collective punishment that has for the past several years been imposed on Gaza. This amounts to a grave breach of Article 33 of the Fourth Geneva Convention, and as such qualifies as a potential Crime Against Humanity. The morbid clarity of criminal intent is further disclosed by Israel's willingness to allow 800 or so Gazans who have dual citizenship and hold a foreign passport to leave Gaza by entering Israel at the Erez Crossing, including 150 with American passports. No other Palestinian residents of Gaza have the option of leaving even if disabled, sick, elderly, or young. The civilian population of Gaza is denied the option of seeking refugee status by fleeing Gaza during this time of intense warfare, and there is no space available within Gaza that might allow Palestinian civilians to become internally displaced until Protective Edge completes its dirty work.

In countries such as Iraq and Syria, we grieve appropriately for the millions becoming refugees or "internally displaced," compelled by the dangers of the raging conflict to seek refuge somewhere in the country that is removed from the immediate dangers of inhabiting the war zone. We can sense the extremity of the humanitarian tragedy in Gaza by realizing that these people whose lives are being acutely jeopardized, have no place to hide from the brutalities of war. There is no doubt that the whole of the Gaza Strip is a war zone. Gazans who have endured many mortal threats and a siege since 2007, currently find themselves in situations of extreme hazard, and yet have no possibility of seeking temporary safety as refugees by crossing an international border. The idea of internal refuge is almost inapplicable given the ferocious nature of Protective Edge that has spared not one corner of the tiny and overcrowded Gaza Strip. To be sure, in response to Israeli warnings to abandon their homes tens of thousands of Palestinians are fleeing south from north Gaza. At present writing, an estimated 17 thousand Palestinians have obtained refuge in the 20 UN-run schools situated throughout Gaza. UNRWA is doing its heroic best to handle these desperate people but its buildings have limited space and lack the facilities to handle properly this kind humanitarian emergency—insufficient bathrooms, no beds, and not enough space to meet the demands.

This is not the first time that this exit challenge has been posed in Gaza. Back in 2008–09 and 2012, Israeli launched major military operations in Gaza, and the issue of the entrapped civilian population was brought to the attention of the UN and the international community, a challenge met as now with scandalous silence. The encirclement of Gaza by Israeli controlled crossings and fences, even worse than in the past due to an Egyptian political leadership that makes no secret of its hostility to Hamas. The overall humanitarian crisis is catastrophic in the risk it poses to the totally vulnerable Gazan social reality.

For some perspective, it is useful to recall that just prior to the Kosovo War in 1999, up to a million Kosovars crossed into Macedonia to escape

anticipated NATO air strikes and because of a credible fear of an imminent ethnic cleansing campaign carried out by Serbian forces then controlling the country. As soon as the war was over and Serbia abandoned
Kosovo, these refugees returned, having safely navigated the dangers of
the war.

In Libya, too, the international community meaningfully responded
in 2011 to the urgent crisis of an entrapped civilian population. In the
Libyan crisis, Security Council members talked piously about relying on
the emergent norm of international law known as the Responsibility to
Protect, or R2P, that validated intruding on Libyan sovereignty by way
of a No Fly Zone that was established to protect the civilian population
of Benghazi facing the vengeance of Qaddafi's forces. This 2011 intervention has been much criticized because the humanitarian justification on
which authorization for the undertaking was transformed immediately
into a controversial regime-changing intervention that raised many ob-
jections. What is most relevant here is that the UN and the member governments of the Security Council acknowledged their responsibility to do
something to protect a civilian population unable to remove itself from
a combat zone. It should not be forgotten in comparing Libya with Gaza
that humanitarian appeals seem much more effective when the country in
question is perceived to have strategic value, especially large oil deposits.

The UN, aside from the admirable field efforts of UNRWA noted
above, and the international refusal to adopt measures protective of the
people of Gaza is unforgiveable, particularly as Gazans are being subjected to severe forms of violence that are approaching genocidal thresholds.
Even so the UN and its leading member governments turn their heads
and look away. Some do worse by actually endorsing Israel's aggression.
This pattern of behavior exhibits either a sense of helplessness in the face
of Israel's military juggernaut or even more disturbingly, a silence that
can be construed as tacitly blessing this infernal entrapment of innocent
and a long victimized people.

International law has little to say. International refugee law avoids
issues associated with any right to escape from a war zone and does
impose a duty on belligerent parties to provide civilians with an exit
and/or a temporary place of sanctuary. International humanitarian
law offers little more by way of protection to an entrapped people, despite the seeming relevance of the Fourth Geneva Convention devoted to the Protection of Civilians in Time of War. There is accorded to
foreign nationals a right of departure with the onset of war, including

even repatriation to an enemy country, but no right of nationals to leave their own country if under attack. And the generalized obligation of an Occupying Power to protect the civilian population is legally subordinated to its security needs, including military necessity, and so is generally of little practical use during an ongoing military operation.

What is evident in relation to the entrapped civilian population of Gaza is that no legal obligation exists to provide for safe havens either within the country experiencing the warfare or beyond its borders. At minimum, this horrible cauldron of violence and vulnerability reveals serious gaps in international humanitarian law, as well as the absence of self-imposed moral constraints that might limit belligerent violence. Such unattended vulnerability to atrocity urgently calls for a supplemental international agreement, perhaps taking the form of a treaty protocol to the Geneva Convention conferring an unconditional right of exit on civilians entrapped in a war zone. There is also a need to make any denial of the right of exit a species of war crime within the purview of the International Criminal Court. It should also be considered whether there should be conferred a right of internal displacement, imposing an obligation upon the Occupying Power, a territorial government, and insurgent actor to establish and respect enclaves set aside for displaced persons and to allow unimpeded civilian departure from war zones so as to take advantage of internal displacement. There are further complications that need to be addressed including whether the territorial government or Occupying Power can invoke security considerations to deny exit and displacement rights to those it has reason to believe are entitled to respect as civilians.

For the present it is enough to observe that the civilian population of Gaza finds itself totally entrapped in a terrifying war zone, and that Israel, the UN, and neighboring governments have refused to accept responsibility to offer some form of humane protection. It is one aspect of the unacceptability of the Israeli military operation from a moral/legal perspective and the related failure of international humanitarian law to lay down suitable rules and procedures that respect the human dignity of civilian innocence so entrapped. Yet, as almost always in such situations, it is the presence or absence of political will on the part of leading geopolitical actors that is the decisive factor in determining whether victimized people will be protected or not. And so it is with Gaza.

Global Justice in the 21st Century (blog), July 16, 2014,
http://bit.ly/1HvHVhj

Egypt's Propagandists and the Gaza Massacre

Joseph Massad

As Israel's murderous machine inflicts terror and death on the Palestinian people with the collaboration of the U.S. government and its principal Arab allies, not least of which is the Saudi clan of 20,000 princes and princesses, a huge campaign of hate on the official and unofficial level has been launched in Egypt.

Egypt's regime is one of the two principal jailers of Gaza Palestinians in the largest concentration camp in the world.

Hosni Mubarak's heir on the Egyptian throne, General Abdulfattah al-Sisi, expressed well the lies that the Egyptian ruling class of thieves has been propagating in Egypt since the anti-Arab and anti-Palestinian campaigns of the mid to late 1970s under President Anwar Sadat.

The uncharismatic Sisi, whose oratorical abilities rival those of Yasser Arafat, announced with much pomp in his July 23 speech marking the anniversary of the 1952 overthrow of the monarchy that Egypt had already sacrificed "100,000 Egyptian martyrs" for the Palestinian cause.

While few people doubt the sacrifices that Egyptian soldiers have made to defend Egypt in the last 67 years, to claim that these sacrifices were made on behalf of Palestine and the Palestinians is the ultimate in hypocrisy.

It is a line of argument that the ruling class of Egyptian thieves has been propagating in order to claim that Egypt's terrible economy and state of poverty are not the product of this class' outright pillage of Egypt with the help of their American and Saudi sponsors since the 1970s, but on account of Egypt's alleged defense of Palestine and the Palestinians and President Gamal Abdel Nasser's alleged commitment to liberate the Palestinians from Israel's colonial occupation.

Tawdry Pillaging Class

Since the 1970s, Palestinians have been subjected to these lies and to the vacuity and utter tawdriness of this Egyptian class of the ignorant and the illiterate. This class' lack of education and worldliness was on full display during the last three years of counter-revolutionary propaganda and agitation on its television stations and in its press.

The form and content of this output would embarrass and scandalize any self-respecting community of intellectuals, journalists and artists,

except that the majority of Egyptian intellectuals, journalists and artists
have either been conscripted or fully bought off to defend this class' interests (though some of those conscripted in support of the regime, especially
academics, started to backpedal more recently and to rewrite their history
denying their cheerleading for it).

The degradation of Egyptian intellectual and aesthetic cultures and
products in the last four decades is a direct outcome of this class' ty-
rannical rule. One only has to sit with these businessmen and women,
or visit their homes, or watch their representation in Egyptian serials
and films and the culture they want to impose through them, or listen
to their conversations in Cairo's five-star hotel bars and restaurants, or
watch their interviews on Egypt's scandalously substandard television
stations, to realize their utter mediocrity on every level of economic and
political thinking and of aesthetic taste, not to mention their ignorance
of Egyptian, Arabic and world literatures and arts, let alone their utter
contempt for Egypt's poor who constitute more than eighty percent of
the population.

That this envious and jealous super-wealthy class resents and be-
grudges the poorest of the poor for their meager possessions, especially
the Palestinians of Gaza, illustrates the kind of moral compass that guides
its actions.

I still remember my horror when I had dinner in Cairo in October
2010 with billionaire Nassef Sawiris, the richest man in the country, when
he announced with much pride to the small dinner party of seven persons
that he keeps three TV screens on at all times, in his office, at home and
while traveling, set to three different U.S. news channels simultaneously
(if memory serves, he listed CNN, CNBC and Fox News) that clearly function as his major sources of education.

Sawiris, who is much less exhibitionist than either of his two older
brothers, seemed in disbelief when I informed him that I opposed the
right-wing policies of U.S. President Barack Obama, both domestic and
foreign, as he seemed unable to conceive of a political position left of
Obama.

In a just-published interview with the pro-Sisi newspaper *Al-Masry
Al-Youm*, Sawiris commended Sisi for lifting fuel subsidies on the poor
(while keeping the price of gasoline for luxury cars down for the rich),
and made a series of neoliberal recommendations, including devaluing
the Egyptian pound further; privatizing public transportation; removing
taxes imposed on the rich (which he claims the government of deposed

president Mohamed Morsi had illegally imposed on his company); shielding ministers and government employees from legal prosecution and allowing coal to be used to fuel cement factories despite the massive opposition of health and environmental activists.

Such measures would surely continue to enrich the rich one percent and impoverish the poor (Nassef's more flamboyant older but poorer brother Naguib just started to write a weekly column for Egypt's *Al-Akhbar* in which he reiterates his brother's neoliberal recommendations. He also calls on Sisi, in a TV interview, to grant Mubarak amnesty and release him from prison).

"Fiction and Fabrication"

What Sisi and this class with which he is allied want to claim is that all of Egypt's wars with Israel were launched to defend Palestine and the Palestinians and that they were hugely costly to Egypt financially and in the lives of soldiers lost. But none of this is true.

In 1956, Israel invaded Egypt and occupied Sinai, and the Egyptian soldiers who were killed died while engaged in defending their country and their land; in 1967, Israel again invaded Egypt and occupied Sinai, and Egyptian soldiers were killed defending their country against foreign invasion; between 1968 and 1970, Israel and Egypt fought the "War of Attrition" in which Egyptian soldiers were killed defending their country against continuing Israeli aggression and the preservation of Israel's ongoing occupation of Sinai, a war that was fought on Egyptian soil; and in 1973, Egypt launched a war to liberate Sinai, *not* Palestine, and Egyptian soldiers were again killed defending their country against foreign occupation.

This leaves us with the 1948 war in which, depending on sources, anywhere from one thousand to two thousand Egyptian soldiers and volunteers were killed. This Egyptian military intervention to stop Zionist expulsion of the Palestinians and the Zionist theft of the land of the Palestinians was launched not by Nasser, who is blamed for his rhetorical support of the Palestinians, but by King Farouq.

As most studies of the motives behind Farouq's and his government's intervention in Palestine attest, it was on account of Farouq's concern about Egypt's leading regional role and fear of Iraqi rivalry and less so as some form of Arab nationalism or solidarity.

These motives aside, most Palestinians do not doubt that the Egyptian soldiers and volunteer fighters who died had indeed died defending

Palestine and the Palestinians even if the soldiers among them were doing so based on orders that sought to defend Egyptian regional hegemony. But this remains the only war where Egyptian soldiers and volunteers died defending Palestine and for whom the Palestinian people and their national movement have expressed much gratitude.

But the way these one to two thousand soldiers and volunteers multiply to the tune of "100,000 martyrs," as Sisi falsely claimed, is the stuff of fiction and fabrication, which the ruling Egyptian class of thieves and their intellectuals-for-hire and paid propagandists in the press have concocted following Sadat's 1978 Camp David accords, which sacrificed the rights of the Palestinian people, including the Palestinians of Gaza, in return for Egyptian non-sovereign, partial police control of Sinai.

This is not to suggest that millions of Egyptians, civilians and soldiers, do not or would not support Palestine and the Palestinians, or that they would not fight for Palestine and the Palestinians, as they often avow and declare that they would; it is to say that aside from the 1948 battles, they have never been given a chance to defend the Palestinians on the battleground. This is precisely what galls the Egyptian ruling class of thieves and what propels the ongoing anti-Palestinian propaganda and hate speech on the television stations owned by this class.

Hearing their propaganda, one would think that it was the Palestinians who had occupied Sinai, not Egypt that had taken over and ruled Gaza from 1948 to 1967 and had laid siege to it intermittently since, imposing a full, continuing siege for the last eight years.

Despite these massive media campaigns, Egyptians are not deterred in their support of the Palestinians, whether by demonstrating against the Sisi regime's complicity in the massacres as they have been doing in the last two weeks, or by sending medical relief convoys to Gaza, which Sisi's soldiers turn back, refusing them passage.

Intellectual Mass Suicide

In this context, it is crucial to understand that this Egyptian ruling class of thieves is the primary enemy not of the Palestinian people, but of most Egyptians whom it oppresses, exploits, robs and humiliates on a daily basis. That the enemies of the Palestinians in Egypt are also the enemies of most Egyptians has recently been obscured by the role played by the cheerleaders of Sisi's regime.

The intellectual mass suicide that the majority of Egypt's intellectuals and artists (Nasserists, Marxists, liberals, and Salafists) have committed in their abdication of their critical faculties when they supported or remained silent on the massacres and repression of the new regime, let alone their silence on the campaigns against the Egyptian poor and the Palestinians, is reminiscent of the suicide committed by Egyptian communists who disbanded their party in 1964 to join Nasser's Socialist Union.

This class extends from the Marxist economist and indefatigably pro-Sisi Samir Amin to much less illustrious figures like novelist and Mubarak critic Alaa al-Aswany, and everyone in between including economist Galal Amin and writers and poets Sonallah Ibrahim, Abd al-Rahman al-Abnudi, Bahaa Taher, and scores more.

The suicide of Egyptian communists in 1964, however, was staged due to the communists' understanding that Nasser's repression, while unwelcome and regrettable, was ultimately aimed to serve their common project of nationalization and socialization of property in order to eradicate Egyptian poverty. It remains unclear what the rationale of Egypt's contemporary intellectuals is in committing suicide in order to support Egypt's ruling class of thieves.

Gaza Massacre Is "Plan B"

That Sisi has outdone Mubarak's policies in allying himself with Israel and coordinating with it against the besieged Palestinians is hardly surprising, since he serves the very same class and interests which Mubarak served. What is different, however, is Hamas' erstwhile quiescence and submission to Mubarak's *diktat* out of a sense of entrapment, which Hamas has since abandoned.

It is now clear that Israel's ongoing slaughter of the Palestinians turns out to be plan B, wherein plan A had been a possible Egyptian ground invasion of Gaza that Sisi's government had threatened to carry out a few months ago after it had destroyed Gaza's lifeline tunnels (and this was before Sisi's sham elections), presumably with Israeli help, with the ostensible purpose to re-install Mohammed Dahlan as Gaza's warlord and get rid of Hamas and Palestinian resistance.

That the Egyptian head of intelligence was on a visit to Israel a few days before Israel's massacres were launched, and that three Israeli intelligence officials visited Egypt a few days later, are only tiny indicators of the high level of coordination between the two countries.

The sadism and narcissism that are traits of mainstream Israeli Jewish colonial culture and which manifest in pervasive street mobs crying "death to the Arabs" and propel segments of the country's colonial

Jewish population to watch from the hilltops and cheer the slaughter of the native Palestinians is only matched by the sadistic and hateful propaganda of the Sisi regime media and that of the Egyptian ruling class of thieves.

Indeed, even while Israel's slaughter of the Palestinians of Gaza continues, the Egyptian army announced on July 27 that it had just destroyed thirteen more tunnels between Gaza and Egypt, presumably as part of its own heroic contribution to the ongoing Israeli oppression of the Palestinians.

As for the "ceasefire" that Sisi offered a week into the Gaza slaughter, which was dictated to him by his Israeli allies, it has been appropriately spurned by the Palestinian people in favor of a valiant military resistance to their Israeli colonial captors' criminality and a courageous political and diplomatic resistance in facing up to their Egyptian jailers' cruelty.

The Electronic Intifada, July 29, 2014, http://bit.ly/WP6W6o

Collective Punishment in Gaza
Rashid Khalidi

Three days after the Israeli prime minister Benjamin Netanyahu launched the current war in Gaza, he held a press conference in Tel Aviv during which he said, in Hebrew, according to the *Times of Israel,* "I think the Israeli people understand now what I always say: that there cannot be a situation, under any agreement, in which we relinquish security control of the territory west of the River Jordan."

It's worth listening carefully when Netanyahu speaks to the Israeli people. What is going on in Palestine today is not really about Hamas. It is not about rockets. It is not about "human shields" or terrorism or tunnels. It is about Israel's permanent control over Palestinian land and Palestinian lives. That is what Netanyahu is really saying, and that is what he now admits he has "always" talked about. It is about an unswerving, decades-long Israeli policy of denying Palestine self-determination, freedom, and sovereignty.

What Israel is doing in Gaza now is collective punishment. It is punishment for Gaza's refusal to be a docile ghetto. It is punishment for the gall of Palestinians in unifying, and of Hamas and other factions in responding to Israel's siege and its provocations with resistance, armed or otherwise, after Israel repeatedly reacted to unarmed protest with crushing

Young boy standing inside the destroyed home of his relatives, the Kaware family, in Khan Yunis. The house was hit with an Israeli drone (the "warning" strike) followed by a second missile that targeted the rooftop. The July 8 attack killed nine members of the family as well as a neighbor who was attempting to rescue the injured. Photo by Eman Mohammed.

force. Despite years of ceasefires and truces, the siege of Gaza has never been lifted.

As Netanyahu's own words show, however, Israel will accept nothing short of the acquiescence of Palestinians to their own subordination. It will accept only a Palestinian "state" that is stripped of all the attributes of a real state: control over security, borders, airspace, maritime limits, contiguity, and, therefore, sovereignty. The twenty-three-year charade of the "peace process" has shown that this is all Israel is offering, with the full approval of Washington. Whenever the Palestinians have resisted that pathetic fate (as any nation would), Israel has punished them for their insolence. This is not new.

Punishing Palestinians for existing has a long history. It was Israel's policy before Hamas and its rudimentary rockets were Israel's boogeyman of the moment, and before Israel turned Gaza into an open-air prison, punching bag, and weapons laboratory. In 1948, Israel killed thousands of innocents, and terrorized and displaced hundreds of thousands more, in the name of creating a Jewish-majority state in a land that was then sixty-five percent Arab. In 1967, it displaced hundreds of thousands of Palestinians again, occupying territory that it still largely controls, forty-seven years later.

In 1982, in a quest to expel the Palestine Liberation Organization and extinguish Palestinian nationalism, Israel invaded Lebanon, killing seventeen thousand people, mostly civilians. Since the late 1980s, when Palestinians under occupation rose up, mostly by throwing stones and staging general strikes, Israel has arrested tens of thousands of Palestinians: over 750,000 people have spent time in Israeli prisons since 1967, a number that amounts to forty percent of the adult male population today. They have emerged with accounts of torture, which are substantiated by human-rights groups like B'Tselem. During the second intifada, which began in 2000, Israel reinvaded the West Bank (it had never fully left). The occupation and colonization of Palestinian land continued unabated throughout the "peace process" of the 1990s, and continues to this day. And yet, in America, the discussion ignores this crucial, constantly oppressive context, and is instead too often limited to Israeli "self-defense" and the Palestinians' supposed responsibility for their own suffering.

In the past seven or more years, Israel has besieged, tormented, and regularly attacked the Gaza Strip. The pretexts change: they elected Hamas; they refused to be docile; they refused to recognize Israel; they fired rockets; they built tunnels to circumvent the siege; and on and on. But each pretext is a red herring, because the truth of ghettos—what happens when you imprison 1.8 million people in a hundred and forty square miles, about a third of the area of New York City, with no control of borders, almost no access to the sea for fishermen (three out of the twenty kilometers allowed by the Oslo accords), no real way in or out, and with drones buzzing overhead night and day—is that, eventually, the ghetto will fight back. It was true in Soweto and Belfast, and it is true in Gaza. We might not like Hamas or some of its methods, but that is not the same as accepting the proposition that Palestinians should supinely accept the denial of their right to exist as a free people in their ancestral homeland.

This is precisely why the United States' support of current Israeli policy is folly. Peace was achieved in Northern Ireland and in South Africa because the United States and the world realized that they had to put pressure on the stronger party, holding it accountable and ending its impunity. Northern Ireland and South Africa are far from perfect examples, but it is worth remembering that, to achieve a just outcome, it was necessary for the United States to deal with groups like the Irish Republican Army and the African National Congress, which engaged in guerrilla war and even terrorism. That was the only way to embark on a road toward true peace and reconciliation. The case of Palestine is not fundamentally different.

Instead, the United States puts its thumb on the scales in favor of the stronger party. In this surreal, upside-down vision of the world, it almost seems as if it is the Israelis who are occupied by the Palestinians, and not the other way around. In this skewed universe, the inmates of an open-air prison are besieging a nuclear-armed power with one of the most sophisticated militaries in the world.

If we are to move away from this unreality, the U.S. must either reverse its policies or abandon its claim of being an "honest broker." If the U.S. government wants to fund and arm Israel and parrot its talking points that fly in the face of reason and international law, so be it. But it should not claim the moral high ground and intone solemnly about peace. And it should certainly not insult Palestinians by saying that it cares about them or their children, who are dying in Gaza today.

The New Yorker, July 29, 2014, http://nyr.kr/1lSQLKv

5

The Pen, the Keyboard, and the F-16: Creative Resistance in the Digital Age

The Israeli onslaught on Gaza in the summer of 2014 will be remembered for many things, including the way in which it was broadcast in real time. Social media, digital art, and infographics all played prominent roles in shaping public perceptions of the assault; these tools were used for propaganda purposes, most notably by Israel, who established entire "war rooms" to aid its hasbara efforts. But they were also used as a means of resistance by Palestinians in Gaza bearing the brunt of the attacks, and by advocates attempting to amplify the voices of besieged Palestinian globally. Critics will argue about the ultimate success of these unconventional efforts, but this much is clear: Palestinian voices were louder, more present, and more expressive than ever before. From a social media-savvy 16-year-old from Gaza or a doctor tweeting from a hospital emergency room strained to the limit, to Palestinian artists in the diaspora re-imagining the viciousness of the offensive, the Palestinian narrative was alive and well and (for the first time) being mainly told in Palestinian voices. Another creative mode of written expression was poetry. Here, we have chosen pieces, written in the most trying of times, as a monument of resistance.

War on Gaza, Social Media and Efficacy of Protest
Hatem Bazian

Israel's summer 2014 war on Gaza will be extensively studied by military and political strategists alike due to the extensive shifts witnessed on the battlefield, government offices, at home and abroad, and more critically the effects brought about by social media. For starters, the Israeli leadership expressed goal of ending Hamas's rule in Gaza was quickly jettisoned as unfolding events demonstrated the folly of such a plan and a narrower aim directed at locating and destroying existing tunnels took center stage. The initial hoped-for Israeli military success, which was politically supported by Arab and Western powers, quickly collapsed as Palestinian resistance on the frontlines managed to withstand the pressure and mounted a sustained response that altered the war's contours.

Yet, a more critical aspect that deserves as much attention is the global response through social media by activists and organizers who managed over the course of the war to alter the highly controlled and managed Israeli military and political narrative. The Israeli narrative dominates the mainstream media outlets but on Twitter, Facebook and other social media avenues, Gaza's story had a Palestinian face to it. What is the impact of social media in this war and how effective were pro-Palestine activists in dominating this medium? More critical are issues relative to the nature of the medium and the prevalence of gory images and whether they provide the lead to greater levels of engagement or have a negative outcome. Lastly, as Israel's war on Gaza intensified, a global protest movement got underway. It is too early to ask questions on the long-term impact of this mobilization. However, the need is to weigh the efficacy of protest and demonstrations and what impacts they have on the unfolding events.

It is too early to assess the overall impacts of Israel's war in Gaza on public attitudes across the world and whether success in the mainstream media is sufficient to keep support for Israel moving forward in the days ahead. The cracks are already visible in the social media space with Twitter and Facebook being dominated by pro-Palestine narratives and contributing to shifts in some mainstream media coverage. For example, NBC initially removed from the region Ayman Mohyeldin, the award-winning news correspondent who personally witnessed the killing by Israel of four boys playing soccer on Gaza's beach and posted a photo of the grieving mother to Twitter. However, after a massive response on social media NBC was forced to change the decision and send the reporter back to the area.

On the other hand, CNN reassigned Diana Magnay, an international correspondent from Israel, to Moscow after she sent a tweet, "Israelis on hill above Sdrot cheer as bombs land on #Gaza threaten to 'destroy our car if I say a word wrong'. Scum." The removal from the area was deemed to be for security and safety concerns but social media and activists on Twitter were able to focus attention on the coverage and the story became for few days one of the most widely shared across the globe. Indeed, CNN's actions and removal of the reporter led to greater attention given to Israelis' response and attitudes during the war on Gaza.

Palestinians' use of social media during the war was very effective; a number of bloggers operating directly from Gaza made for an open and uncensored channel of reporting becoming a window into the daily lives and the impacts of the war on the ground. This steady Gaza information source became important in countering the erasure or obfuscation of the Palestinian narrative in the mainstream press, which was spoon-fed by the Israeli public relations infrastructure. The Palestinian success in social media led Israel to attempt a response by offering to pay students to work on posting positive stories about it and countering the Palestinian narrative coming out from activists narrating Gaza's suffering. Taking this step on a governmental level was a clear indication on the one hand of the success of Palestine's activists in this medium and on the other a sign of the utter failure of Israel's ability to keep its carefully crafted war narrative intact outside the controlled mainstream media.

However, one consequence of Palestine's activists' heavy reliance on social media is the overuse of gory images and prevalence of photos documenting almost every case of death. While it is important to record and document each death in Gaza for possible future legal investigation and to ascertain the cause of death, social media activists' use of these photos to shock more people into action on behalf of Palestine is highly problematic and objectifies the individuals whose images are utilized. Death is painful and Palestinians are dispossessed of agency alive and likewise in death.

I am not here blaming individuals who are sharing these images to bring about a human response; rather it is the overall colonial structure that makes the approach paradigmatic of how Palestinians are approached. The problem is colonization and the continued occupation that makes the life of a Palestinian subject to contestation while alive, dead, and post-death. We must find ways to uplift Palestine and Palestinians at all times without having to objectify them so as to get the needed support. I am not here dealing with the Islamic legal and ethical treatment of the dead body, for the issues at hand are beyond discussing the religious norms.

It is far more powerful to construct a full picture of the lost Palestinian life with a narrative focusing on him or her as a human being with family, friends, and potential that was brought to an end by Israeli violence. Indeed, if we only focus on images of Palestinian dead bodies, then we are reducing the full life of an individual or a family to the crime itself. We should resist this reduction and seek to draw the full picture and insist on it at all times. I am fully aware of the pain and difficulties witnessing the daily suffering of the Palestinians, but let us resist the dehumanization by keeping them alive even after the moment of death.

The above also brings me to the protest movement that erupted after the Israeli attacks on Gaza. Across the world activists and organizations mobilized heavily to protest Israeli crimes and urged governments to take the needed actions to end this assault on a captive and imprisoned population. Parts of Western Europe, South Africa, Latin and South America witnessed the largest protests, a fact that has not been seen since the mass mobilization in 2003 against the U.S. invasion of Iraq. The demonstrations were unable to shift some governments' positions in the short period, however the same can't be said in the long run as the effects of these efforts would have to show a bleed-in effect in the upcoming elections in England and other countries facing the voters this coming fall for conclusive evidence to emerge.

Protests and putting massive numbers of people in the streets is important in the face of governments who are refusing to alter or be critical of Israeli policies or even domestic related issues. For example, Martin Luther King, the Civil Rights Movement and the anti-Vietnam war efforts had very strong and sustained protest movements that in the long run helped shift public opinion and as a result brought about a change in policies. Thus, the lesson is not whether protest and demonstrations are effective or not but how to bring about a sustained effort and also engage in complementary strategies that take the numbers in the streets and transform them into political muscle to change policies and bring an end to unjust laws affecting Palestinians abroad and people of color at home.

In the days ahead, we collectively have to think seriously about the needed steps that can transform the thousands in the streets into a source of political empowerment that can bring about a change in policies pertaining to the unconditional support extended to Israel. The U.S.

government continues to support Israel's position right or wrong, which means that Palestinians are expendable and Muslim voices in America have no value or power. For sure the time has come for Muslims and Arabs in America and their allies to take their numbers, resources and political worldview seriously and begin to effectuate a sustained protest movement on the outside and a focused inside political strategy to bring an end to this one-sided support. As a Muslim, my own conscience is heavy knowing daily that my own taxes are purchasing the bullets for Israel to use in killing the Palestinians. I feel this is my own responsibility and all Muslims in America should put maximum effort to bring this to end; otherwise we are part of the problem.

Islamic Horizons, September–October 2014, pp. 28–30,
http://bit.ly/1I91jEg

Social Media: The Weapon of Choice in the Gaza-Israel Conflict
Yousef al-Helou

When 16-year-old Palestinian Farah Baker began tweeting about the bombs falling around her, she could never have guessed that she would rise to such prominence. But in the space of just a few weeks, her followers on Twitter jumped from 800 to 207,000, with people hungry for a first-hand, personal account of what was transpiring in Gaza. Baker is just one of the Palestinians turning to social media platforms such as Facebook and Twitter to share photos of the destruction in the Gaza Strip and disseminate information, updates, and posts.

Even when the power was out, citizen journalists managed to post pictures of dead bodies, destroyed neighborhoods, and injured people to the outside world. Photography has always been a powerful force, but the Gaza conflict was one of the first wars to be photographed mainly by amateurs and social media platforms, allowing those images to spread far and wide at the click of a button, helping the people of Gaza win hearts and minds, and subsequently causing unprecedented outrage against Israel. In demonstrations around the world, such photos were enlarged and carried by demonstrators, demanding that their respective governments take action to halt Israel's onslaught.

"I noticed that most of the Western media supports Israel, so also some people abroad believe that we Palestinians are the murderers and that it is us who started the attacks on Israel. This is not right. I felt I had to do something to help Gaza. I used Twitter as a weapon to share what exactly happens in Gaza by posting links of recorded clips of bombs, photos of the smoke to make people who follow me feel as if they are living in Gaza, to let them know we are the victims," Farah Baker said.

No doubt reporting in a war zone like Gaza is risky, even if you take all required precautions. Of the 2016 Palestinians killed in the current Israeli assault, 14 were journalists, including a foreign reporter who worked for local and international media outlets. Simultaneously, a number of buildings housing media offices and outlets were attacked.

Israel is ranked 96th in the world on the "Press Freedom Index"—a report compiled by Reporters without Borders—because of the Israeli military's targeting of Palestinian journalists in the occupied Palestinian territory. This ranking was published before the start of Israel's third war on Gaza, called "Operation Protective Edge."

"Since the start of the Gaza blockade in 2006, a new generation of Palestinians has come to prominence in Gaza. Articulating their message in fluent English through blogs and Twitter, they conveyed their message to the world as a means to break their isolation, not only from the outside world but also from the rest of the occupied territories in the West Bank and the capital of East Jerusalem," said Abed al-Nasser Abu Oun, a TV correspondent and radio presenter at a local radio station.

As the war progressed, it was an online battle of narratives—between heavily funded Israeli state media outlets, represented by Israeli spokespersons of the Israeli government and the army with decades of experience—versus Palestinian citizen journalists who only had their own laptops, smartphones, and cameras.

Some citizen journalists from Gaza argue that they were even able to win the cyberwar, and reach the public in the West, by repackaging, commenting on, and distributing content in innovative ways, tweeting updates a lot faster than other media outlets.

"Most of the Western corporations and outlets are biased in favor of Israel, so they totally mislead people by fabricating news, showing Palestinians' destroyed homes as Israeli ones. This attitude sparked uproar and disgust toward those news channels—namely Fox News. Alternatively, Palestinian activists firmly focus on revealing the reality through social media tools," said Maram Humaid, a social media activist.

The use of social media also forged connections with international media organizations, which contacted Gaza residents and citizen journalists with questions and interview requests.

Twitter became a platform for tens of thousands of regular people who have an opinion to share, for those who wish to challenge someone else's point of view, or those who simply want to share updates and their own personal feelings on the human cost of Israel's war. Many of these messages can be viewed under the hashtags #GazaUnderAttack and #PrayforGaza.

"Many people—young and old alike—are using social media to report on their immediate circumstances in ways that the mainstream media cannot. We see this shifting coverage and understanding of events from Gaza to Ferguson. In both places, tweets from local residents have offered immediate news to those watching from elsewhere. In some cases, citizen journalists have greatly challenged the narratives of more established sources," said Joe Catron, an American pro-Palestine activist in Gaza.

Citizen journalists can publish their own work, analysis, and breaking news in a free, uncensored and unfiltered way, unlike professional reporters of the mainstream media who have to stick to their corporations' editorial policy and guidelines.

One of the motivating factors that drives more citizen journalists to volunteer dismantling information is due to the unfair media coverage of the Palestinian narrative.

"The rise of the internet has helped to reconstruct the fragmentation of Palestine, as it is a way for Palestinians to reconnect and break their isolation. I think the effect of the social media boom among young Palestinian social media activists somehow succeeded in changing public perception of the Palestinian in the West," said Majed Shuplaq, a Palestinian journalist.

Citizen journalism from Palestine is especially valuable for those who are looking for information that has not been filtered through a Western agenda. Social media has definitely weakened the Israeli narrative, as Palestinians are able to connect directly with overseas audiences and tell the stories that they feel are important.

Hundreds of thousands of tweets exchanged reports, opinions, and challenges to mainstream news reports and to each other. There were of course, many other tags that hosted additional discussions. In hindsight, it seems that Twitter hosted the most open and democratic discussions, compared with other social media venues.

Middle East Eye, August 21, 2014, http://bit.ly/1CHAiok

In Asymmetric Twitter War over Gaza, Palestinians Are Winning

Belal Dabour

A figure comparing hashtag use was omitted for space considerations.

As Israel's relentless bombardment of Gaza continues, another fierce battle also rages.

As soon as the first bomb fell on Gaza, thousands of Palestinian and Israeli Twitter users engaged in what appears to be a virtual fight.

On one side are the hundreds of Palestinian citizens using Twitter to document the horrifying impact of Israeli attacks that have so far killed more than two thousand people and injured eleven thousand more.

Everyone in his or her area posted photos and videos of houses being blown up and provided evidence-packed witness to atrocities that regular media outlets fail to reach or deliberately ignore.

On the other side are the pro-Israel users, whose focus remains mainly on denying everything claimed by the Palestinian side—the colonized and occupied side—and failing to provide evidence in the process.

Many resort to explicitly racist and anti-Muslim statements in order to dehumanize Palestinians and justify killing them.

This explains why they are rightly labeled by many as "trolls" or "apologists."

Palestinians Gaining Online Support

Just like the war on the ground, this virtual war, too, looks asymmetric. This time, however, the asymmetry is in favor of the Palestinians, a very obvious fact if we compare hashtag activity, followers, and interaction counts.

A number of Palestinian Twitter users quickly gained thousands or tens of thousands of new followers from people eager to learn first hand what is happening in Gaza.

Each of them is a potential new supporter of justice even after the Israeli aggression ends.

Israeli Twitter users, at least the dozens that I encountered myself, barely have tens or in some cases a few hundred followers. And many are even too lazy to change the egg-shaped profile picture Twitter provides for new users.

Winning Hashtags

The hashtags used by people expressing support for Palestinians scored a definite win. Over the last month, since July, 22 the hashtag #GazaUnderAttack was mentioned in more than 4.1 million tweets, according to the social analytics service Topsy.

Meanwhile, the hashtag #IsraelUnderAttack, used predominantly by supporters of the Israeli attack on Gaza, garnered a mere one percent of that, or just 47,000 tweets.

Hashtags used by supporters of Palestinian rights have had millions more mentions than those used by supporters of the Israeli massacre in Gaza.

This vast difference has been consistent since the July 7 start of the Israeli assault, and has been observable for other popular hashtags including #PrayForGaza and #ISupportGaza versus #PrayForIsrael and #ISupportIsrael.

The level of enthusiasm, persistence and accuracy that Palestinian Twitter users continue to show is remarkable especially when compared to the Israel supporters.

It is even more amazing given that the Israeli government and government-funded organizations have to offer financial incentives or set up special social media "war rooms" in order to farm online propaganda.

Unmediated Truth

But what is all this activity really about? What is developing here on Twitter exceeds mere story-telling. For more than six decades, Palestinians have been denied the right to offer their narrative of the conflict in Palestine.

Corporate media subservient to the agendas and policies of Western governments have adopted the Israeli narrative and, without question, promoted it.

As shown by the large protests against the BBC over its unfair and biased coverage of Gaza, outrage at and mistrust of traditional media has reached unprecedented levels.

But now, Palestinians have found a new, unmediated, and easy-to-use platform in which they can freely express themselves without feeling pressured to use a compromising language.

Here, a photo (properly sourced, of course) is enough to tear apart the biggest of lies, and a video suffices to make an Israeli general think twice before he hops on a plane.

From Support to Action

What we are beginning to see here is a new experience, where the Palestinian and Israeli narratives finally confront each other with no go-between, and so far it seems the Palestinians are winning.

While tweets themselves can't necessarily change the world, they reflect and influence a broader trend that is going to have a big impact.

Comparing the pro-Palestine protests that accompanied the Israeli attacks on Gaza in 2008, 2012, and 2014, one can see that with social media, voices in Gaza have more prominence and access than ever. This does have an effect on public opinion.

With time, this change in public opinion, especially in the West, is going to weigh on politicians too.

It is already happening as the recent resignation of the British minister Sayeeda Warsi shows.

Moreover, new recruits are joining and promoting the boycott, divestment and sanctions (BDS) campaign.

For example, the bombing of the Islamic University of Gaza and UNRWA schools sparked outrage against Israel, and will undoubtedly spur support for academic boycott.

In the future, these cases might be used against Israeli leaders in criminal courts or serve as a basis for possible persona non-grata rulings barring them from travel.

Furthermore, the online calls for the International Criminal Court to investigate the Israeli assault on Gaza could transform into street movements, putting real pressure on the international community to not stay silent and watch while Israeli leaders get away with their crimes once again.

This has already happened with the calls for an arms embargo on Israel when earlier this month British activists occupied an Israeli arms factory in Birmingham, chaining the doors shut and hanging a banner on the roof which read: "UK: Stop Arming Israel."

Only days later, the UK government announced that it would suspend arms exports to Israel if "significant hostilities" resumed.

This is a small step—and the UK has yet to act on it—but it would not have happened at all without grassroots pressure building up over a long time.

For the first time, we are seeing the Palestinian reality get through and overwhelm Zionist propaganda.

Perhaps the most important victory of all will be attained years from now, when history comes to say its word: it will undoubtedly favor the truth.

Until that day comes, Palestinian activists will continue to mobilize all platforms available to build support for their just cause.

The Electronic Intifada, August 21, 2014, http://bit.ly/1ohxowo

Selection of Tweets, July 5–August 26
Farah Baker (@Farah__Gazan)

Farah Baker is a teenage student in Gaza whose tweets garnered much attention during the attacks.

July 5: An F16 bombed at suhoor time for Muslims.

July 7: It's a messy night in every single part in

July 7: Have I lost my legs!! I can't walk! I still can't move!! I thought the bomb was at the garden.

July 7: The situation at my area now: the power is cut, i can hear nothing but the bombs, f16s and the radio, the only light i see is the bomb's.

July 7: Whatever happens we won't turn our backs and leave

July 9: Israel still bombing! Oh my god i can bear no other bomb! I'm breathing hardly and shaking. This is enough.

July 9: Another massive bomb 5:44 am. Oh now I started crying :'(

July 10: I swear I smile involuntarily when I remember that I'm Palestinian. I am proud <3 :D

July 10: Someday I'll become a lawyer and I'll focus on Palestine and all oppressed countries. I'll focus on human rights. I'll spread justice.

July 11: Warships shot poor fishermen boats. They have nothing to hunt by so they'll get no money.

July 11: The number of drones in the sky is higher than the stars number.

July 11: 6:15 am. This is not a good morning at all. The sky is raining rockets.

July 12: Israel bombed a house and a mosque while muslims were praying taraweeh. 17 martyrs and more than 35 injuries in these 2 shells.

July 12: Gazans donate blood to save others lives <3

July 16: My relatives when bombed when they were playing football in the seaport near their shop! WHY?!

July 19: OMG! That wasn't an f16! It was a new type used for wars called f22.

July 20: Massacre in al #shujaia_holocaust last night and no ambulances or fire engines could reach them until morning

July 21: Since the first hours in the morning until now 4:10 pm, warships haven't stopped shooting at all.

July 21: Today, Israel bombed civilians house while they were preparing for a feast and they killed the mother and her 7 children.

July 21: Israel must know this: You can burn up our mosques and our homes and our schools, but our spirit will never die.

July 21: #Gaza is beautiful and its citizens r cute and lovely. If you come to Gaza, trust me u'll love th city. Gaza and ppl don't deserve this war.

July 22: My 6 yrs old sister have witnessed 3 wars!

July 23: As soon as we started having futoor(breaking fast) warships started bombing.

July 23: The power is finally back after being cut for 23 hours.

July 23: If you want to find a safe place in #Gaza do NOT stand beside a CHILD #GazaUnderAttack #AJAGAZA #Gaza

July 25: The power had been cut for 35 hours.

July 25: A hospital in Beit Hanoun just been bombed.

July 25: The sun looks sad.

July 25: If I could stop this...

July 25: If I could bring happiness back...

July 26: 73 bodies were found under the rubble during searching in the ceasefire and they still searching for more.

July 27: Hello, I'm Farah Baker. I live in #Gaza and Hamas is NOT using me as a human shield

July 28: Okay, on the first day if Eid Al-Fitr 10 children were killed while they were playing on a swing! Oh yeah the swing could kill Israelis.

A father looking for his 11-year-old son finds him in the morgue. The child was killed along with 16 other children from Gaza Beach camp who were struck by Israeli shelling while playing on the beach on the first day of Eid al-Fitr, the holiday that marks the end of Ramadan.
Photo by Ezz Al Zanoon.

July 28: Bombing continues in all parts of #Gaza strip and there are many wounded. This is our Eid #GazaUnderAttack #AJAGAZA #ICC4Israel

July 28: They are bombing heavily in my area. This is the worst night in this war. I just want you to know that I might martyr at any moment.

July 28: This is in my area. I can't stop crying. I might die tonight.

July 28: I AM NOT SAFE AND I CAN'T GET OUT OF THE HOME BECAUSE THEY'RE BOMBING IN MY AREA.

July 28: I AM CRYING AND CAN'T STAND BOMBS SOUND! I'M ABOUT TO LOSE SENSE OF HEARING.

July 28: I'm 16yrs old and have witnessed 3 wars, as I see, this is the hardest one.

July 28 : ALTHOUGH THIS NIGHT IS THE WORST FOR ALL GAZANS, WE WILL STAY STRONG AND RESIST.

July 29: I COULD SURVIVE LAST NIGHT!! I AM ALIVE!! Alhamdulillah.

July 29: Daddy who's a dr. says that th hospital's operating rooms r full & there r ppl dying bc there is no room to conduct operations.

July 29: 2nd day of power cut: food in the fridge rotted, water on th verge of force bc we can not run the motor, Mobile Charge almost finished

July 30: I went out to visit my grandma today, I discovered that at least one building was bombed in every single street.

July 30: 48 hours without electricity ...

July 30: HUGE MISSILE JUST LIT UP THE AREA AND ROCKED THE HOUSE.

August 3: I miss the sea, I miss my friends, I miss ice cream, I miss happiness and joy. I MISS MY ORDINARY LIFE.

August 6: I wanna thank every single human being who stood with me and supported me, I wish I can do sth 4 u. I love u very much, u made me stronger.

August 6: This 16 years old teenager has survived three wars, and her heroes are ppl who stood with her n tough days.

August 20: If I were mr. muscles, I would break all the rockets, tanks, warplanes and warships and throw them away.

August 20: My school bus is shelled :(

August 24: My dreams turned from travelling to Spain and learning guitar to staying alive!

August 24: Rockets are falling in huge quantities, they're falling like the rain and making strong orange light in the sky.

August 24: The house is jumping! Huge attack.

August 25: The day 51 of the war: 2131 martyrs most of them are women and children.

August 25: The smoke smell is sneaking to the house and made the area foggy.

August 25: ISRAEL CAN FIND NOTHING TO BOMB, SO IT'S HEADED TO BOMB TOWERS WHICH ALL ITS RESIDENTS ARE CITIZENS.

August 25: Make protests and revolutions against what is happening in #Gaza, don't keep watching. Bring humanity back.MOVE MOVE MOVE #GazaUnderAttack

August 25: A car just passed, when I heard its sound I jumped over my bed! I thought that was a rocket falling sound.

August 25: Wake me up when humanity is back. I guess I will never wake up.

August 26: IOF [Israel Occupation Forces] is calling us on phone.

August 26: Celebrations in Gaza because the cease fire just begun.

Tweets from a Doctor in Gaza, July 26
Belal Dabour (@Belalmd12)

Belal Dabour is a young Palestinian doctor who works in Shifa Hospital, Gaza. A temporary "humanitarian" ceasefire was announced on July 26 to allow the Gaza emergency services to go to some of the places worst hit by Israel to try to recover bodies from neighborhoods blown to smithereens.

07:58:51 At the dark of night Israel bombed Al-Najjar family house in Khanyounis. At least 8 members of the family were killed, half of them children.

14:51:08 So far the medics have recovered 60 bodies from the areas they reached during the ceasefire. In 2 hours alone the death toll reached 940!

15:16:18 Mohammed Al-Abadla, one of 2 medics Israel murdered in one day, yesterday.

16:25:21 All across history the only colonial movements which succeeded were the ones which exterminated all of the original population.

16:26:20 The Zionist movement failed to do so, and therefore Israel is bound by laws of history to be defeated and give Palestinians their rights..

19:30:13 Here there were homes and dreams. Here there was Life, but Israel didn't like that.

03:48:21 Hamas fighters' strict compliance during the ceasefire is proof that what IOF claimed were "command and control centers" were just homes.

03:50:15 Home targeting is the utmost form of collective punishment Gazans had to endure during the 3 wars Israel waged against #Gaza.

15:02:26 The world needs to comprehend that Gaza has had enough siege and it's not going back to that. We've had enough power shortages up to 60%!

15:03:31 We've had enough drinking water that is basically sewage. We've had enough living on donations. Enough of unemployment rates above 40%!

15:05:04 We've had enough of Israel counting how many calories we can get. Enough humiliation on the borders. Enough being treated as terrorists!

15:54:24 Bombardment near by.. I felt the shock wave.

18:34:33 Never blame the victim for speaking up. Never blame the oppressed for standing to their oppressor.

Palestine Unbound (Excerpt)

Steven Salaita

Editors' note: Palestinian American Steven Salaita is an activist and academic whose tweets during the war were described by the University of Illinois as lacking in "civility" and used as a pretext for firing him before he taught his first class. The following tweets (published in Journal of Palestine Studies *44, no. 1 (Autumn 2014), p. 199) are a sample of his war commentary.*

July 26: We can argue into eternity, but in the end this is what matters most: the people in #Gaza are there because they're not Jewish.

July 26: Cheyennes will have to be roundly whipped—or completely wiped out—before they will be quiet—Chivington Sounds awfully familiar #Gaza

July 27: I'm pretty sure anybody can buy those #Hamas rockets at nearly every interstate exit in South Carolina.

July 28: #Israel's attack on #Gaza is a "war" in the same way that cannibalism is "dining with a friend."

July 29: All these dead children in #Gaza, yet Michelle Obama hasn't even seen fit to do a hashtag publicity stunt.

July 30: It's common for colonizers to show disrespect to the dead in addition to the living. Just ask any Native nation.

July 31: Arab Rulers: Maintaining relations with #Israel as it destroys #Gaza symbolizes why everybody recently revolted against your sorry asses.

August 1: I'm absolutely shocked that #Israel broke the ceasefire, said not a single person in the entire world.

Palestinian Artists Illustrate the Deadly Realities in Gaza
Mariam Elba

It's hard to find the words to encapsulate how infuriating and sorrowful the situation is getting to be in Gaza. As of this writing, over 750 Palestinians—the overwhelming majority are civilians—have been killed in Gaza. Over a quarter are believed to be children. Facing the most difficult of circumstances, we are seeing the resilience of Palestinian youth through the simplest, yet most powerful of mediums: creative arts intervention.

A Palestinian blogger from Gaza, Refaat Alareer has been collecting digital altercations of photos of Israeli airstrikes exploding over their communities. Within the clouds of smoke and debris, are various pictures. Some contain nationalist Palestinian symbols, others simple drawings of faces. These faces range from having solemn expressions to those that are crying over the destruction below them.

This is a trending artform called "smoke art photography." One of these young Palestinian artists, Bushra Shanan, a graphic designer from Hebron in the occupied West Bank, captioned one of her photos (see page 216): "This is how they see it, this is how we see it." These works of art are a way for these Palestinians to tell their own stories, an opportunity to show what western media won't allow them to. These artists are challenging the portrayal of Palestinians in mainstream media and taking it upon themselves to change it.

These photos have been shared widely on social media and are windows into the dreams and imagination of Palestinian youth living under constant siege. Many of these works are anonymous. These images remind us of how we looked up at the clouds as children to see shapes of animals,

Art by Bushra Shanan.

dragons, people, faces—anything one's imagination could conjure. It's also a grim reminder that under this destructive black cloud there are people who are affected by this persistent violence. It's almost as if these faces are looking at Gaza, surveying the damage and mourning over what had happened.

This is not the only time we have seen Palestinians turn reminders of their besiegement into art. We can look to examples such as Palestinians in the West Bank turning the tear gas canisters shot at them into potted plants, or young Palestinians practicing parkour using the dense neighborhoods they live in as obstacles.

This is how these young people want to be represented and remembered. Not as mere numbers. Not as mangled corpses lying in concrete rubble. But as children that see shapes and figures and pictures even in the most horrific and brutal of circumstances. They are reminding the rest of the world that they too are people who value life and want to live as the rest of the world does: quietly. These altered photos are one of the most vital examples we have of how Palestinians in Gaza are coping with the consistent presence of death surrounding them.

Waging Nonviolence, July 24, 2014, http://bit.ly/1lMzH5v.

Three Poems for Gaza
Nathalie Handal

Gaza

Once in a tiny strip
dark holes swallowed hearts
and one child told another
withdraw your breath
whenever the night wind
is no longer a land of dreams

The Gazans

I died before I lived
I lived once in a grave
now I'm told it's not big enough
to hold all of my deaths

Tiny Feet

A mother looks at another—
a sea of small bodies
burnt or decapitated
around them—
and asks,
How do we mourn this?

World Literature Today, July 29, 2014, http://bit.ly/1xvs1U6

Palestine, Summer 2014

Kim Jensen

There are things that allow you
to take leave of the earth:
the sea quarantined
behind cement and wire
chains   of signifiers
that men have been here—
gun mounts and barbed towers
a crested wave in the shape
of a warped neck.

There are things
that allow you to take leave:
four small children with frozen faces
grey from the dust of rubble
the color red blossoming
beneath motionless heads
in Shuja'iya   Rafah   little Salma
swaddled in blood. The Bakr boys   fleeing on the beach
hovering above the sand   Don't ask me
to wait   to see   what happens
when they land.

This is how you take leave
of ancient cities
that rose in the gilded mist of imagination.
You take leave as a monk does
singing in chants and madrigals.
You take leave in a spiral motion, a lyric wish
in formal passage—so that perhaps
your absence
may be noted.

The UN Counted the Number of Our Dead
Samah Sabawi

The UN counted the number of our dead
Thank you for that
But we know how to count

The UN published reports and factsheets
Detailing 51 days of "hostilities"
Provided footage and documentaries
The massacres were televised
2131 killed...1.8 million terrorized
110,000 displaced...
495 children slaughtered...dead
And the UN said
"There is nothing more shameful
Than killing sleeping children"
Grave concerns were expressed
Rivers of tears were shed
The UN counted the number of our dead
Thank you for that
But we know how to count

The UN issued denunciations
Using words like "indiscriminate"
"disproportionate"
And even "abomination"
The UN huffed and puffed
And called for an investigation
And they counted...and counted...and counted...
...the number of our dead
Thank you for that
But we know how to count

We have counted our dead and displaced
Since 1948
We have counted demolished homes
And uprooted trees
Detentions
Fatalities
Injuries

Revoked permits
Exiled refugees
We have counted settlements
That spread like a disease
We have been counting for years
Towers and walls
Checkpoints and wars
And we know how to count
Resolutions and declarations
Statements and denunciations
Press releases and condemnations
War crimes and violations
So thank you for counting United Nations
But we know how to count

Ferguson and Gaza

Zeina Azzam

They tried to make us invisible:
the silencing bullets invaded,
disappeared without fear
into our flesh.

The killer and the instrument
have no words,
just tear gas and F16s
and unknowable means.

Our bodies, like our maps,
filled with holes.

Our eyes sting, burn.
Injustice everywhere smarting
like smoke
in the air we breathe.

In Ferguson,
officers in gear
imitating soldiers
conjuring a killing field.

In Gaza
drones watch and thrum
there is nowhere to run.
People explode, houses collapse,
soldiers imitate themselves.

I am not invisible.
I've been the eyelash in your eye
the stone in your shoe
the heartburn in your heart
burning, fashioning words that
you chew and chew
—a bitter, strange fruit
you cannot swallow.

Ferguson is our new word—
it's been on our tongues
with Intifada, Soweto, Tiananmen,
Tahrir, Occupy, Occupy...
In Gaza, we're occupied,
we speak Ferguson like we've been there.
We have brothers and sisters in Missouri.
We tell them how to resist
because it's in our blood to resist.

Yes, let's make the police uncomfortable,
the soldiers squirm,
the reporters struggle to censor or understand.
Ferguson is our word to speak, shout, sew on our flags
as we hoist them high in the sky.
As Michael Brown fell to the ground:

My hands are up, don't shoot me
My food has run out, don't evict me
My face is brown, don't choke me
My baby is crying, don't tear gas me
My family is homeless, don't jail me
My flag is flying, don't arrest me
My job is gone, don't erase me
My son is dead, don't torture me
My door is broken, don't rape me

My school was bombed, don't dismiss me
I have nowhere to go, don't starve me

My hands are up, don't shoot me

My hands are up, don't forget me.

From Dawn to Dusk
Lina H. Al-Sharif

Caught between a rock
and Gaza.
Gaza is a hard place.
Boxed into the trenches of abyss.
Jawed between the teeth of darkness.
Slowly filtered of life.
Sea left to salt.
Remembered when the night gnaws the dusk.
Forgotten when the dawn makes the almonds husk.
Dusted, trumped, rusted, crushed.
Like a piece of rusk.
The dim din.
The ticking bomb.
The sand clock.
The Pandora box.
Gaza is a rock.
coarse, hoarse.
Gaza is a hard place.
Rose and fought.
Filters in light.
Remembered with pride.
Forgot to recline.
From dawn to dusk...
when crushed like a rusk
When the almonds husk
Gaza never succumbs.

An Unjust World
Nour ElBorno

I was asked to talk to the world
In the language they know
About the truth.

They say I must try to wake them up.
Make them see and listen.
I say "No."

A world that needs someone to tell them,
"It's wrong to kill children and women."
Must rest and discuss global worming, with an "o."

I'd rather save my voice
To comfort the child,
And the mother that mourns,
The man who saw his house turn
From shelter to ash,
And the bodies of his family burn along.

I refuse to waste what is left of me
On defending my right to exist.

The world was told so many times;
It decided to keep the dark,
And blow out the candles instead:
Who needs light when darkness takes over;

It is an unjust world
I refuse to take part in.

I'd rather stay under the wreck
With the memories I have built
Than stand on a stage,
And show my rage.

My people are dying,
And you are trying
To be convinced:
You give reasons why murder is okay;

You give speeches when a child being an orphan is fine;
When bombing a hospital is the only choice left.

You ask me to tell the world what?
Wake up?

Dude they are a hopeless case.
Why?
Because they need reasons to be convinced
Why a human must be allowed to exist.

I no longer seek refuge in the world
I hereby announce myself an outworld.
And my people and I, hell yeah, will never cease to exist.

Seafaring Nocturne
Lena Khalaf Tuffaha

Across the sea floor
limbs curl through ink clouds,

settle near an old trunk
spilling its treasures.

Sodden maps surrender
their borders and silver frames

tarnish. Currents swallow
dark clots and over Gaza the rain

sorties over new monuments
of ash, open wounds of rubble.

Waves buckle under
the weight of swollen

vessels, flayed carcasses, hauling
hundreds of lives

to shorelines where no one
looks forward to their arrival,

relentless survivors, white-knuckle
grasping at stars, reaching

for the buckle of Orion's
belt, cleft of his boot.

Even on nights when
there is no anchor, the brine

of a dream consumed

by the sea, salt like shards
on parched lips is gentler

than the sulfur of prayer,
the dry scorch of waiting for mercy.

This Miraculous Terrorism
Omar J. Sakr

For Shayma

My tears are ineffective bombs,
Hamas-hurled, Israel-born. If only
I had more funding, state-of-the-art
GPS navigation, I could guide them

to bless the right soldiers, the ones
without guns, untrained and still young,
the little snakes-to-be, the ones dying.
How is it that I can hear their screams

and feel their mourning, their subtle ghosts,
even though I sit deaf, hands folded,
eyes closed, an ocean away? The flashes
of cameras, and the twitching of fingers

(accompanied by the sterile antiseptic drawl
of reporter-speak, desert dry), can only account
for so much. Why am I crying so fucking hard?
When my tears dry up, when I am emptied of loss

will the US kindly resupply my stock? Sorry,
this isn't—I'm not trying to be—I'm just tugging
on this invisible line tying my chest to Palestine;
I don't know when it got there, or which fisherman

sunk his hook so deep. But it isn't just one line
is it? No, it's a multitude, a madman's cat-cradle
criss-crossing the world, set to twang
every time someone says the word 'Muslim',

the label on the net I was caught in from birth.
It's been getting tighter and tighter every year,
and now our skin is fetish-marked fishstocking
and we are all marred as one. Maybe this is why

as these children die, and men and women burn
beneath this name, this dog-tag embedded in our eyes,
I feel their grief, their death, as if it were my own. It is
my name too, it is my grief too, it is my heart too, it is

my children too, and my death toll forever. That accounts
for some of it, but not all. I hear the air sirens in Tel Aviv,
I hear the death-chants on the streets, I taste their fear,
as a distant echo, as the other side to this bitter coin.

Right now though, as I sit here shaking and weeping,
I cannot escape the call of my name shouted so often,
ringing in the shrill music of missiles singing. I cannot
stop thinking about Shayma Sheikh Khalil, 5 days old,

prematurely born via caesarean section
on July 26, 2014, 10 minutes after her mother died
in an Israeli airstrike. They called her a "miracle baby"
for surviving, for being pulled out of familial death

and into life. However, she died
July 30, 2014, after the power plants in Gaza
were attacked and her incubator shut off.
I could not write those words—

thank god for copy + paste, thank god for reporter-speak
otherwise you'd have only my trembling, my aching
grief, my tears to translate into meaning. Shayma
is merely a pebble in a blood-strewn avalanche:

over 1300 dead. 433 a week. 61 a day. Two an hour.
Such efficiency of horror. Such methodical death
tearing gaping holes in this fishing net, letting the bodies
rise to the surface to line the streets like grisly buoys.

I cannot think anymore. I cannot speak anymore.
I cannot feel anymore, or see through the shame.
When even miracles are killed in their infancy
in their first blue blush of life,

can you imagine what comes next? Dare you even try?

Scratched That [blog], http://bit.ly/1bMOAKn

6

51 Days Later, and Counting: The Untenable Status Quo

Another assault ends with a cease-fire, and suddenly there is a slow and steady stillness, a numbing status quo. We have counted the dead and recounted the massacres and surveyed the damage and tallied the cost of reconstruction. We have heard the rebuttals of the carefully crafted spin. We have the figures to assist us in making sense where there is no sense to be found, as though an explanation would provide closure. But after the smoke clears, who will remember the dead? And what happens when the lenses of the cameras turn elsewhere, and gaze of the global community is no longer absorbed by Gaza's burning images on their screen? And how will those left behind live, rather than merely survive? Who will be there to pick up the pieces, to cradle the children, and to heal an entire society violently ruptured by an onslaught that deliberately aimed to fracture livelihoods, destroy productivity, and deprive a new generation of any chance of prosperity? This chapter takes stock of where things stand in the immediate aftermath of the assault and explores the long-term impact of repeated assaults on Gaza.

How Israel Is Turning Gaza into a Super-Max Prison

Jonathan Cook

It is astonishing that the reconstruction of Gaza, bombed into the Stone Age according to the explicit goals of an Israeli military doctrine known as "Dahiya," has tentatively only just begun two months after the end of the fighting.

According to the United Nations, 100,000 homes have been destroyed or damaged, leaving 600,000 Palestinians—nearly one in three of Gaza's population—homeless or in urgent need of humanitarian help.

Roads, schools and the electricity plant to power water and sewerage systems are in ruins. The cold and wet of winter are approaching. Aid agency Oxfam warns that at the current rate of progress it may take 50 years to rebuild Gaza.

Where else in the world apart from the Palestinian territories would the international community stand by idly as so many people suffer—and not from a random act of God but willed by fellow humans?

The reason for the hold-up is, as ever, Israel's "security needs." Gaza can be rebuilt but only to the precise specifications laid down by Israeli officials.

We have been here before. Twelve years ago, Israeli bulldozers rolled into Jenin camp in the West Bank in the midst of the second intifada. Israel had just lost its largest number of soldiers in a single battle as the army struggled through a warren of narrow alleys. In scenes that shocked the world, Israel turned hundreds of homes to rubble.

With residents living in tents, Israel insisted on the terms of Jenin camp's rehabilitation. The alleys that assisted the Palestinian resistance in its ambushes had to go. In their place, streets were built wide enough for Israeli tanks to patrol.

In short, both the Palestinians' humanitarian needs and their right in international law to resist their oppressor were sacrificed to satisfy Israel's desire to make the enforcement of its occupation more efficient.

It is hard not to view the agreement reached in Cairo this month for Gaza's reconstruction in similar terms.

Donors pledged $5.4 billion (Dh19.8bn)—though, based on past experience, much of it won't materialize. In addition, half will be immediately redirected to the distant West Bank to pay off the Palestinian Authority's mounting debts. No one in the international community appears to have suggested that Israel, which has asset-stripped both the West Bank and Gaza in different ways, foot the bill.

The Cairo agreement has been widely welcomed, though the terms on which Gaza will be rebuilt have been only vaguely publicized. Leaks from worried insiders, however, have fleshed out the details.

One Israeli analyst has compared the proposed solution to transforming a third-world prison into a modern U.S. super-max incarceration facility. The more civilized exterior will simply obscure its real purpose: not to make life better for the Palestinian inmates, but to offer greater security to the Israeli guards.

Humanitarian concern is being harnessed to allow Israel to streamline an eight-year blockade that has barred many essential items, including those needed to rebuild Gaza after previous assaults.

The agreement passes nominal control over Gaza's borders and the transfer of reconstruction materials to the PA and UN in order to bypass and weaken Hamas. But the overseers—and true decision-makers—will be Israel. For example, it will get a veto over who supplies the massive quantities of cement needed. That means much of the donors' money will end up in the pockets of Israeli cement-makers and middlemen.

But the problem runs deeper than that. The system must satisfy Israel's desire to know where every bag of cement or steel rod ends up, to prevent Hamas rebuilding its homemade rockets and network of tunnels.

The tunnels, and element of surprise they offered, were the reason Israel lost so many soldiers. Without them, Israel will have a freer hand next time it wants to "mow the grass," as its commanders call Gaza's repeated destruction.

Last week Israel's defense minister Moshe Yaalon warned that rebuilding Gaza would be conditioned on Hamas's good behavior. Israel wanted to be sure "the funds and equipment are not used for terrorism, therefore we are closely monitoring all of the developments."

The PA and UN will have to submit to an Israeli database the details of every home that needs rebuilding. Indications are that Israeli drones will watch every move on the ground.

Israel will be able to veto anyone it considers a militant—which means anyone with a connection to Hamas or Islamic Jihad. Presumably, Israel hopes this will dissuade most Palestinians from associating with the resistance movements.

Further, it is hard not to assume that the supervision system will provide Israel with the GPS co-ordinates of every home in Gaza, and the details of every family, consolidating its control when it next decides to attack. And Israel can hold the whole process to ransom, pulling the plug at any moment.

Sadly, the UN—desperate to see relief for Gaza's families—has agreed to conspire in this new version of the blockade, despite it violating international law and Palestinians' rights.

Washington and its allies, it seems, are only too happy to see Hamas and Islamic Jihad deprived of the materials needed to resist Israel's next onslaught.

The *New York Times* summed up its concern: "What is the point of raising and spending many millions of dollars...to rebuild the Gaza Strip just so it can be destroyed in the next war?"

For some donors exasperated by years of sinking money into a bottomless hole, upgrading Gaza to a super-max prison looks like a better return on their investment.

Jonathan Cook: The View from Nazareth (blog), October 27, 2014,
http://bit.ly/1Ex9Csy

Under Siege: Remembering Leningrad, Surviving Gaza
Ayah Bashir and Esther Rappaport

In the state of siege,
Time becomes space transfixed in its eternity,
In the state of siege,
Space becomes time that has missed its yesterday and its tomorrow.

—Mahmoud Darwish, *Under Siege*

Overview

How does one communicate what life is like under siege? Much has been written to describe the besieged Gaza Strip yet Al-Shabaka Policy Member Ayah Bashir and Guest Author Esther Rappaport bring new insights and perspectives in this Roundtable. Ayah Bashir lives under the siege of Gaza at the present time; Esther Rappaport's family lived under the siege of Leningrad during World War II. Ayah and Esther came to know each other through social media during the Summer 2014 attack on Gaza and first thought of writing this piece during this war. In their reflections and analysis of the two sieges they ably communicate the stark reality of life under siege. The reflections of each of the two authors are given in their own voice. They also provide some additional factual information and background, and this part of their discussion, conversation, and argument is presented in the voice of a "narrator."

Ayah Bashir and Esther Rappaport: We are in agreement that this text is not a normalization project. It is based on our mutual belief and political message that the siege as well as the illegal Israeli occupation of 1967 must come to an end and that Palestinian refugees must be able to return to their towns and villages. We strive to achieve Palestinians' rights as enshrined in international law and we aim for equal rights for both Palestinians and Israelis.

What Is a Siege? Leningrad and Gaza

Esther Rappaport: My mother's birth city, Leningrad, was under German siege for 2.5 years during World War II. Early in the siege, a fire broke out in the emergency food supply storage facilities, leaving the city essentially without food. Throughout the siege, the Soviet government tried to smuggle food supplies into the city via Lake Ladoga and by airplanes but because of unceasing German bombardment and shelling very few of those supplies were safely delivered. The population was subjected to extreme starvation, which killed around one million people. Some resorted to eating pets and dead bodies, others scraped wallpaper off the walls to consume the potato starch glue that had some nutrients.

Midway through the siege, a narrow pathway was opened up, making it possible to evacuate the most vulnerable population groups out of the city. This pathway, leading through the frozen Lake Ladoga, became known as The Road of Life but was also often referred to as The Road of Death, because it was so dangerous. My grandfather, who was then about 40, died of a minor illness in besieged Leningrad, as a result of the lack of food and medical supplies, and was buried in a mass grave. After his death, my mother, grandmother and uncles were evacuated from the city via the Road of Life/Death with the kindergarten that my grandmother worked for.

Ayah Bashir: Few outsiders realize what the siege is like. The Gaza Strip, the place where I have lived all my life, has been under a brutal ongoing siege since 2007. After Hamas seized control of Gaza in 2006, Israel, aided by Egypt, sealed off the passages, i.e. the six crossings with Israel and the

Rafah crossing with Egypt, and tightly controlled the exit and entry of people and all goods including humanitarian and medical supplies.

Our deprivation of our basic rights under the siege has not only been physical but also mental and psychological. For example, when I was in high school in 2006, I had big dreams of academic life at the university. I did my best to get a very high Grade Point Average (GPA) so that I could fulfill my dream of studying at Birzeit University in the West Bank. My GPA was 98.6%. However, like many other students I was unable to leave Gaza and had to accept this fact. Doing my BA studies in Gaza, I suffered from the shortage of both electricity and books. The university's library was limited to the literary writings of Charles Dickens and Shakespeare and held no contemporary literature or texts on women's studies, the field in which I am very interested. Books are among the many thousands of items whose entrance into Gaza is severely restricted. I finished my BA in English Literature without being able to buy a single novel or book. We constantly depended on photocopying and online resources. Due to Israel's siege and occupation the educational system in Gaza takes us back to the Middle Ages.

Narrator: Under international humanitarian law (IHL), a siege is not prohibited per se in armed conflicts. However, combatants must respect other provisions of IHL as well as of international human rights law, such as not starving the enemy civilian population and not imposing collective punishment. The siege of Gaza has been widely defined as collective punishment, which is prohibited under Article 50 of the Hague Regulations of 1907 and Article 33 of the fourth Geneva Convention). The ICRC confirmed in 2010 that the closure constitutes collective punishment and violates Israel's international law obligations.

Ayah Bashir: The position of international law is of course controversial for me personally in the sense that a siege is not prohibited outright. However, international law clearly identifies the Gaza Strip as being occupied and subject to an illegal siege where collective punishment and war crimes are continuously perpetuated by Israel. Hence, it is clearly a problem for me that so many people, organizations, donors and decision makers tend to treat Gaza as if it is a humanitarian issue. Gaza's problem is political: the root causes of the "conflict" rather than the specific humanitarian challenges have to be tackled and international law must be applied if the world wants to see any sustainable positive change in the life of the Palestinians. It is politics that has been impeding the enforcement of law with regard to Palestine/Israel since 1948.

Esther Rappaport: Although I am very concerned about Gaza and consume all the information I can get, it is difficult to form a clear sense of what daily life is like there under the siege. The information that comes through is limited and often inaccurate (for example, we know which aid items are theoretically allowed in but have no way of knowing what actually gets delivered). Unlike the West Bank, which I visit regularly and can learn first-hand about the harsh realities on the ground, I cannot visit Gaza. Although many journalists report from Gaza, they tend to focus on political issues while aid organizations typically only report on the most urgent humanitarian concerns. I think this lack of information is part of the siege: Gaza is cut off from the world in such a way that it is hard to know what is happening there.

Ayah Bashir: It was so clear from our exchanges that Esther reads a lot about Gaza and is very well aware of the facts, politics and information here. However, she was often very surprised to hear what I had to say about the suffering of the people in Gaza. The truth is that although information is available, it does not reflect the detailed reality that people are living in Gaza. Even for people here it is sometimes incomprehensible and unimaginable.

For example, as part of my work with an international non-governmental organization (NGO), I went to Khuza'a before the latest attack to interview a beneficiary who was identified as a success story: She had been able to plant a wonderful garden with a variety of trees as well as vines. After the attack, I went again to see her. Everything was destroyed! I was expecting to see the remnants of the trees, but to my great astonishment I couldn't even find burned trunks: It was as if this land had never had trees on it! I was thinking that if I had not seen it by my own eyes I would never have believed or imagined that there had been life here.

Narrator: Under a siege, life is reduced to existence or survival. Economic development and trade are kept to a minimum and residents are forced to rely on humanitarian aid. Culture stagnates as few have the resources or mental space for anything beyond the mundane. The future becomes unimaginable and hope is hard to maintain.

In Leningrad, the siege was part of a world war. The powerful Soviet army was fighting against the German army, and the residents believed that at some point the war would end and the siege would fall. Gaza doesn't have an army but only guerilla groups and the siege does not take place during a declared state of war. It is, rather, the chronic state of events and part of the deadly systematic routine of oppression that the occupying power is forcing on the Palestinian population. Eighty percent of Gazans are refugees from other locations in historical Palestine (the part that is now Israel). They are entitled by international law to their right of return to their places of origin yet they are unable to realize this right. The siege has gone on for seven years and there is no end in sight.

Yes, It Is Similar to the Holocaust

Esther Rappaport: I think being under a siege is similar to being in a Jewish ghetto during the Holocaust. You cannot come in or out very easily, living conditions are extremely hard, your life is not worth much and you can be killed or starve at any point. Both the international Jewish community and Germany have in fact recognized the similarity between a siege and the Holocaust: In 2009, the Jewish survivors of the Leningrad siege were recognized by Germany as Holocaust survivors and received financial compensation after a lengthy struggle led by the Claims Conference, a Jewish organization that fights to obtain compensations from Germany for Holocaust survivors. I am not sure why only Jews from among the residents of Leningrad received the recognition and the compensation, even though the conditions were identical for Jews and non-Jews in the besieged city; I believe this is due to the fact that no one fought on behalf of the non-Jewish survivors the way the Claims Conference fought for the Jews.

Perhaps being in Gaza during an Israeli military operation is even worse than being in a ghetto, and more like being in a concentration camp, since any Gaza civilian, no matter what age she or he is, what their political affiliations are or where they are situated, can be killed or maimed any second and there is literally nowhere to flee for safety.

I am aware that many Jews experience it as offensive and hurtful when the Palestinian suffering is compared to the Holocaust. As a psychologist who regularly treats post-trauma victims, I understand these reactions and do not wish to hurt anyone's feelings. Nonetheless, I think that the objective similarities between some aspects of the Holocaust survivors' experiences and some aspects of the besieged Gaza population's experiences are profound and cannot be ignored.

Because both my parents have been recognized as Holocaust survivors, I feel entitled enough to the Holocaust heritage to make this claim.

Ayah Bashir: Reading about Leningrad, I wholeheartedly felt that I could relate to the experience of horror. It has been always so perplexing for me to understand how the same descendants of Jewish people who historically have suffered remarkably as a nation are capable of dehumanizing us. The Nazis tried to starve Leningrad as Hitler's strategic decision was to bypass Leningrad and strangle the city into submission, instead of attacking it directly. Israel, I feel, is doing both: Killing Palestinian civilians in frequent massacres as well as slowly and collectively making our life unbearable by denying our most basic needs, such as the need for water supply and electricity. I remember my aunt saying, during a "humanitarian truce" in the latest aggression on Gaza, "Why are they calling it a truce as if we—the ones still living—were not also dying during this period? We are dying, but slowly, without medicine, adequate food, electricity and cooking gas."

Gaza is now in near-absolute darkness with most households receiving only up to four hours of power per day as Israel's direct and repeated bombings have badly damaged the only power plant in Gaza and the electricity infrastructure. I clearly remember the nights when the only source of light was coming from artillery flares illuminating the sky. At that time, it was a great privilege to have your phone charged so that you could check up on a friend or a relative. I recall the long painful moments when we were disconnected not only from the world, but also from each other. Not only could I not go out to hug my closest friend who fled her house in Al-Shuja'iya because of the continuous bombings—I could not even call her as I did not have the electricity to charge my phone. It was also rare to have enough water to wash. Leningrad was also cut off from both water and electricity in the winter of 1941–42.

Esther Rappaport: Hundreds of thousands of Leningraders were killed or died of cold or starvation as the daily bread ration was 125 grams (4.4 ounces) per person in December 1941. In Gaza, most people are not literally starving but the Israeli government thinks it has the right to control the residents' intake of food, deciding precisely how much food they deserve to receive, of what kind and how frequently. Immediately after imposing the siege on Gaza, a senior Israeli official described Israel's planned response. "It's like a meeting with a dictician. We have to make them much thinner, but not enough to die." Since then, the Israeli Health Ministry has been calculating the Gazans' daily caloric needs—a form of control that I find disgusting.

Ayah Bashir: Israel ruled that Gazans needed a daily average of 2,279 calories—requiring 170 trucks a day. That was the theory. The reality is that what has been allowed in is much less than half of these minimum requirements.

How Economies Function—Or Not—Under Siege

Narrator: In Leningrad, non-war-related industry and trade were kept to a minimum at the time of the siege. Some residents went to work and others did not; on some occasions, stores continued to carry merchandise not required for survival even including luxury items, but both industry and trade were far below the pre-war levels. For food supplies, the military and the civilian population alike depended on the rations issued by the government.

Although Israel's official reason for the siege of Gaza is security-related in order to prevent or counter the Hamas rocket fire into Israeli territory, Israeli official statements suggest that one of the purposes of the siege is to prevent the development of the Palestinian economy.

The Israeli government has been quoted as stating, "A country has the right to decide that it chooses not to engage in economic relations or to give economic assistance to the other party to the conflict, or that it wishes to operate using 'economic warfare'."

In Gaza, unlike in Leningrad, there is no attempt to literally physically starve the population. Rather, the population is being starved metaphorically: reduced to a minimalist existence and kept dependent with no end in sight, with no hope of sustainability, autonomy or growth.

In practice, the Gazan economy has been made inoperable by the siege. Exports are not allowed, except for limited and intermittent exports of agricultural products that have to be carried out under strict Israeli control. The three military operations in seven years have left Gaza in ruins and a large portion of its population exists in a state of perpetual humanitarian crisis, depending on aid and with no prospects of economic sustainability.

Ayah Bashir: For example, in Deir al-Balah where I live in the central Gaza Strip the Al-Awda Factory was entirely destroyed in the recent attack. This factory had manufactured sweets, biscuits and ice cream since 1977. It employed over 400 workers in three shifts, 24 hours a day. Now the factory is gone and all the workers are unemployed.

Narrator: According to the United Nations Office for the Coordination of Humanitarian Affairs (OCHA), 178,000 Palestinians are directly affected by the restrictions on access to the land and sea in Gaza. Restrictions on the land cover 62.6 km^2, which represents 35% of Gaza's agricultural land and 17% of the entire territory. The Internal Displacement Monitoring Centre has estimated an annual loss of 75,000 tons of agriculture output (some $50 million). At the same time, Israel continues to benefit from both Gaza and the West Bank as major captive markets for its products by preventing possible alternatives to Israeli merchandise.

Ayah Bashir: Before the Summer 2014 attack, a large percentage of the population had access to food and water through a vouchers assistance scheme. After the massacre and the intolerable humanitarian devastation as people lost their homes and possessions, many have had to obtain even their clothes through vouchers issued by NGOs.

The Israeli and Egyptian blockade of Gaza has led to skyrocketing unemployment resulting in despair, depression, drug addiction, and recently fatal attempts at migration as people have drowned while attempting to flee Gaza by sea. Prolonging and tightening the existing siege on Gaza is not about destroying Hamas, disabling tunnels, or stopping rocket fire into Israel. It has always been about Israel's control over our lives, land, and borders. And it has been about killing more of us.

Significantly, this strategy is not new. We have endured a long history of massacres, decades of systemic ethnic cleansing, 47 years of military occupation, and apartheid policies and forced displacement since 1948. All this continues to this day. However, the latest massacre, genocide, holocaust—call it what you may—of Gaza in 2014, is the most ferocious one I have ever witnessed with my own eyes. The deliberate targeting and ruthless slaughter of defenseless civilians, the majority of whom are refugees, the massacre of entire neighborhoods as in Al-Shuja'iya, Khuza'a, and Rafah, and the obliteration of houses: All are deeply shocking.

What is happening in Gaza is multigenerational trauma. Years of war and aggression have affected everything—human beings, houses, infrastructure, land, trees, animals, livelihoods, hospitals, medical supplies, schools, mosques, factories, water resources and even Gaza's only power plant. All of this was already in bad condition before the summer of 2014 as a direct result of the seven-year-long siege imposed by Israel and enforced by Egypt.

Resistance, Escape, and the Political Climate

Narrator: When Leningrad was under siege, the powerful and well-organized Soviet army fought on behalf of the besieged civilian population. The civilian population, including children, was also mobilized by the city and state governments to assist in the resistance efforts, e.g., by producing ammunition and erecting anti-tank barriers.

With respect to Gaza, claims are often made that the militias use the civilian population as human shields, e.g., by firing rockets out of civilian areas. These claims are then used as justifications for attacks against civilians. But based on the example of Leningrad, the situation of siege itself makes it difficult to make sharp distinctions between the military and the civilian population: The civilian population as a whole, collectively subjected to extreme hardship by the siege, will ardently mobilize to support the resistance efforts in any way it can. The besieged population's support for those fighting to end the siege on their behalf was near absolute in Leningrad, despite the fact that the government was oppressive. It is substantial in Gaza's case as well, particularly during military operations. Because the siege is intolerable, the population views ending it as the most urgent goal and is willing to ignore, for the time being, the rulers' other deficiencies.

Escape from the besieged Leningrad was hard and so is fleeing besieged Gaza. To be evacuated from Leningrad, one needed to ride over a frozen lake with the risk of sinking if the German army's bombardment broke the ice. (No tunnels could be dug out of Leningrad because the land is frozen most of the year.) To flee Gaza, one needs to be one of the few who are able to prove special circumstances (e.g., those who have received a scholarship to study abroad may be issued a permission to leave via Israel), have the luck to be allowed into Egypt through the Rafah crossing, which is opened sporadically and inconsistently, or travel to Egypt through the tunnels—tunnels that Egypt has since destroyed. Terrifyingly, precisely during those times when Gaza becomes most dangerous—i.e. during Israel's military operations—the exits shut down completely and leaving becomes near-impossible. At other times, Israel's policy of issuing permits is somewhat conflicted: on the one hand, there is a desire to encourage emigration, on the other, an equally strong desire to deny Gazans freedom of movement.

Ayah Bashir: I think it is so dehumanizing and humiliating to view us, the Palestinians of Gaza, as miserable. It is true that we suffer enormously and survive catastrophic conditions, but we are also people who resist for our dignity and justice. We all pray that we don't become one of Gaza's numbers. After surviving the 2008–09 onslaught on Gaza, during which I felt so powerless, I joined the Palestinian movement for Boycott, Divestment and Sanctions (BDS) on Israel that gave me a renewed sense of optimism and sense of power. I also survived the ruthless assault on Gaza in 2012. The Israeli horror of 2014 coincided with the 9th anniversary of the

BDS call and the 10th anniversary of the International Court of Justice's Advisory Opinion on the illegality of Israel's apartheid wall in the occupied West Bank. Not only does Israel's brutality intensify the growing BDS movement, it also shatters the illusion that the Israel of today has any intention of achieving a just peace.

Esther Rappaport: I wish that people in Israel and in the West were more aware of the non-violent resistance to the Occupation and the Siege that so many Palestinians practice. Unfortunately, the only form of resistance coming from Gaza that the world pays any attention to is rocket fire: When that is happening, Gaza is in the news and the world becomes aware of its existence, its plight, and its desire for change. Once, however, a ceasefire is achieved, the world sighs with relief, as if the problem was now solved, and forgets all about Gaza. It is intolerable that nothing else that the Palestinians of Gaza say or do manages to break the walls of complacency and indifference.

Al-Shabaka: The Palestinian Policy Network (al-shabaka.org),
http://bit.ly/1DgSy4E

Investigators: Israel Fired on Civilians Carrying White Flags
Charlotte Silver

The Israeli military opened fire on a mass march of civilians who were carrying white flags and calling out "peaceful, peaceful" as they tried to exit Khuza'a village in southern Gaza, which had been under siege for three days, corralling them back into the village.

Those who were trapped in the village had tried to coordinate a safe evacuation with the International Committee of the Red Cross, but Israel's shelling would not let up.

This is one of the many disturbing findings from one of the only international and independent fact-finding missions that Israel has allowed to access the Gaza Strip since the August 26 ceasefire that ended 51 days of intensive bombing.

Last week the mission published "No Safe Place," a more than two hundred-page report on their findings from their forensic investigation. The mission's aim was to assess the types, causes and patterns of injuries and deaths and to collect evidence for potential use in local or international justice mechanisms.

The investigation devotes special attention to the siege on Khuza'a, detailing the attempts civilians made to flee Israeli fire and finding that the army used people as human shields, executed civilians at close range, and intentionally neglected mortally wounded children. During the four days of heavy bombardment of the village, scores were critically injured. While the report refers to twelve deaths specifically, it says the total number of casualties remains unknown.

The report also finds that most of those who were killed during the summer assault were crushed to death, frequently in their homes, and often with other members of their family by their side. More than 142 families lost at least three members in a single strike. Recent casualty counts estimate the total killed as at least 2,257 and as high as 2,310.

Organized by Physicians for Human Rights-Israel and Gaza-based Al Mezan Center for Human Rights, the investigation team consisted of international experts from the fields of forensic pathology, emergency medicine, pediatrics and health and human rights.

The delegation interviewed 68 injured patients and reviewed 370 digital images and records of those killed and the report includes transcripts of interviews with injured civilians and medical professionals. While limited in scope and access, the report concludes that evidence suggests several serious violations of human rights and international humanitarian law.

All of Gaza a Battlefield

The report confirms what was reported at the time: indiscriminate and total bombardment of the Gaza Strip.

While in some cases the Israeli military dropped warning leaflets or sent "warning strikes" or "roof taps," this did not save lives as there were no clear boundaries of where the battlefield was. The army targeted possible escape routes, ambulances carrying wounded people, and individuals attempting to flee.

Hospitals Overwhelmed

The mission found that the rate of injury and death overwhelmed the capacities of hospitals in the Gaza Strip, and the destruction of medical facilities further undermined medical workers' ability to adequately treat patients. Doctors testified that they were forced to take shortcuts like not using sterile gloves or sterile gauze and had use makeshift suture material. Some patients reported that they found maggots in their wounds after leaving the hospital.

For those needing rehabilitation, their options are now worse. Gaza's sole public rehabilitation hospital, al-Wafa, was completely destroyed during the war. And while there are other private or nongovernmental medical rehab facilities, there is a lack of cohesion in providing services to the population in part because many international groups refuse to coordinate with Hamas government authorities.

Psychological Trauma

The majority of the 68 patients interviewed suffer insomnia, flashbacks, nightmares, screaming, loss of appetite, weight loss, depression and unstable emotional states.

Doctors and nurses said that the trauma they saw was not just from the attacks, displacement, threats of joblessness and poverty, but also the sense of total isolation from the rest of the world. Those interviewed said that Gaza's dire situation affects individuals' life choices, like whether or not to get married and have children.

Medics Under Attack

Yousef al-Kahlout, a 32-year-old medic with the Palestine Red Crescent Society, said Israel's tactics posed a danger more grave last summer than in previous wars. Ambulances came under repeated attack and first responders were put at risk by Israel's method of striking a single target multiple times in close succession, a method called "double tapping."

The report adds that the Israeli military would often refuse to coordinate with the International Committee of the Red Cross to allow local medics into an area to evacuate casualties, forcing them to enter dangerous areas at their own risk.

Even when the Israeli military would coordinate with the Red Cross to allow Red Crescent staff to enter an area, medics would come under fire.

Powerful Explosives Used Indiscriminately

Huge numbers of injuries and deaths last summer were caused by the indiscriminate use of large amounts of powerful explosives, the report states.

One weapon used to inflict such destruction is called an "explosive barrel" by local residents and "Tzefa Shirion" (Viper Armor) by the Israeli military. Its stated purpose is to clear landmines for advancing troops, but

Israel used it in at least two neighborhoods in Gaza: Khuzaʻa and Khan Younis. The device can be rolled out from a tank or dropped from the sky; as the barrel rolls forward, its explosives are detonated and a corridor is created for the military.

The mission also found evidence corroborating the use of flechette shells, which indiscriminately spray thousands of tiny darts, and evidence suggesting the use of Dense Inert Metal Explosives (DIME), an experimental weapon that was previously used in Israel's 2008–2009 military attack on Gaza. Doctors also found computer chips with SONY markings embedded in bodies like shrapnel.

The publication ends by encouraging the pursuit of justice, while also acknowledging the deep sense of pessimism Palestinians have towards any international mechanism to deter Israel's constant attacks on Gaza. One head nurse at al-Shifa hospital said: "Many felt that 'another report' documenting their pain and suffering would be ineffective in addressing the root causes of the morbidity and mortality they experience daily."

The Electronic Intifada, January 28, 2015, http://bit.ly/1CsRMTZ

Revealed: Gaza Orphans Israel Trip Was Government-Backed PR Stunt
Ali Abunimah

An Israeli initiative to exploit a group of Palestinian orphans from Gaza to burnish Israel's blood-soaked image backfired on Sunday when Hamas, the Palestinian political and military resistance movement, put a stop to it.

A group of children whose parents were killed in the Israeli assault on Gaza last summer and several adult chaperones were about to pass through the Erez crossing into Israel on Sunday to be greeted by Israeli officials and a media throng.

But Hamas officials halted the visit. According to a statement posted on Facebook by the interior ministry in Gaza, security services stopped "37 children of martyrs from departing to the lands occupied in 1948 [Israel] for a suspicious visit to several settlements and occupied cities." It said the step was taken "to protect the culture of our children and our people and protect them from the policy of normalization."

But it appears the children—though they were the props—were not the target.

The visit was the brainchild of an Israeli operative deeply involved in settlements in the occupied West Bank, working closely with the Israeli government.

It involved Palestinian counterparts in Israel with ties to the ruling Likud party and the Zionist political establishment.

It is unlikely that the non-governmental organization in Gaza that helped coordinate the visit was aware of these facts when it agreed to take part.

Priceless Propaganda

The children had been scheduled to visit the Palestinian town of Kafr Qasim and the Bedouin forced-resettlement town of Rahat. They were also to be received by Palestinian Authority *de facto* leader Mahmoud Abbas in Ramallah.

But the week-long visit would also have provided Israel with priceless photo opportunities of happy, smiling Gaza children at the zoo in the Tel Aviv suburb of Ramat Gan, as well as several Israeli settlements.

Such propaganda would have provided a marked counterpoint to the indelible images from the summer of some of the more than five hundred children killed and thousands injured and terrorized by Israel's attack.

Israeli media, public relations officials and international media sympathetic to them, including the BBC and AP, have presented Hamas' action as preventing hapless orphans from making what Reuters termed "a rare goodwill visit to the Jewish state."

Exploiting Orphans

Many commenters on social media have noted that Israel advocates fully supportive of the siege of Gaza and of restrictions that routinely prevent Palestinian students, medical patients and loved ones of prisoners passing through Erez, were suddenly outraged that this particular group of children had been stopped.

Marian Houk, a journalist currently based in Ramallah, said it was "hard to understand" Israel's decision to allow the orphans in to "visit kibbutzes, a zoo" and Mahmoud Abbas, while it had recently "refused to allow a man from Gaza to visit his dying 18-month-old son in the West Bank, and then refused to allow him to attend the funeral."

The story of Israel's refusal to let Bakr Hafi visit his young son, Emir, who died on 14 December, was told by *Haaretz*.

The *Electronic Intifada's* Rami Almeghari reported last year on the case of twelve-year-old Amal Samouni, who has shrapnel in her skull from Israel's 2009 attack on Gaza, and was denied permission to travel through Erez for treatment in the West Bank.

Not surprisingly, news of the visit provoked a fierce outcry from Palestinians on social media.

Refaat Alareer, the Palestinian writer and educator in Gaza, tweeted, "I would categorically refuse for my nephew, whose father Israel murdered, to go to be brainwashed by some liberal Israelis."

In July, Alareer wrote a moving tribute to his brother Mohammed, who played a beloved children's character on Palestinian TV and who was killed by Israel's indiscriminate shelling of Gaza City's Shuja'iya neighborhood.

"Israel is so vulgar and despicable it murdered my niece Raneem's dad and now Israel wants to use [children like] her for propaganda," Alareer added.

"Look kid, this is where the Israeli artillery was stationed when it bombed your house, cool, right? Love us! We just killed ur parents," Twitter user @ANimer quipped, imagining an exchange between one of the orphans and his Israeli hosts.

Settlement Promoter Behind Visit

Media have identified the organizer of the initiative as Yoel Marshak, an official of the Kibbutz Movement. Kibbutzim are Zionist communal settlements whose influence and popularity peaked in the mid-twentieth century.

Although they took over much land from Palestinians ethnically cleansed in 1948—atrocities in which many kibbutz members participated—kibbutzim long enjoyed a progressive, or even socialist image in the West due to their collectivist ideology. This was used for years to effectively market Zionism to a poorly informed or credulous international audience.

Reuters labels Marshak a "peace activist," but a more accurate descriptor might be "land-theft activist." He is himself an agent encouraging Jewish settlement in the occupied West Bank on behalf of the Israeli government.

Marshak presents the hosting of the orphans as utterly selfless. "We initiated this to plant seeds of peace," Marshak told the English-language *Times of Israel*.

"In a few years, when these children become the leaders of the Gaza Strip, they will remember this positive experience well and know that they can live in peace, nation next to nation. We don't have to fight and kill, we can also hug and extend our hand in friendship."

Marshak told the Arabic-language website *Lakom* that the visit is "the least that we can offer these orphans whose families were killed by our army."

He also denied any political connotations for the visit.

"To turn this into a political act ahead of the Israeli elections [in March] is to exploit the pain of these orphans," Marshak told *Times of Israel.*

Backed by Defense Ministry

But in the Hebrew-language media, Marshak is more frank about the propaganda value of the children for Israel's bloodstained reputation.

"There is only profit in this visit: the innocent children, who are rescued for a week from the closure and stress and get some days of holiday and a trip, and the State of Israel, which happens upon the opportunity to show the children against who and what their parents were fighting, and to gain points in the hostile world opinion," Marshak told the Israeli publication *Ynet.*

"The trip was meant to show a positive face of Israel," *Haaretz* also reported, citing Marshak.

When asked, "On whose behalf are you working?" Marshak makes clear that this was no individual initiative, but one with high-level state support.

"It is important to say that I am acting—and I stress this—as an agent of the Kibbutz Movement, and as a volunteer," he told *Ynet.* "And moreover, I am not acting alone. Working with me, in full and dedicated cooperation, are the regional staff in the south, and people from the ministries of absorption, education and defense, and there is full and supportive back-up from the Secretary of the Kibbutz movement, Eitan Broshi."

No Palestinian can move through Erez without clearance by Israeli intelligence services, so the very fact that the visit was approved at all confirms official interest and involvement.

"The Shin Bet [security service] had given the green light for the children and their five minders to enter Israel," Marshak told AFP.

Blocking mothers

Marshak has not always been a supporter of humanitarian contact and passage across Israeli-imposed borders.

In 2010, Marshak was one of the organizers of an action to prevent Palestinian prisoners in Israeli jails receiving family visits.

"Campaigners to free captured Israeli soldier Gilad Shalit blocked entry to the Hadarim prison near Netanya on Tuesday in an attempt to prevent mothers of Palestinian inmates visiting their sons," *Haaretz* reported at the time.

Marshak was unabashed in defending this vindictive collective punishment to achieve his goals. "We want to kick-start the process and avert a situation in which talks freeze and we lose Gilad," Marshak told the paper, referring to the Israeli occupation soldier captured by Gaza-based Palestinian resistance fighters in 2006 and released in an October 2011 prisoner exchange.

Helping Steal Palestinian Land

Marshak's claims of high-level support are entirely credible. In 2010, *Haaretz* reported that Marshak headed a Kibbutz Movement task force to encourage demobilized Israeli soldiers to move to settlements in the occupied West Bank, particularly in the Jordan Valley, where the indigenous Palestinian population has been almost completely pushed out by settlers.

Marshak told *Haaretz* that years earlier, "his unit launched a project to settle kibbutz members in evacuated military installations near Yitav, a kibbutz north of Jericho, in cooperation with the Prime Minister's Office."

The goal, Marshak said, "was to keep state lands"—appropriated from Palestinians—"in the hands of Jews and provide security to individuals sent there by the state and the Kibbutz Movement."

Last year, Marshak forcefully defended Israeli colonization in the occupied West Bank, declaring that even if there were a two-state solution, it would not result in the settlements he has helped reinforce being removed.

"I do not see any situation where they remove hundreds of thousands of residents from their homes," Marshak told the Israeli publication *Arutz Sheva*.

Palestinian Partners in Israel

Among those waiting for the orphans on the Israeli side of the Erez crossing was Malik Freij, a Palestinian citizen of Israel and director of "Candle for Peace and Brotherhood," a non-governmental organization based in the town of Kafr Qasim.

At Erez, Freij posed with a banner, pinned to the Israeli bus that was supposed to collect the children, emblazoned with the name of his organization in Arabic and Hebrew.

In Arabic only, the banner states "Gaza's orphans...our children," and, adding insult to injury, "Breaking the siege on Gaza."

Freij has been quoted in numerous media reports lamenting Hamas' blocking of the orphans and presenting the effort as entirely humanitarian.

"There was a plan, it was approved by authorities in Gaza. It was approved from the charity [in Gaza]," Freij claimed in an interview on Israel's i24 News television.

"But unfortunately there is media here. It would look like Israel wanted to use them, that Israel killed their parents and wants to use the children. This is a mistake," Freij added.

Freij told media that his organization sent truckloads of aid into Gaza during the Israeli assault last summer, and had previously hosted a small number of orphans.

He has been less open, however, about his and his organization's ties to Israel's Zionist ruling parties and establishment.

According to its official Israeli registration documents, Candle for Peace and Brotherhood was founded by Freij, Yishai Zandani, Jaafar Khaled Abdul, Said Sarsour, Shawqi Sarsour, Amin Issa, and Atif Qrinawi.

No financial reports appear to be available since its founding in 2002.

Ties to Likud

But what is remarkable are the ties several Candle for Peace and Brotherhood founders have to Likud, the ruling party of Prime Minister Benjamin Netanyahu.

The name Yishai Zandani comes up in Internet searches as a minor-league Likud activist. Atif Qrinawi, by contrast, has demonstrated much bigger ambitions. Qrinawi is a former member of Likud and was sixty-seventh on the party's candidate list at the 2006 election. In Israel's 2013 election, Qrinawi ran as the head of his own party, "Hope for Change."

In an interview with Reuters, Qrinawi predicted he would win ten of the 120 seats in Israel's parliament, wiping out the traditional Arab parties (his party won no seats). He even offered to form an "unprecedented" electoral pact with Likud, bringing the Arab public to them.

Asked if he would have been prepared to join a government led by Netanyahu and his key political ally Avigdor Lieberman, who is particularly notorious for his anti-Arab racism, Qrinawi replied, "I'm ready to sit in any coalition."

The Good Arab

Candle for Peace and Brotherhood director Malik Freij has been less overtly political, though there is plenty of evidence of him currying favor with Israel's establishment. In 2010, Freij was part of an abortive delegation—along with Marshak—that planned to go to Gaza to appeal for the release of the Israeli prisoner of war Gilad Shalit.

Almakan, a website that often runs sympathetic reports about Freij, revealed that in 2012 he paid a private visit to Shaul Mofaz, leader of Israel's Kadima party. The purpose of the visit, according to *Almakan*, was to "congratulate [Mofaz] on his courageous decision to join the coalition government led by the Likud."

Mofaz, Israeli army chief of staff during the second intifada and later defense minister, is most notorious among Palestinians for his advocacy and execution of massive violence that has claimed thousands of Palestinian lives. Since 2002, victims of Mofaz have been seeking, without success, to bring him to justice for war crimes.

In a similar vein in 2009, Freij wrote an email to Marshak introducing himself and offering fawning congratulations for the settler activist's assumption of a higher function in the Kibbutz Movement.

In seeking out and flattering the likes of Mofaz and Marshak, Freij appears to willingly inhabit a role long cultivated by Israel since the 1950s: the "good Arab" who accepts his inferior place in the prevailing order and is prepared to get along with the Zionist state. In return he can achieve a little bit of status and patronage to distribute to other obedient Arabs.

Freij appears in many YouTube videos promoting his various endeavors. In one 2011 video, for instance, he boasts about how, through his appeals to the Israeli defense ministry, he was able to get permission for a Palestinian woman in the West Bank to enter Israel to marry her fiancé.

In the video, he claims Palestinian citizens of Israel come to him from all over the country for such assistance, while he decries the alleged failure of the existing Arab political parties.

Freij did not respond to an email address found for him online, and a phone number connected with his name was not answered. No organizational contact information for Candle for Peace and Brotherhood was located.

Gaza Counterpart

By using his organization as the front for the orphans initiative, Freij appears to have been providing another service to the Israeli establishment, but the scheme still needed a counterpart in Gaza.

The partner for the planned visit was Yaboos Charitable Society, a Palestinian social services agency based in the southern Gaza Strip city of Rafah.

Yaboos has strongly denied that its involvement in the orphans visit had any "normalization" or political goal whatsoever. Khalid Abu al-Aramneh, Yaboos' program and communications director, told Ma'an News Agency that his organization received an invitation from Candles for Peace and Brotherhood, a "Palestinian organization in Kafr Qasim," to sponsor a number of orphans on a recreational visit to Kafr Qasim, Umm al-Fahm and Rahat—predominantly Palestinian towns in present-day Israel.

The mere name of Kafr Qasim would have had great Palestinian nationalist cachet: all Palestinians know it as the site of the notorious 1956 massacre of dozens of unarmed villagers by Israeli forces.

Al-Aramneh said there was never any intention to visit Israeli settlements or strengthen ties with Israel, as Israeli media have claimed. He added that based on the invitation, his group coordinated with the "concerned authorities" in Gaza—almost certainly a reference to Hamas—to arrange for the travel of the children Yaboos nominated.

Al-Aramneh said that once the bus carrying the children arrived at the Gaza side of the crossing and Israeli media began to report that the children would be visiting Israeli settlements, his organization's board of directors decided "after several consultations" to cancel the visit, given that the "security services at the crossing confined their position by advising them not to proceed with the trip."

Earlier in December, the Israel-based Arabic-language website *Lakom* published an image of a letter from Yaboos' board of directors welcoming the invitation from Candle for Peace and Brotherhood and sending greetings from the people of Gaza to their counterparts in Kafr Qasim.

Although the text is difficult to read due to the poor quality of the image, the October letter addresses Candle for Peace and Brotherhood and the people of Kafr Qasim as fellow Palestinians tied by the "blood of the martyrs and the soil of the nation."

The letter states specifically that orphaned children would be visiting "the village of Kafr Qasim," and no other destination is listed. It makes no reference to, and shows no awareness of, any involvement of any Zionist organizations and no "goodwill" toward Israel whatsoever.

The letter corroborates al-Aramneh's characterization of Yaboos' perception of the initiative as being entirely one of solidarity from Palestinians in Israel to Palestinians in Gaza with no connection to Zionist entities. A conclusion from Yaboos' explanation combined with the evidence from the letter is that the charity was in effect tricked in a kind of bait-and-switch.

It should be noted that no organization in Gaza could knowingly publicly associate itself with a visit supported by Israeli officials and settlement bodies such as the Kibbutz Movement and hope to maintain any local credibility or support.

Hasbara

While it is clear that Marshak was—as he himself stated—working with the Israeli government, it is difficult to determine where the orphans scheme was hatched.

The Jewish Agency's ubiquitous online propagandist Avi Mayer immediately took to Twitter to try to play down any official Israeli role or intent to use the children for *hasbara*—or official propaganda.

"What's notable about this incredible humanitarian initiative is that organizers made absolutely no effort to draw attention to it," Mayer tweeted.

"The laughable notion that this trip was an Israeli PR ploy is belied by the fact that no one knew about it until Hamas crushed it," he added.

What Mayer didn't explain is how all the journalists gathered on the Israeli side of Erez knew to be there to wait for the children. Moreover, advance notice of the "humanitarian" visit would have been completely counterproductive resulting—as it did—in cancellation. The propaganda value of the children would have been realized only once they were through Erez.

For the same reason, the Kibbutz Movement did not send the invitation to the children's charity in Gaza directly, but used Malik Freij's Likud-linked Candle for Peace and Brotherhood as an apparently patriotic Palestinian front.

While this cynical ploy failed, Israel's spinners are trying to make the most of it with Mayer slamming Hamas' "incredible cruelty" in disallowing the visit.

What remains unchanged is that 900,000 children—half the population of Gaza—are still under a tight siege in deteriorating conditions.

Imprisoned as they are in a ghetto, Israel affords Gaza's children fewer rights than the Tel Aviv zoo animals the orphans did not get to see.

The Electronic Intifada, December 29, 2014, http://bit.ly/1vDaxOX

Uncovering the Truth in Khuza'a
Ruairi Henchy

As one of the coldest winters in recent history across Palestine and the Middle East starts to break, and people begin to look toward the spring, the inhabitants of Khuza'a in the Gaza Strip are still reeling from the effects of the July–August 2014 war. The approximately one and a half month conflict left 2,205 Palestinians dead, mostly unarmed civilians, whereas 71 Israelis died, the vast majority of them soldiers.

The asymmetric conflict mostly consisted of the Israeli army's intensive bombardment of the Gaza Strip by land, sea and air. However, for short periods of the conflict, Israeli soldiers did enter and occupy some areas of Gaza. As soon as the ground troops entered, however, they were met with stiff opposition from all of the Palestinian resistance groups, and within a matter of days, the IDF had already sustained its most significant casualties since the 2006 war with Lebanon. These losses drew a fierce backlash from Israel, who reverted to intense bombardment and demolition of entire neighborhoods in order to avoid clashing with the Palestinian militant groups at close quarters on the ground. One such area was the town of Khuza'a, east of Khan Yunis in the southern Gaza Strip.

The *Palestine Monitor* spoke with Walid Rouk, a local from Khuza'a working with the charity Freedom Aid, to hear more about what happened there and the efforts to return to normal life since the war ended. Walid explains that the population of Khuza'a is about 15,000 people, 84 of whom were killed during the war. This small village lost more people during last summer's violence than the entire state of Israel.

Rouk recounts with pride how Yasser Arafat awarded his town a certification, along with the West Bank city of Jericho, for being the most beautiful places in Palestine. Khuza'a was an important agricultural area in Gaza, renowned for its olive groves and lemon trees. It was one of the quietest areas in the notoriously overcrowded Gaza Strip, and was well provided for in infrastructure with good telecommunications, electricity and water services.

All of this was wiped out in four short days when the Israeli army entered and occupied the area with tanks and infantry. Thousands fled in the face of the invasion, carrying their loved ones and whatever few prized possessions they could lug along with them. Walid stayed with his family and neighbors for two weeks in a United Nations school, and he paints a harrowing picture of the scenes he encountered on returning. The Khuza'a of his youth was no more. Ninety percent of the buildings were completely destroyed by bulldozers and tanks. This included his old school, all but two of the town's mosques and all but one room of his old house lay in ruins. The town graveyard had even been blown to smithereens—there was no safe haven in Khuza'a for the living or the dead.

Indeed, Walid tells of how the stench of death haunted the air as he returned to what used to be his home town. Most of the residents had fled, but during the initial evacuation, he had already seen neighbors and friends, many carrying white flags, being shot at from behind by the advancing Israeli soldiers and artillery. Moreover, some of the old and infirm were unable to run and could not be evacuated in time. Nobody who remained in the village was left alive after the Israeli army's four-day occupation. So when Walid and others returned, the unburied remains of many of their neighbors had already been baking in the summer heat for two weeks, in the streets and beneath the rubble. They lay where they fell.

One such case, which has shot to prominence as of late, is the death of 74-year-old Ghalya Abu Rida. The Israeli military released a photo of an IDF soldier giving Ghalya a drink of water. She was later found dead. Ahmed Qdeh, a journalist from Al-Aqsa TV and a local from Khuza'a claimed to have witnessed this event. "During the aggression, an Israeli soldier approached the old woman and took a photo for another soldier while giving her water. They then executed her by shooting her in the head from a distance of one meter and let her bleed until she died," said Qdeh.

An Israeli English language blog, *Israelly Cool*, dismissed the story as lies and "a Palestinian Blood Libel." Walid Rouk, however, corroborates Qdeh's account, saying that he visited the area around Ghalya Abu Rida's home after returning to Khuza'a. He spoke to her neighbours and family about what happened; "I went to see her family at her old home and they showed me the medical report from Nasser Hospital in Khan Younis. The report said she was shot from one meter away and the bullet was lodged inside of her head," Rouk claimed.

This alleged summary execution is one of the many cases being looked at closely by groups such as Human Rights Watch and Amnesty International as instances of possible war crimes committed by the Israeli army in Khuza'a and elsewhere in Gaza during the Operation Protective Edge in the summer of 2014. Both parties have been prevented from sending their international experts to Gaza to document the facts, but have been slowly gathering information through the limited operations they already have extant in Gaza.

Walid trembles when he speaks about what happened in Khuza'a, condemning the lack of humanity of the world toward his people. "No media covered what happened, there was no camera from anywhere covering Khuza'a. This is a war against humanity, not just Palestinian people," he told the *Palestine Monitor* over the phone.

This is what led him and his friends to set up the Humans of Khuza'a Facebook page, to record some of these stories and share them with the world. With the ongoing work being done to document potential war crimes in the area and the Palestinian Authorities recent moves to join the International Criminal Court, perhaps the horrors of Khuza'a will be belatedly relayed to the world through these fora.

Palestine Monitor, 27 January 2015, http://bit.ly/1CsVmNK

A Call from Gaza: Make Israel Accountable for Its Crimes in Gaza—Intensify BDS!
Gaza Civil Society Organizations

From the ruins of our towns and cities in Gaza, we send our heartfelt appreciation to all those who stood with us and mobilized during the latest Israeli massacre. In the occupied West Bank, Israel has embarked on one of its largest illegal land grabs in decades by confiscating another 1000 acres of Palestinian land to expand its illegal colonies. Now, our battle to hold Israel accountable for its fresh war crimes and crimes against humanity has begun. The outcome of this battle to end Israeli impunity will determine whether Israel's latest assault will be yet another stage in Israel's "incremental genocide" of Palestinians or the turning point that will bring an end to Israel's status as an entity above the law—the world's dangerous pariah. The outcome of this battle depends on you.

Two months after its 2008–09 massacre in Gaza, Israel's prize was an upgrade in trade relations with the European Union. By 2012, western powers in cooperation with the UN Secretary General had effectively prevented all investigation by the United Nations and the International Criminal Court (ICC) into the war crimes and crimes against humanity that Israel committed during the attack.

During the most recent massacre, on August 2, 2014, three days after the occupation forces bombed the designated UN humanitarian shelter in Jabaliya refugee camp, killing 20 civilians and wounding at least 150 people as they slept, the U.S. Congress approved $225 million in additional military aid to Israel. The following day, the occupation forces bombed another UN shelter in Rafah killing ten civilians and injuring dozens. Also during the massacre, Germany sold Israel an attack submarine with nuclear capability, and Britain refused to freeze its arms sales to Israel. These and other forms of criminal complicity from world governments and official bodies pave the way for Israel's ongoing genocidal attacks. It is up to people of conscience and all those who seek peace with justice worldwide to make sure this complicity ends now.

We urge you to stand with the Palestinian people in its entirety and to demand that Israel be held accountable for the war crimes and crimes against humanity it has committed and continues to commit against the Palestinian people everywhere. We urge you to intensify boycott, divestment and sanctions (BDS) campaigns to further isolate Israel economically, militarily, academically and culturally.

Intensify BDS against Israel in all fields, including by taking the following actions:

1. Working to have arrest warrants issued against Israeli war criminals and for them to be tried before your courts.
2. Pressuring governments to impose a comprehensive military embargo on Israel.
3. Pressuring governments to suspend all free trade and bilateral agreements with Israel until it complies with international law.
4. Building effective direct action against Israel and Israeli companies, such as the inspiring Block the Boat actions that prevented Israeli ships from unloading in California and Seattle, and the occupations of Israeli weapons company Elbit Systems' factories in the UK and Australia.

5. Working within trade unions to raise awareness about Israel's regime of oppression and engaging in effective BDS measures such as stopping handling of Israeli goods, divesting trade union funds from Israel and complicit companies, and boycotting complicit Israel trade unions. The trade union movement has a proud history of successful campaigning against apartheid in South Africa, and the Congress of South African Trade Unions has joined Palestinian trade unions in calling for trade union action to end Israel's impunity.

6. Holding to account those corporations and retailers that support and profit from Israel's regime of occupation, colonialism and apartheid, including by boycotting their products and taking creative and direct action. The Palestinian BDS National Committee (BNC) has suggested a list of corporate criminals to target: http://www.bdsmovement.net/make-an-impact.

The majority of the world's people are waking up to the reality of Israel's rogue regime of oppression and racism. For the rest of what is supposed to be the International year of solidarity with the Palestinian people, demand an end to Israel's criminal impunity. Stand with Gaza, and act for freedom, justice and peace in Palestine.

Issued by the Palestinian BDS National Committee (BNC) and the following Gaza organizations/unions:

Palestinian General Federation of Trade Unions
University Teachers' Association in Palestine
Palestinian Non-Governmental Organizations
    Network (Umbrella for 133 orgs)
Medical Democratic Assembly
General Union of Palestine Workers
General Union for Health Services Workers
General Union for Public Services Workers
General Union for Petrochemical and Gas Workers
General Union for Agricultural Workers
Union of Women's Work Committees
Pal-Cinema (Palestine Cinema Forum)
Herak Youth Movement
Union of Women's Struggle Committees
Union of Synergies—Women Unit
Union of Palestinian Women Committees
Women's Studies Society

Working Woman's Society
Palestinian Students' Campaign for the Academic Boycott of Israel
Gaza BDS Working Group
One Democratic State Group

BDS Movement, September 5, 2014, http://bit.ly/1rRtH6Y

One Thing They Can't Bomb
Ned Rosch

The great Indian writer Arundhati Roy once said, "The trouble is that once you see it, you can't unsee it. And once you've seen it, keeping quiet, saying nothing, becomes as political an act as speaking out. There's no innocence. Either way, you're accountable."[1]

For a brief but remarkable nine days in November, 2014, I had the privilege of being part of a Washington State Physicians for Social Responsibility health delegation to Gaza. To be there so soon after last summer's brutally devastating war on the people of Gaza was to catch a glimpse—through the stories we heard and the destruction we saw—of the grotesque horror of those 51 days. The destruction was everywhere, the grief universal, the trauma intense.

"Scared our turn might be next, my husband and I sat our 4 children, ages 9–15, down and we and our kids each talked about what we would do if a bomb hit and we were the only survivor of our family. I felt I needed to have that conversation because the possibility seemed so real and as a mother, I needed to know that our children had a plan." Rawya, who translated for a training that I did with 15 school counselors, shared this with me over a cup of tea during a break. She, the counselors, the children they see, and according to the counselors, it's safe to say, everyone is traumatized. When Israeli jets were heard overhead one evening while we were in Gaza City, the re-stimulated fear was palpable.

On the way into Gaza City, we saw haunting skeletons of homes, people living in bombed out buildings, and mosques, hospitals and factories reduced to rubble. Etched in my mind probably forever will be what we witnessed in heavily bombed neighborhoods of Beit Hanoun, Shuja'iya and Khuza'a. It's hard to find words that adequately describe the utter devastation. People are living in makeshift structures of cardboard and blankets surrounded by rubble. Even though I'd seen these images online, somehow the impact of witnessing families squatting next to what was everything they had owned and what in a matter of seconds had been absolutely wiped out took my breath away, as did a busted up large slab of concrete with names spray painted on it of family members buried under the mounds of debris, a woman sitting on the rubble staring vacantly off in the distance, and a wedding party celebrating amidst ravaged buildings.

And yet, through all the trauma, there is resistance and resilience. An incredibly vivacious woman named Reem in a refugee camp told me she just can't think any more about the future. "All I have," she said, "is today and that's OK as it's filled with opportunities to help people." Reem is opening centers in some of Gaza's most destroyed areas, centers where children play, read, sing, learn French, plant seeds in paper cups—to maybe get a taste of what a "normal" childhood might be like. Very little is normal in Gaza as almost 8 years of siege and 3 wars in the past 6 years have devastated the economy, wrecked the environment, and ripped apart people's hopes that things will someday get better, that there is a future.

People intuitively understand that literally over-the-top stress levels in Gaza are strangling them and their traumatized loved ones. An end to the Israeli siege, freedom and justice for Palestinians would go an incredibly long way towards alleviating the stress, but at least until then, people are hungry for ways to reduce continuous traumatic stress disorder. I was struck by the eagerness of so many people to learn about meditation, relaxation techniques, visualization and yoga to reduce stress. So, in close collaboration with the Gaza Community Mental Health Program (our delegation's host agency) and the Center for Mind-Body Medicine's Gaza Project, two organizations for which I have the deepest respect, I was privileged to facilitate a series of experiential stress reduction workshops.

Taking place in impoverished refugee camps, under-resourced schools, overwhelmed Red Crescent Society clinics, and inundated mental health centers, these workshops were unusually emotional and powerfully interactive. I was honored to lead workshops for wonderful and committed healthcare providers and other public servants who sensitively serve others while doing their best to somehow tend to their own profound loss and grief.

In the first workshop I did with an inspiring and hugely overworked group of school counselors, I suggested at one point that they visualize a beautiful place that they could share with their families and others they love. When I asked what that place looked and felt like, the most common response was that it was hard to push out of their heads the horrors of the summer to find a place of beauty. The second most common reply was that the place they envisioned was safe—extremely safe. From then on I always described the visualized place as not only beautiful but extremely safe and calm, qualities virtually impossible to come by in Gaza.

The yoga portion of my workshops typically included a divider down the middle of the room totally separating women from men as traditionally men should not watch women doing things like, well, yoga! I was generally at the head of the divider so that everyone could see me demonstrating how to do the poses. I kept my eyes focused on the men so even though the women could see me, I "couldn't" see them. The following comments after the final relaxation pose of my first workshop in a ramshackle hotel overlooking the Mediterranean reflect the feedback I heard after every workshop:

"In the 2008–2009 war, I lost my son. A teacher from France taught me some yoga which helped me heal and which I did every day until this summer's war when I just couldn't do anything. This workshop and how it made me feel reminded me that I need to continue my healing."

"Ever since this summer's war, I've had a weight on my chest. I released a part of it today."

In a growing body of research, yoga has demonstrated remarkable effectiveness in assisting people to reduce overwhelmingly high stress levels, especially those dealing with posttraumatic stress disorder. In the December 2014 edition of the *Journal of Clinical Psychiatry*, researchers under the leadership of Bessel van der Kolk, MD, published "Yoga as an Adjunctive Treatment for Posttraumatic Stress Disorder," a study exploring the efficacy of yoga to decrease PTSD symptomatology.

The primary outcome measure was that yoga significantly reduced PTSD with effect sizes comparable to well-researched psychotherapeutic and psychopharmacologic approaches. The study went on to say that yoga may improve the functioning of traumatized individuals by helping them to tolerate physical and sensory experiences associated with fear and helplessness and to increase emotional awareness and affect tolerance.

While going through my 200-hour yoga teacher training program, I always dreamed of someday integrating my passion for yoga with my commitment to activism—especially the struggle for justice in Palestine. Little did I know at the time that utilizing yoga to explore stress reduction would swing open a door to Gaza and be my ticket to meaningfully connecting with its amazing people. All of us who practice yoga know that it can be exceptionally cathartic—its effects experienced not just in the physical realm, but in the emotional sphere as well. The combination of meditation, movement and relaxation in my Gaza workshops burst open emotional dams from which stunningly powerful stories poured forth—on occasion more than I could bear.

Virtually everyone had a story that broke my heart, and each drama revealed another layer of what it is like to live in Gaza, striving for some semblance of dignity in spite of a suffocating siege, tens of thousands of bombs, and a world that seems apathetic to holding Israel accountable.

Yasser, a gentle soul and the executive director of Gaza Community Mental Health Program, our host agency, lost 28 members of his extended family in this summer's bombings. No one in Gaza was spared from knowing someone who was killed or injured in the brutal Israeli assault. Yasser said his family speaks of 28 empty chairs!

Ramadan's family, which lived in Shuja'iya, is now ten people less. One of the deceased was a young girl who was rescued after somehow surviving for 10 days under a massive pile of concrete and rebar, only to die in the hospital two days later. Her name was Yasmin. "I can't get Yasmin and the thought of what her last days were like out of my mind," Ramadan shared, tears wetting his shirt.

"I'm 38 years old. I'm a doctor. I have nothing. Because the clinic has no money, I work as a volunteer. How can I get married and start a family without money?" Salim was sweet, thoughtful and depressed. Half the people in Gaza are unemployed, and many haven't received salaries for six months, a year, or longer.

Everyone yearns for the borders to open so they might be able to work, travel, study abroad, or get medical care not available in Gaza due to the shortage of everything caused by the Israeli siege, but most assert they would return. "Just like a fish can't survive out of water, we can't live out of Gaza for too long. At some point, we need to return," explained Walaa.

Imad, a nurse who works full time and hasn't been paid for a year, invited us to meet his wife and eight children in their modest but comfortable apartment. According to Imad, this was the first time foreigners had ever been in his apartment. When asked how they survive with no income and so many mouths to feed, Imad explained that everyone in Gaza does what they can to help others out since really they're all pretty much in the same boat. He then shrugged his shoulders and pensively posed the question we heard often, "What can we do?"

A couple of days after leaving Gaza, I bumped into Amani in the Old City of Jerusalem. It was great to see someone from Gaza as the intensity of my experiences there were searingly fresh and vibrant. In her mid-20s, Amani, for the first time in her life, was out of Gaza. It's striking that

262   Gaza Unsilenced

Gazans are imprisoned in an area that is only 25 miles long and 5-8 miles wide (smaller than the Portland metro area!). I was happy to see her, but her happiness was that she was able to shop! Her shopping wasn't just for souvenirs, as not much is getting into Gaza. The tunnels that had become the commercial highways through which practically everything—from cars to sheep to pasta—traveled, have been sealed.

A marvelous facilitator, who does support groups for children, invited me to a group she runs for 5 year olds who lost their homes—and more— in the bombing. I sat in the circle with the children as they chose happy or sad faces to represent how they felt. One girl said she took a sad face because her grandfather was killed by a bomb. Others took sad faces because they had bad dreams. The facilitator told me that her own 10-year-old daughter pleaded with her during the war, "Don't leave me alone. I want to die together."

So, there's more than enough stress, grief and sadness to go around, but there is also an undeniable quality and remarkable amount of love, generosity, and samud (steadfastness). Ramadan, who translated for me at a workshop and who is working on a Ph.D. in psychology, pointed out that just as lots of folks may only appreciate their health when they become sick and no longer have it, Palestinians may feel the lack of a homeland more intensely, having so brutally lost it. "Others have a physical homeland, a place they live in or visit. Our homeland lives in our hearts," Ramadan explained over coffee to the sound of the waves beating on the shore. "It's the smell of our grandparents."

While walking through the devastation of Khuza'a, witnessing homes, apartment buildings and a school totally leveled, I was approached by a middle-aged man who politely offered me a large manuscript covered with the dust of blown-up homes. When I asked him what it was and why he wanted to give it to me, he motioned for me to follow him across the street to a huge mound of debris. As we climbed up the pile, he pulled out his phone and showed me a picture of quite an attractive home—his home. He explained that we were standing on that home and that absolutely everything had been destroyed except for the manuscript, his doctoral dissertation, which was a literary critique of the works of Ezra Pound and T.S. Eliot. This professor, who had lost it all, was insisting that I take what remained of a life. I'll never know for sure why. Maybe it was Palestinian hospitality that required him to give this guest something, and that was all he had to give. Perhaps he wanted me to take it to a safe place as he well knew that nothing was safe in Gaza. Possibly this professor was saying that in spite of all the destruction the Israelis could unleash at will, there is one thing they can never destroy: ideas—not only about Pound and Eliot, but also about the restoration of justice to a people who have suffered unimaginable levels of brutality and dispossession.

I'm struggling with many things now, not the least of which is finding words to express the intensity of the experience of getting to know, in some small but profoundly meaningful way, a number of unforgettable and beautiful people in Gaza, and catching a glimpse into the harsh reality of their lives.

It's difficult to make sense of how the occupation and siege of Gaza which is slowly but steadily crushing the life of 1.85 million people can be happening and how the world is doing so little to stop it. But Imad's question, "What can we do?" echoes in my head often. Some of what I can do is clear: a stronger commitment to 1) as Arundhati Roy says, speaking out, asserting the Palestinian struggle more broadly and more often, as we Americans are so deeply complicit in the ongoing Nakba (Arabic word for catastrophe which historically has referred to the ethnic cleansing of 1948); and 2) BDS, or Boycott, Divestment and Sanctions against Israel, a growing civil society non-violent movement similar to the one that helped to bring down apartheid in South Africa. More of what I can do will surely emerge with time as I continue to think about Walaa, Yasser, Rawya and all the other incredible people I met who want nothing more than to live.

In Gaza, I left behind friends and more than a piece of my heart.

We Shall Live to Tell the Stories of War Crimes in Gaza
Hana Baalousha

In all Hollywood action films, when the enemy uses a civilian as a human shield, the policeman drops his gun and lets the enemy go in order to save the civilian. The innocent person's life is always depicted as more important than the enemy's death.

Clearly these morals are only for movies. The morals on the ground in Gaza, however, are totally different. Israel shoots and bombs children and young people, leaving them to bleed to death in front of their parents while bombarding ambulances that try to reach them.

In this horrendous aggression against Gaza, every Palestinian is a target and age isn't an issue. As I hold my three-month-old Jolie close to my chest, I recall the pictures of babies her age with face injuries that hide their beauty and innocence, and others dead with amputated limbs, heads emptied from their contents, or burnt bodies.

As I squeeze her little defenseless body between my arms, I hear the voice of my cousin's husband saying, "I found the leg of my son coming out of the wreckage."

He lost his pregnant wife and two sons, four and six years old. I recall the picture of a man carrying the parts of his son's body in a plastic bag, a human body that he raised and cherished had been turned—in a blink of an eye—into a pile of flesh gathered from under the rubble by an army that justifies it by saying "mistakes happen."

"We're sorry for any accidental civilian deaths but it's Hamas that bears complete responsibility for such civilian casualties," Benjamin Netanyahu has said.

Since July 7, there have been more than 1,650 Palestinians killed in Gaza. Approximately 1,300 civilians slaughtered by Israel—not Hamas.

Does anyone seriously believe that these deaths were accidental?

No Safe Place

I recall the pictures of the four Baker family boys, all aged between nine and eleven. Killed by an Israeli missile on July 16, their bodies were thrown all over the beach in front of a hotel mainly populated by journalists. The kids were playing on the beach in an attempt to take some time out of this chaos and enjoy their childhood. But they were not allowed to do so.

Resistance fighters aren't stupid enough to launch rockets in front of a hotel where every single person carries a camera around the clock. In Gaza, there is no safe place.

As I comb my baby's hair with my fingers, I imagine the three kids feeding their pigeons on the roof of their house the next day (July 17). They were killed along with their pigeons.

The voice of a boy about ten years old—or so it appears from his voice in a video clip—echoes in my ears: *Yemma, wen shebshebi?* ("Mom, where are my slippers?"). He shouted this while paramedics searched his house in an attempt to evacuate the family along with any others injured.

With the Israeli warplanes loudly hovering overhead, randomly hitting everywhere and the family fearfully trying to leave the targeted neighborhood in which he lives, his main concern was his slippers. He did not want to run in the street barefoot, and he repeated his question again. He is just a child.

Holiday in Gaza

Two years ago, I started a new job teaching Arabic to native speakers of English in the United Kingdom. My icebreaker on the first day was a question. I asked the students what they did that summer. Some said they spent the holiday visiting family in Jordan or Egypt. Others went on holiday in Europe.

Others even said they went on tour from Jordan to London to Paris. I had to hide my surprise.

I thought, "Who are these people?" Definitely not Gazans. This is not how we holiday in Gaza. The best we can do is go to the beach. Not this summer. We get killed there.

Today, I'm trying to imagine what memories of this summer the students I know in Gaza will have to recount. One has lost an arm, and the other has lost a brother. A third has become homeless and a fourth has become an orphan. One may not be able to share his story because he lost his life.

Lost Everything

During the onslaught, Ramadan, a month when we Muslims abstain from food and drink from dawn to dusk, came to an end. Eid al-Fitr is the first day after Ramadan, and it is usually a day of celebration.

Mothers cook delicious meals and bake special cookies. Children wear new clothes, buy candy and new toys and go to playgroups; they visit relatives and friends along with their parents to congratulate them for the end of this month which we spent worshipping God.

Children wait for this day all year long. They prepare their new clothes and count the days until they can put them on.

This year, there was no such day. No new clothes. No cookies. No toys. No candy. No playgroups. No family visits. Thousands of houses no longer stood in place. Thousands of families who still had their houses no longer lived in them.

They escaped the Israeli war machine and sheltered in schools. Mothers did not cook or bake luxury foods because, inside the schools, they waited for charitable organizations to send them basic staples. Hundreds of children neither wore new clothes nor bought new toys because they had lost the people who bought them these clothes, and those with whom they usually celebrated.

Some have lost everything, their family and their house. Others had to spend this special day alone on a cold bed in a hospital.

On the first day of Eid, ten children were killed in a playground.

No words can justify what is happening to children today in Gaza. Nothing can justify killing the innocence of our babies and children. And nothing can justify the world's silence.

As long as this bloodshed continues, the whole world will be an accomplice in these war crimes. As long as we live, we shall not forgive.

And we shall live to tell the story.

The Electronic Intifada, August 2, 2014, http://bit.ly/1lposDn

Who Benefits from Billions Pledged for Gaza Reconstruction?
Maureen Clare Murphy

A donor conference hosted in Cairo on Sunday to raise funds for the reconstruction of war-devastated Gaza has boasted $5.4 billion in pledges from various Western and Arab governments.

Yet Israel is the true beneficiary of this aid money. The self-declared international community has once again footed the reconstruction bill as it arms Israel with the weaponry and ensures it the impunity that only rewards its brutal onslaught on Gaza and essentially guarantees its repetition.

"This is the third time in less than six years that together with the people of Gaza, we have been forced to confront a reconstruction effort," an exasperated U.S. Secretary of State John Kerry stated at the conference, as though this summer's bloodshed was something other than inevitable given all those arms Washington lavished on Israel, along with the monetary aid and diplomatic cover since the large-scale assaults in November 2012 and winter 2008–2009.

Parties involved in the donor conference are making only the most minimal efforts to pretend that the priority is the survivors in Gaza, where more than one in every thousand of the nearly 1.8 million Palestinians there, most of whom are refugees, were killed.

The Palestinian Authority, based in the occupied West Bank city of Ramallah, has already announced that half of the pledges raised at Sunday's conference will not even make it to Gaza.

Burned fishing boat on a Gaza beach, August 7, 2014. Israeli shelling cost the fishing industry about $3 million in July. The industry has been hard hit by repeated Israeli restrictions on fishing areas (from six to three nautical miles from the coastline).[2]
Photo by Mohammed Asad.

Gaza Pledges Diverted to Ramallah

Instead, those funds will be diverted to the Palestinian Authority's budget for unspecified purposes.

Though the PA did not say how it will spend the money raised at the Gaza reconstruction conference that it earmarked for itself, "the security sector has grown faster than any other part of the Palestinian Authority" in the past decade, as noted by Sabrien Amrov and Alaa Tartir in a recent policy brief published by the Palestinian think-tank Al-Shabaka.

Last year, 26 percent of the PA's budget was spent on security (compared with just 16 percent for education, nine percent for health and a minuscule one percent on agriculture, historically the backbone of the Palestinian economy). Forty-four percent of PA civil servants are employed in the security sector—more than any other, Amrov and Tartir point out.

The Palestinian Authority—which has already blocked efforts to bring Israeli war crimes in Gaza this summer before the International Criminal

Court—is led by Mahmoud Abbas, who recently described collaboration with Israeli occupation forces in the West Bank as "sacred."

PA Seizes Opportunity

More than forty Palestinians have been killed by Israeli forces in the occupied West Bank so far this year; fourteen were killed during the equivalent period in 2013. "Security coordination" is obviously not concerned with securing the preservation of Palestinian lives.

As pointed out by Amrov and Tartir, "the armed resistance that was once considered an inseparable part of the Palestinian struggle for self-determination is being dealt with by the PA as a form of dissent that needs not just policing but eradication and criminalization."

The current paradigm of security coordination, state Amrov and Tartir, is "to criminalize resistance against the occupation and leave Israel—and its trusted minions—in sole possession of the use of arms against a defenseless population."

As the Palestinian Authority, which serves as the policing arm of the Israeli occupation, positions itself as the executor of Gaza's reconstruction, this will surely be used as an opportunity for those who seek to dismantle the armed resistance (which defended Gaza and demonstrated greater discipline and tactical capability than it did during any prior confrontation with Israel).

Though the PA has jockeyed for this role to sideline the Hamas leadership in Gaza, any attempts to rebuild are subject to Israel's ultimate authority.

(It is worth noting that the Palestine Liberation Organization told the Ma'an News Agency on Sunday that no date has yet been set for implementing reconstruction projects in Gaza.)

Reminding observers who is really in charge, West Bank-based PA ministers including Prime Minister Rami Hamdallah were initially denied permits by Israel to visit Gaza, which remains under closure and economic siege imposed by Israel and enforced by donor conference host Egypt.

"More than 50 Years to Rebuild"

The international aid agency Oxfam warned last week that money pledged at the global donor conference "will languish in bank accounts for decades before it reaches people, unless long-standing Israeli restrictions on imports are lifted."

As the importation of basic construction material into Gaza has been prohibited with few exceptions since 2007, and the supply tunnels under the border with Egypt largely destroyed, Palestinians are unable to rebuild.

Oxfam added that "under current restrictions and rate of imports it could take more than 50 years to build the 89,000 new homes, 226 new schools, as well as the health facilities, factories and water and sanitation infrastructure that people in Gaza need."

No matter how much money international donors raise for reconstruction, Israel determines what gets in and out of Gaza.

Truckloads of construction materials brought in to Gaza last month were "designated for projects pre-approved by Israeli authorities and to be implemented by international organizations in Gaza," the United Nations Agency for the Coordination of Humanitarian Affairs notes in a recent weekly monitoring report.

Israel's total stranglehold on Gaza's economy also applies to exports—only two truckloads of which were permitted through the Israeli-controlled commercial crossing last month, the first trucks of exports since June.

Accountability or Complicity

The Palestinian Boycott, Divestment and Sanctions National Committee (BNC) condemns the failure to bring meaningful pressure on Israel to end the siege that had brought the economy to its knees even before the destruction it wrought on Gaza this summer—during which 419 businesses and workshops were damaged, with 128 completely destroyed.

"Donor money pledges are no substitute for holding Israel accountable for its grave violations of international law, including war crimes and crimes against humanity, and achieving justice for the Palestinian victims," the BNC stated on Sunday.

"Israel's blockade and repeated military assaults against the occupied Gaza Strip are part and parcel of systematic Israeli efforts to permanently separate the tiny Gaza Strip from the West Bank and 'get rid' of its large Palestinian population, most of them refugees of the 1948 Nakba with unresolved rights and claims in Israel," the statement adds.

The BNC criticizes international agencies including the United Nations and the International Committee of the Red Cross for operating "within the confines of Israel's policy of separation and collective punishment."

Without also adopting a comprehensive and binding military embargo on Israel, donor states, international agencies and nongovernmental organizations are complicit in an unjust and illegal policy of collective punishment, the BNC makes clear. And there is no mechanism of accountability to the Palestinian public.

Abandoning Gaza

Given all of these realities, it is tragic but unsurprising that young Palestinians in Gaza, facing unemployment rates as high as 60 percent, have lost hope and are putting their lives in the hands of smugglers in a bid to reach Europe and a future.

"This has never happened before...Even in the worst of times, people never considered abandoning the Gaza Strip," Sara Roy, who has studied Gaza's economy for three decades, told Bettina Marx in an interview for *Deutsche Welle*.

"The middle class has largely been wiped out," Roy said.

Even the deliberate sinking of a ship carrying an estimated 500 passengers—many of them Palestinians from Gaza, the vast majority of whom are presumed to have drowned—off the coast of Malta last month hasn't stemmed the mass migration from the Strip via clandestine tunnels.

In August 2012 the United Nations issued a report studying whether Gaza would be a livable place in the year 2020. But Gaza's unlivable reality is already here.

The Electronic Intifada, October 14, 2014, http://bit.ly/1qwbrKw

Editors' Afterwords

Re-humanizing Gaza
Laila El-Haddad

We Palestinians from Gaza are frequently spoken of as heroes. We've grown accustomed to pats on the back and praise for our courage and bravery. But speak to average people in Gaza and chances are they'll roll their eyes. Not because there isn't indeed a spirit of steadfastness in Gaza; historically, it has been a thorn in the side of any army that dared to invade it. But because such reductionist characterizations, well-intentioned as they may be, assume no frailty and thus, no humanness. Even this most basic of human characteristics, undesirable as it may be, is denied the Palestinian of Gaza.

Such depictions further the dehumanization of Palestinians. By failing to see Gaza as a polity with many debates raging, many views being aired, we ourselves contribute to the dehumanization or un-humanization of Gaza. If the blockade persists, we think, "But they can handle that, right? They're Gazan!" If the borders close we say, "But they must be used to this by now; the border always closes." Instead of viewing Palestinians as human beings, we see them as abstractions.

We have turned Gaza into a legend before the story has even ended.

The simple truth is, people cope because they have to. In desperate and impossible times, people either survive or perish.

Granted, the conditions Gaza is subject to are more extreme perhaps than any other on earth. It is a territory more surveilled, more enclosed, more perversely de-developed and debilitated than any other.

One can't help but wonder then, is it something about Gaza that makes it unique, where other peoples might have long perished or at the very least acquiesced? Are there some core values or social bonds that enable them to react the way they do?

There are. And its precisely these things that Israel's ongoing blockade intends to fracture: normality, basic freedoms, sustainability, entrepreneurship, prosperity.

But Palestinians insist on existing, and simple everyday acts, like going to school or cooking traditional meals become acts of resistance.

In 2010, I met a farmer in Gaza's ravaged northern village of Beit Hanun, the breadbasket of Gaza, gently planting row upon row of olive saplings in his land, after taking a break and drenching himself with the hose. We talked briefly, touching on the debate regarding sustainably grown rain-fed agriculture like olives vs. water-intensive cash crops. "I could have left this land and given up. But I'm planting these trees for the third consecutive time. Three different times, the Israelis have demolished my farm, and cleared it of its fruitful trees. But if I walk away, if I decide one day to stop replanting those trees, fruitless as they may be, then I have nothing. I've lost."

So it's no wonder we react in awe.

But Palestinians in Gaza say, time and again, we don't want your sympathy, we want your sanctions! We don't want your anger, we want your action!

Feeling horrified or sad or even proud of Gaza is not going to help anyone. Speaking and building bridges with students, who comprise more than half the population and who are categorically banned from traveling to pursue their higher educations, just might, as could supporting young entrepreneurs, whose prospects are blocked from every angle.

How can we support and sustain that strength and those networks—and not merely reconstruct infrastructure—when the guns fall silent? How can we invest in re-building a generation of young people, in healing the wounds that go far beyond the visible scars and amputated limbs, instead of reconstructing buildings?

There are no easy answers, but the quest begins by asking the right questions and knowing where to look. Perhaps this book provides a starting point. We hope to have provided you a starting point in this book.

In eastern Shija'ia, school children pass through neighborhoods reduced to rubble (November 16, 2014). Residents were displaced to temporary camps, which provide no shelter from the winter cold.
Photo by Mohammed Asad.

When Will We Go Back Home?
Refaat Alareer

I Will Be Back. I Promise.

The last time my niece Raneem, 4, saw her Dad was when the Israeli shells were falling on the heads and houses of more than one hundred thousand Palestinians in Shija'ia. My brother Mohammed took the time to help guide many families to shortcuts in a desperate attempt to escape the flying shrapnel and debris.

Mohammed kept close to his wife, his son Hamza, 1, and his daughter Raneem. "I will be back. Soon," he assured his weeping kids and worried wife. "I will be back. I promise." Bringing his family and many others to a relatively safer place, he thought he should go back to help others evacuate.

My brother Mohammed never came back.

He never came back. Not because he did not keep his word, but rather because the Israeli occupation has developed a policy of destroying people and their relationships. Israel made sure my brother Mohammed and a couple thousand Palestinians would never get to see their family members ever again.

Ever since, Raneem has been asking about her Dad. "When will Dad come back? Why does Baba not come back?" she keeps asking. Only watery eyes and pained hearts answer her quizzical looks. However we try to distract her, nothing replaces a father, let alone a loving father who made his small family his own world.

I Wish I Had Not Come

We thought that taking Raneem to see the pile of rubble that was once our house might help her understand something until my elder brother's nephew, Mohammed, 6, went to see the house with his father. Mohammed kept nagging for more than a month. He wanted nothing but to go to Shija'ia and see our house. When he was there, when he saw all the destruction and ruins, little Mohammed dangled his head and said, "I wish I had not come."

Taking Raneem and the little ones to see the pile of rubble our house was turned into is now out of the question. We are only counting on a speedy reconstruction process that will mitigate the pain and return the kids to their house.

I Hate Dad. He Never Comes Back!

A month after the Israeli onslaught, Raneem must have realized that her Dad would not be coming back again. She approached my mother and said, "Teta, I dislike my Dad. He does not come back."

My mother has not recovered from Raneem's remark. It was like her son was killed twice. But I can only imagine the psychological damage that has already caused Raneem, who has developed a tendency toward absent-mindedness, to talk to herself. Two months ago her Mom found her giggling and mumbling. When asked what she was doing, Raneem said, "My Dad gave me candy." Her tiny fist remained clenched for a long time.

Why We Stayed

But why did so many stay behind? Why did the people of Shija'ia refuse to leave despite Israel's propaganda warning? This issue is not as simple as Zionist parrots and trolls suggest. A Palestinian man's house is his castle. Literally. Leaving was not an option when in 2008–2009 most of the people Israel murdered were in the city center where Israel suggested they go. Leaving was not an option because Israel wanted more than 150,000 people to leave their houses and go to the streets and schools, where Israel also targeted them.

Leaving was not an option because we still remember the 1948 ethnic cleansing massacres against the Palestinians. Because leaving for Israel means that Palestinians never come back. People stayed because it's their lands and their houses, and because we refuse to be dictated to by an occupier and a mass murderer.

People stayed because simply finding peace and protection in one's own house is a very human act. And for that Israel sought to punish the whole Gaza Strip. It was clear for us that Israel was tracing mobile signals and destroying houses where mobile signals emitted even if the signal came from a mobile phone whose owner forgot it at home in the rush to escape Israeli shells.

The Shija'ia Massacre

When I read the comments that Israel was planning to carpet bomb Shija'ia like it did to some areas in South Lebanon in 2006, I thought people were kidding. But it turned out Israel had this childish, though hateful, grudge against Shija'ia since the fifties. Shija'ia was the last area to fall under Israeli occupation in 1967. Shija'ia has always produced fighters and civil servants and defenders of human rights. Shija'ia was a thorn in Israel's throat in the first and second intifadas.

Executions and Bragging

We all know Salem Shamaly because his execution was caught on camera. There are many Salems in Shija'ia. I know of at least 5 others, 4 of whom are my relatives, who were shot at close range. They were not allowed to leave their houses. Neither the Red Cross nor ambulances were allowed to evacuate them. My distant cousin Samy Alareer tried to leave the house to seek help for his two brothers, Hassan and Abdulkarim, and his son Fathi, who were injured by the random systematic shelling. On his way to fetch help, Samy was shot dead. The other three were found dead in their house with empty bullet cases all over the place.

Israeli officials were quick to brag about the death and destruction they brought upon Shija'ia. Hundreds were slain and injured, many of whom will be disabled forever. Avichay Adraee, the Israeli army's spokesman in Arabic, bragged on Twitter that the Israeli army dropped 120 one-ton bombs on Shija'ia in the first two weeks alone. Add to that the hundreds of shells and mortars with their huge error radius.

Resistance

I do not have the words to do justice to the unyieldingly valiant, lion-hearted fighters of Palestine. They remained steadfast with what little weapons and strong faith in their rights they have in the face of the most inhumanely heinous occupation the world has known.

However, there is one thing the whole world should know: in face-to-face combat, far fewer Palestinian fighters were killed than Israeli soldiers. The Israeli heavily armed elite troops supported with tanks, planes, and high-tech equipment were squealing when faced with Shuja'iya's modestly trained and minimally armed resistance fighters who defended their homes and families with skill and determination. Israel's response was to randomly, yet systematically, destroy houses and shell densely crowded areas. Palestinian fighters rose to the challenge of battle imposed upon them. And they fought honorably and well. They fearlessly stood for their people.

Rebuilding Gaza

The cost of putting up a defense in Gaza is that all Palestinians in Gaza are being punished. Israel has tightened the siege on Gaza. Egypt has tightened its siege on Gaza. The Palestinian Authority has tightened its siege on Gaza. The stupidity those parties are displaying is unprecedented. Collective punishment against Palestinians has never worked. And the rules of logic say doing the very same things and expecting different results is foolishness. But Israel in its arrogance, the PA's Mahmoud Abbas in his cravenness, and Arab regimes in their complicity seem to have agreed that a good Gaza is a starved Gaza.

With the delay of reconstruction and the clear complicity of Abbas and his cronies and the UN and its army of mercenaries living off the Palestinian plight, Raneem and Hamza and tens of thousands will never get to go back to the house where they lived their happiest days ever with the most loving person they will ever meet. Raneem will have to live with the horrible memories of seeing her house become a pile of rubble.

*A family returns to its home in Shija'ia with the few belongings given to them by
relief organizations. At the height of the assault, 500,000 Palestinians were
displaced; two months later, 100,000 remained in temporary accommodations.[1]
Photo by Mohammed Asad.*

Whitewashing Israel

The likes of my niece Raneem and little nephew Mohammed are purposefully being punished by Israel and the international community—first by
destroying their houses and lives, and then by providing Israel with the
impunity and excuses it wants, and finally by delaying the process of justice. They want these little kids to live in ruins and destruction. Ironically
Palestinian children are expected to grow up and like Israel or see a future
where peace can be achieved when the murderers of their parents and de-
stroyers of their houses go unpunished and unaccountable.

Unless Israeli war criminals are brought to justice and the occupation
ends, my fear is that these children will grow up feeling that they were be-
trayed by the world. We owe it to them to change that vision.

Names of the Dead

July 8: Hafeth Mohammad Hamad, 26; Ibrahim Mohammad Hamad, 26; Mahdi Mohammad Hamad, 46; Donia Mahdi Hamad, 16; Fawziyya Khalil Hamad, 62; Soha Hamad, 25; Mohammad Shaban, 24; Ahmad Nael Mahdi, 16; Mohammad Habib, 22; Ahmed Mousa Habib, 16; Amjad Shaban, 30; Khader al-Basheeleqety, 45; Saqr Aayesh al-Ajjoury, 22; Mohammad Ayman Ashour, 15; Riyadh Mohammad Kaware, 50; Hussein Yousef Kaware, 13; Bassem Salem Kaware, 10; Mohammad Ibrahim Kaware, 50; Suleiman Salam Abu Sawaween, 22; Bakr Mohammad Joudeh, 50; Ammar Mohammad Joudeh, 26; Siraj Eyad Abdul-Aal, 8; Rashad Yassin, 27; Abdul-Hadi Soufi, 24.

July 9: Sahar Hamdan (al-Masry), 40; Mohammad Ibrahim al-Masry, 14; Amjad Hamdan, 23; Hani Saleh Hamad, 57; Ibrahim Hani Saleh Hamad, 20; Mohammad Khalaf Nawasra, 4; Nidal Khalaf Nawasra, 5; Salah Awad Nawasra, 24; Aesha Najm al-Nawasra, 23 (pregnant); Hamed Shihab; Hatem Abu Salem; Amal Yousef Abdul-Ghafour, 20; Nariman Jouda Abdul-Ghafour, 18 months; Yasmin Mohammad Matouq, 4; Rafiq al-Kafarna, 30; Abdul-Nasser Abu Kweik, 60; Khaled Abu Kweik, 31; Mohammad Mustafa Malika, 18 months; Hana Mohammed Fuad Malaka, 28; Mohammad Khaled an-Nimra, 22; Ibrahim Daoud al-Bal'aawy; Abdul-Rahman Jamal az-Zamely; Mazin Faraj Al-Jarba; Marwan Eslayyem; Naifa Mohammed Zaher Farajallah, 80; Raed Mohammed Shalat, 37; Ibrahim Ahmad Abdin, 42; Mustafa Abu Murr, 20; Khaled Abu Murr, 22; Salima al-Arja, 53; Miriam Atiya al-Arja, 9.

July 10: Abdullah Ramadan Abu Ghazal, 5; Ayman Adham Yusef al-Hajj, 16; Baha Abu al-Leil, 35; Salem Qandil, 27; Amer al-Fayyoumi, 30;

Mahmoud Lutfi al-Hajj, 58; Bassema Abdul-Fatteh Mohammad al-Hajj, 48; Asma Mahmoud al-Hajj, 22; Fatima Mahmoud al-Hajj, 12; Saad Mahmoud al-Hajj, 17; Najla Mahmoud al-Hajj, 29; Tareq Mahmoud al-Hajj, 18; Omar Mahmoud al-Hajj, 20; Suleiman Saleem Mousa al-Astal, 17; Ahmed Saleem Mousa al-Astal, 24; Mousa Mohammed Taher al-Astal, 50; Ibrahim Khalil Qanan, 24; Mohammad Khalil Qanan, 26; Ibrahim Sawali, 28; Hamdi Badea Sawali, 33; Mohammad al-Aqqad, 24; Ismael Hassan Abu Jame, 19; Hussein Odeh Abu Jame, 75; Mohammad Ehsan Ferwana, 27; Raed az-Zourah, 32.

July 11: Sahar Salman Abu Namous, 3; Ahmed Zaher Hamdan, 24; Ala Abdul Nabi; Shahrman Ismail Abu al-Kas, 42; Mazin Mustafa Aslan, 63; Bassam Abul-Rahman Khattab, 6; Abdul-Halim Abdul-Moty Ashra, 54; Mohammad Samiri, 24; Rami Abu Mosaed, 23; Abdullah Mustafa abu Mahrouq, 22; Saber Sokkar, 80; Hussein Mohammad al-Mamlouk, 47; Nasser Rabah Mohammad Sammama, 49; Anas Rezeq Abu al-Kas, 33; Sami Adnan Shaldan, 25; Salem al-Ashhab, 40; Mahmoud Waloud, 26; Hazem Ba'lousha; Mohammad Kamel al-Kahlout, 25; Odai Rafiq Sultan, 27; Mohammad Rabea Abu- Hmeedan, 65; Wisam Abdul-Razeq Hasan Ghannam, 31; Mahmoud Abdul-Razeq Hasan Ghannam, 28; Kifah Shaker Ghannam, 33; Ghalia Thieb Ghannam, 57; Mohammad Munir Ashour, 26; Nour Marwan an-Ajdi, 10; Raed Hani Abu Hani, 31; Joma Atiyya Shallouf, 25.

July 12: Ibrahim Nabil Hamada, 30; Hasan Ahmad Abu Ghush, 24; Ahmad Mahmoud al-Bal'awy, 26; Ali Nabil Basal, 32; Mohammad Bassem al-Halaby, 28; Mohammad Sweity (Abu Askar), 20; Rateb Subhi al-Saifi, 22; Azmi Mahmoud Obeid, 51; Nidal Mahmoud Abu al-Malsh, 22; Suleiman Said Obeid, 56; Mustafa Muhammad Inaya, 58; Ghassan Ahmad al-Masri, 25; Mohammad Arif, 13; Mohammad Ghazi Arif, 35; Ghazi Mustafa Arif, 62; Ahmad Yousef Dalloul, 47; Fadi Ya'coub Sukkar, 25; Mohammad Ahmed Basal, 19; Rifat Syouti*; Anas Yousef Qandil, 17; Islam Yousef Mohammad Qandil, 27; Mohammad Edrees Abu Sneina, 20; Abdul-Rahim Saleh al-Khatib, 38; Husam Thieb ar-Razayna, 39; Ola Wishahi, 31; Suha Abu Saade, 38; Mohammad Edrees Abu Sweilem, 20; Mohammad Abdullah Sharatha, 53; Qassem Jaber Odah, 16; Nahedh Naim al-Batsh, 41; Baha Majed al-Batsh, 28; Qusai Issam al-Batsh, 12; Aziza Yousef al-Batsh, 59; Ahmad Noman al-Batsh, 27; Mohammad Issam al-Batsh, 17; Yahia Ala Al-Batsh, 18; Jalal Majed al-Batsh, 26; Mahmoud Majed al-Batsh, 22; Majed Sobhi al-Batsh; Marwa Majed al-Batsh, 25; Khaled Majed al-Batsh, 20; Ibrahim Majed al-Batsh, 18; Manar

Majed al-Batsh, 13; Amal Hussein al-Batsh, 49; Anas Ala al-Batsh, 10; Qusai Ala al-Batsh, 20; Khawla al-Hawajri, 25; Rifat Youssef Amer, 36; Mohannad Yousef Dheir, 23; Shadi Mohammad Zorob, 21; Imad Bassam Zorob, 21; Mohannad Yousef Dheir, 23.

July 13: Qassem Talal Hamdan, 23; Rami Abu Shanab, 25; Mohammad Salem Abu Breis, 65; Hijaziyya Hamed al-Hilo, 80; Ruwaida Abu Harb Zawayda, 30; Fawziyya Abdul-al, 73; Hussein Abdul-Qader Mheisin, 19; Maher Thabet Abu Mour, 23; Moussa Shehda Moammer, 60; Hanadi Hamdi Moammer, 27; Saddam Mousa Moammer, 23; Moayyad al-Araj, 3; Husam Ibrahim Najjar, 14; Laila Hassan al-Odaat, 41; Ezzeddin Bolbol, 25; Haitham Ashraf Zarb, 21.

July 14: Hamid Suleiman Abu al-Araj, 60; Mohammad Yasser Hamdan, 24; Abdullah Mahmoud Baraka, 24; Tamer Salem Qdeih, 37; Ziad Maher an-Najjar, 17; Mohammad Shakib al-Agha, 22; Ahmed Younis Abu Yousef, 22; Kamal Atef Yousef Abu Taha, 16; Ismael Nabil Ahmad Abu Hatab, 21; Atwa Amira al-Amour, 63; Ziad Salem ash-Shawy, 25; Sara Omar Sheikh al-Eid, 4; Omar Ahmad Sheikh al-Eid, 24; Jihad Ahmad Sheikh al-Eid, 48; Boshra Khalil Zorob, 53; Adham Abdul-Fattah Abdul-Aal, 27.

July 15: Ismael Fattouh Ismael, 24; Khalil Sh'aafy; Abdullah Mohammad al-Arjani, 19; Sobhi Abdul-Hamid Mousa, 77; Suleiman Abu Louly, 33; Saleh Said Dahleez, 20; Yasser Eid al-Mahmoum, 18.

July 16: Ahed Atef Bakr, 10; Zakariya Ahed Bakr, 10; Mohammad Ramiz Bakr, 11; Ismail Mahmoud Bakr, 9; Mohammad Kamel Abdul-Rahman, 30; Husam Shamlakh, 23; Abdul-Rahman Ibrahim Khalil as-Sarhi, 37; Hamza Raed Thary, 6; Mohammad Taisir Abu Sharab, 23; Farid Mahmoud Abu-Daqqa, 33; Khadra Al-Abed Salama Abu Daqqa, 65; Omar Ramadan Abu Daqqa, 24; Ibrahim Ramadan Abu Daqqa, 10; Usama Mahmoud Al-Astal, 6; Hussein Abdul-Nasser al-Astal, 23; Kawthar al-Astal, 70; Yasmin al-Astal, 4; Kamal Mohammad Abu Amer, 38; Akram Mohammad Abu Amer, 34; Mohammad Ismael Abu Odah, 27; Mohammad Abdullah Zahouq, 23; Ahmed Adel Nawajha, 23; Mohammad Sabri ad-Debari; Ashraf Khalil Abu Shanab, 33.

July 17: Ismail Youssef al-Kafarna; Ahmad Reehan, 23; Mohammad Mahmoud Al-Qadim, 22; Salem Saleh Fayyad, 25; Fulla Tariq Shuhaibar, 8; Jihad Issam Shuhaibar, 10; Wasim Issam Shuhaibar, 9; Yassin al-Humaidi, 4; Abed Ali Ntheir, 26; Mohammad Shadi Ntheir, 15; Mohammad Salem Ntheir, 4; Said al-Abadla, 71; Rahaf Khalil al-Jbour,

4; Hamza Hussein al-Abadala, 29; Salah Saleh ash-Shafe'ey; Abdullah Salem al-Atras, 27; Bashir Mohammad Abdul-Al, 20; Mohammad Ziyad Ghanem, 25; Mohammad Ahmad al-Hout, 41; Mohammad Abdul-Rahman Hassouna, 67; Zeinab Mohammad.

July 18: Nassim Mahmoud Nassier, 22; Karam Mahmoud Nassier, 20; Amal Khader Ibrahim Dabbour, 40; Ismail Yousef Taha Qassim, 59; Naim Mousa Abu Jarad, 23; Abed Mousa Abu Jarad, 30; Siham Mousa Abu Jarad, 26; Raja Oliyyan Abu Jarad, 31; Haniyya Abdul-Rahman Abu Jarad, 3; Samih Naim Abu Jarad, 1; Mousa Abul-Rahman Abu Jarad, 6 months; Ahlam Mousa Abu Jarad, 13; Mahmoud Ali Darwish, 40; Rani Saqer Abu Tawila, 30; Husam Musallam Abu Issa, 26; Ahmad Ismael Abu Musallam, 14; Mohammad Ismael Abu Musallam, 15; Wala Ismael Abu Musallam, 13; Imad Hamed E'lawwan, 7; Qassem Hamed E'lawwan, 4; Sarah Mohammad Bustan, 13; Rezeq Ahmad al-Hayek, 2; Ismail Ramadan al-Loulahi, 21; Ghassan Salem Mousa Abu Azab, 28; Ahmad Salem Shaat, 22; Mohammad Salem Shaat, 20; Amjad Salem Shaat, 15; Hammad Abdul-Karim Abu Lehya, 23; Mohammad Abdul-Fattah Rashad Fayyad, 26; Mahmoud Mohammad Fayyad, 25; Ahmad Fawzi Radwan, 23; Mahmoud Fawzi Radwan, 24; Bilal Mahmoud Radwan, 23; Monther Radwan, 22; Hasan Majdi Mahmoud Radwan, 19; Mohammad Sami as-Said Omran, 26; Hani As'ad Abdul-Karim Shami, 35; Mohammad Hamdan Abdul-Karim Shami, 35; Mohammad Saad Mahmoud Abu Sa'da; Ra'fat Mohammad al-Bahloul, 35; Wala al-Qarra, 20; Abdullah Jamal as-Smeiri, 17; Ahmad Hasan Saleh al-Ghalban, 23; Hamada Abdullah Mohammad al-Bashiti, 21; Yousef Ibrahim al-Astal, 23; Husam Musallam Abu Aisha, 26; Hamza Mohammad Abu Hussein, 27; Ala Abu Shabab, 23; Mohammad Awad Matar, 37; Bassem Mohammad Mahmoud Madhi, 22; Mustafa Faisal Abu Sneina, 32; Imad Faisal Abu Sneina, 18; Nizar Fayez Abu Sneina, 38; Mohammad Talal as-Sane, 20; Majdi Suleiman Jabara, 22; Faris Juma al-Mahmoum, 5 months; Omar Eid al-Mahmoum, 18; Salmiyya Suleiman Ghayyadh, 70; Saleh Zgheidy, 20; Ahmad Abdullah al-Bahnasawi, 25.

July 19: Mohammad Atallah Odah Saadat, 25; Ahmad Mahmoud Hasan Aziz, 34; Mahmoud Abdul-Hamid al-Zweidi, 23; Dalia Abdel-Hamid al-Zweidi, 37; Rowiya Mahmoud al-Zweidi, 6; Naghm Mahmoud al-Zweidi, 2; Mohammad Khaled Jamil al-Zweidi, 20; Amr Hamouda, 7; Mohammad Riziq Mohammad Hamouda, 18; Yousef Kamal Qabdurra Hamouda, 29; Mohammad Abdul-Rahman Abu Hamad, 25; Mohammad Rafiq ar-Rohhal, 22; Mohammad Ziad ar-Rohhal, 6; Said

Ali Issa, 30; Mohammad Ahmad Abu Zanouna, 37; Momen Taysir al-Abed Abu Dan, 24; Abdul-Aziz Samir Abu Zaitar, 31; Mohammad Ziad Zabout, 24; Hatem Ziad Zabout, 22; Maali Abdul-Rahman Suleiman Abu Zeid, 24; Abdul-Rahman Mohammad Odah, 23; Tariq Samir Khalil al-Hatou, 26; Ahmad Abu Thurayya, 25; Abdullah Ghazi al-Masri, 30; Ayman Nasri an-Na'ouq, 23; Fadal Mohammad al-Bana, 29; Aqram Mahmoud al-Matouq, 37; Ayad Ismail al-Raqqab, 26; Yahia Bassam as-Serry, 20; Mohammad Bassam as-Serry, 17; Mahmoud Rida Salhiyya, 56; Waseem Rida Salhiyya, 15; Mustafa Rida Salhiyya, 21; Mohammad Mustafa Salhiyya, 22; Ibrahim Jamal Kamal Nassr, 13; Rushdi Khaled Nassr, 24; Mohammad Awad Faris Nassr, 25; Raed Walid Laqan, 27; Mohammad Jihad al-Qara, 29; Rafat Ali Bahloul, 36; Bilal Ismail Abu Daqqa, 33; Mohammad Ismail Sammour, 21; Eyad Ismael ar-Raqab, 26; Mohammad Ahmad as-Saidi, 18; Mohammad Fathi al-Ghalban, 23; Mahmoud Anwar Abu Shabab, 16.

July 20: Aya Bahjat Abu Sultan, 15; Yusef Shaaban Ziada, 44; Jamil Shaaban Ziada, 53; Shoeban Jamil Ziada, 12; Soheiib Abu Ziada; Mohammad Mahmoud al-Moqaddma, 30; Salem Ali Abu Saada; Fatima Ahmad Abu Jame', 60; Sabah Abu Jame', 35; Razan Tawfiq Ahmad Abu Jame', 14; Jawdat Tawfiq Ahmad Abu Jame', 13; Aya Tawfiq Ahmad Abu Jame', 12; Haifaa Tawfiq Ahmad Abu Jame', 9; Ahmad Tawfiq Ahmad Abu Jame', 8; Maysaa Tawfiq Ahmad Abu Jame', 7; Tawfiq Tawfiq Ahmad Abu Jame', 4; Shahinaz Walid Muhammad Abu Jame', 29; Fatmeh Taysir Ahmad Abu Jame', 12; Ayub Taysir Ahmad Abu Jame', 10; Rayan Taysir Ahmad Abu Jame', 5; Rinat Taysir Ahmad Abu Jame', 2; Nujud Taysir Ahmad Abu Jame', 4 months; Batul Bassam Ahmad Abu Jame', 4; Soheila Bassam Ahmad Abu Jame', 3; Bisan Bassam Ahmad Abu Jame', 6 months; Sajedah Yasser Ahmad Abu Jame', 7; Siraj Yasser Ahmad Abu Jame', 4; Noor Yasser Ahmad Abu Jame', 2; Yasmin Ahmad Salameh Abu Jame', 25; Yasser Ahmad Muhammad Abu Jame', 27; Fatima Riad Abu Jame', 26; Husam Husam Abu Qeinas, 7; Mohammad Yusef Moammer, 30; Hamza Yousef Moammer, 26; Anas Yousef Moammar, 16; Fathiyeh Nadi Marzouq Abu Moammer, 72; Hosni Mahmoud al-Absi, 56; Suheib Ali Joma Abu Qoura, 21; Ahmad Tawfiq Mohammad Zanoun, 26; Hamid Soboh Mohammad Fojo, 22; Najah Saad al-Deen Daraji, 65; Abdullah Yusef Daraji, 3; Mohammed Rajaa Handam 15; Raed Mansour Nayfa; Fuad Jaber; Mohammad Hani Mohammad al-Hallaq, 2; Kenan Hasan Akram al-Hallaq, 6; Hani Mohammad al-Hallaq, 29; Suad Mohammad al-Hallaq, 62; Saje Hasan Akram al-Hallaq, 4; Hala

Akram Hasan al-Hallaq, 27; Samar Osama al-Hallaq, 29; Ahmad Yassin; Ismael Yassin; Ibrahim Salem Joma as-Sahbani, 20; Aref Ibrahim al-Ghalyeeni, 26; Osama Khalil Ismael al-Hayya, 30; Hallah Saqer Hasan al-Hayya, 29; Umama Osama Khalil al-Hayya, 9; Khalil Osama Khalil al-Hayya, 7; Rebhi Shehta Ayyad, 31; Yasser Ateyya Hamdiyya, 28; Esra Ateyya Hamdiyya, 28; Akram Mohammad Shkafy, 63; Eman Khalil Abed Ammar, 9; Ibrahim Khalil Abed Ammar, 13; Asem Khalil Abed Ammar, 4; Eman Mohammad Ibrahim Hamada, 40; Ahmad Ishaq Yousef Ramlawy, 33; Ahmad Sami Diab Ayyad, 27; Fida Rafiq Diab Ayyad, 24; Narmin Rafiw Diab Ayyad, 20; Husam Ayman Mohareb Ayyad, 23; Ahmad Mohammad Ahmad Abu Zanouna, 28; Tala Akram Ahmad al-Atawy, 7; Tawfiq Barawi Salem Marshoud, 52; Hatem Ziad Ali Zabout, 24; Khaled Riyadh Mohammad Hamad, 25; Khadija Ali Mousa Shihada, 62; Khalil Salem Ibrahim Mosbeh, 53; Dima Adel Abdullah Eslayyem, 2; Dina Roshdi Abdullah Eslayyem, 2; Rahaf Akram Ismael Abu Joma, 4; Shadi Ziad Hasan Eslayyem, 15; Ala Ziad Hasan Eslayyem, 11; Sherin Fathi Othman Ayyad, 18; Adel Abdullah Salem Eslayyem, 29; Fadi Ziad Hasan Eslayyem, 10; Ahed Saad Mousa Sarsak, 30; Aisha Ali Mahmoud Zayed, 54; Abed-Rabbo Ahmad Zayed, 58; Abdul-Rahman Akram Sheikh Khalil, 24; Mona Suleiman Ahmad Sheikh Khalil, 49; Heba Hamed Mohammad Sheikh Khalil, 13; Abdullah Mansour Radwan Amara, 23; Issam Atiyya Said Skafy, 26; Ali Mohammad Hasan Skafy, 27; Mohammad Hasan Skafy, 53; Ala Jamal ed-Deen Barda, 35; Omar Jamil Sobhi Hammouda, 10; Ghada Jamil Sobhi Hammouda, 10; Ghada Ibrahim Suleiman Adwan, 39; Fatima Abdul-Rahim Abu Ammouna, 55; Fahmi Abdul-Aziz Abu Said, 29; Ghada Sobhi Saadi Ayyad, 9; Mohammad Ashraf Rafiq Ayyad, 6; Mohammad Raed Ehsan Ayyad, 6; Mohammad Rami Fathi Ayyad, 2; Mohammad Raed Ehsan Akeela, 19; Mohammad Ziad Ali Zabout, 23; Mohammad Ali Mohared Jundiyya, 38; Marah Shaker Ahmad al-Jammal, 2; Marwan Monir Saleh Qonfid, 23; Maisa Abdul-Rahman Sarsawy, 37; Marwa Salman Ahmad Sarsawy, 13; Mos'ab el-Kheir Salah ed-Din Skafi, 27; Mona Abdul-Rahman Ayyad, 42; Halla Sobhi Sa'dy Ayyad, 25; Younis Ahmad Younis Mustafa, 62; Yousef Salem Hatmo Habib, 62; Fatima Abu Ammouna, 55; Ahmad Mohammad Azzam, 19; Ismael al-Kordi; Tariq Farouq Mahmoud Tafesh, 37; Hazem Naim Mohammad Aqel, 14; Mohammad Nassr Atiyya Ayyad, 25; Omar Zaher Saleh Abu Hussein, 19; Ziad Ghaleb Rajab ar-Redya, 23; Wael Bashir Yahia Assaf, 24.

July 21: Manwa Abdul-Baset as-Sabe, 37; Kamal Balal al-Masri, 22; Fadi Azmi Buryam; Ayman Salaam Buryam; Salaam Abdul-Majeed Buryam; Bilal Jabr Mohammad al-Ashab, 22; Zakariya Masoud al-Ashqar, 24; Abdullah Matroud Abu Hjeir, 16; Ahmad Sofyan Abu Hjeir, 23; Abdul-Karim Hamad Abdul-Karim Hjeir, 33; Ahmad Salhoub, 34; Raed Issam Daoud, 30; Somoud Nassr Siyam, 26; Bader Nabil Siyam, 25; Mustafa Nabil Mahrous Siyam, 12; Ghaida Nabil Mahrous Siyam, 8; Dalal Nabil Mahrous Siyam, 8 months; Ahmad Ayman Mahrous Siyam, 17; Kamal Mahrous Salama Siyam, 27; Mohammad Mahrous Salaam Siyam, 25; Ibrahim Deib Ahmad al-Kilani, 53; Yassr Ibrahim Deib al-Kilani, 8; Elias Ibrahim Deib al-Kilani, 4; Susan Ibrahim Deib al-Kilani, 11; Reem Ibrahim Deib al-Kilani, 12; Yasmeen Ibrahim Deeb al-Kilani, 9; Taghrid Shoeban Mohammad al-Kilani, 45; Aida Shoeban Mohammad Derbas, 47; Mahmoud Shoeban Mohammad Derbas, 37; Sura Shoeban Mohammad Derbas, 41; Aynas Shoeban Mohammad Derbas, 30; Lamia Eyad al-Qisas; Nismaa Eyad al-Qisas; Arwa al-Qisas; Aya Yassr al-Qisas; Aisha Yassr al-Qisas; Aliya Siyam; Fayza Sabr Siyam; Samia Siyam; Rajae Hammad Mohammad, 38; Ahmad Khale Daghmash, 21; Mahmoud Hasan an-Nakhala; Saleh Badawi, 31; Kamal Mas'oud, 21; Mohammad Samih al-Ghalban; Majdi Mahmoud al-Yazeji, 56; Mayar al- Yazeji, 2; Anas al- Yazeji, 5; Yasmin Naif al-Yazeji; Safinaz al-Yazeji; Tamer Nayef Jundiyya, 30; Kamel Jundiyya, 32; Rahma Ahmad Jundiyya, 50; Ahed Kamal Mohammad Jundiyya, 31; Mohammad Mahmoud al-Maghrebi, 24; Ibrahim Shaban Bakron, 37; Yousef Ghazi Hamdiyya, 25; Motaz Jamal Hamdiyya, 18; Aaed Jamal Hamdiyya, 21; Yasmin al-Qisas; Shireen Mahmoud Salaam Siyam, 32; Atiya Yusef Dardouna, 26; Shahinaz Walid Mohammad Abu Hamad, 1; Husam Abu Qeinas, 5; Karim Ibrahim Atiya Barham, 25; Nidal Ali Daka, 26; Nidal Jamaa Abu Asy, 43; Fadi Bashir al-Ablala, 22; Ahmad Suleiman Abu Saoud, 34; Raed Ismail al-Bardawil, 26; Younis Ahmad Younis Sheikh al-Eid, 23; Fatima Ahmad al-Arja.

July 22: Ahmad As'ad al-Boudi, 24; Raed Salah, 22; Ahmad Nassim Saleh, 23; Mahmoud Ghanem, 22; Ebtehal Ibrahim ar-Remahi; Yousef Ibrahim ar-Remahi; Eman Ibrahim ar-Remahi; Abdullah Ismael al-Baheessy, 27; Hasan Khader Baker, 60; Fatima Hasan Azzam, 70; Mariam Hasan Azzam, 50; Mona Rami al-Kharwat, 4; Soha Na'im al-Kharwat, 25; Ahmad Salah Abu Siedo, 17; Mohammad Khalil Aref Ahl, 65; Ahmad Issam Wishah, 29; Ahmad Kamel Abu Mgheiseb, 35; Raed Abdul-Rahman Abu Mgheiseb, 35; Nader Abdul-Rahman Abu Mgheiseb,

35; Ahmad Mohammad Ramadan, 30; Rawan Ziad Jom'a Hajjaj, 28; Mos'ab Nafeth al-Ejla, 30; Tareq Fayeq Hajjaj, 22; Ahmad Ziad Hajjaj, 21; Hasan Sha'ban Khamisy, 28; Ahmad Salah Abu Seedo, 17; Amjad al-Hindi; Atiyya Mohammad Abdul-Raziq, 34; Hamada 'Olewa; Salem Khalil Salem Shemaly, 22; Ibrahim Sobhi al-Fayre; Rafiq Mohammad Qlub; Mahmoud Salim Daraj, 22; Naji Jamal al-Fajm, 26; Salwa Abu Mneifi; Mos'ab Saleh Salama, 19; Mahmoud Suleiman Abu Sabha, 55; Suleiman Abu Daher, 21; Haitham Samir al-Agha, 26; Mohammad Mousa Fayyad, 36; Mohammad Jalal al-Jarf, 24; Hani Awad Sammour, 27; Ibrahim Sammour, 38; Abdullah Awni al-Farra, 25; Ahmad Abu Salah; Mohammad Abdul-Karim Abu Jame'; Atiyya Mohammad Hasan ad-Da'alsa, 34; Ibrahim Nasr Haroun, 38; Radhi Abu Hweishel, 40; Obeida Abu Hweishel, 15; Yousef Abu Mustafa, 27; Nour al-Islam Abu Hweishel, 12; Yousef Fawza Abu Mustafa, 20; Ahmad Ibhrahim Shbeir, 24; Mustafa Mohammad Mahmoud Fayyad, 24; Yasmeen Ahmad Abu Mour, 2; Samer Zuheri Sawafiri, 29; Khalaf Atiyya Abu Sneima, 18; Khalil Atiyya Abu Sneima, 20; Samih Abu Jalala, 64; Hakima Nafe' Abu 'Adwan, 75; Najah Nafe' Abu 'Adwan, 85; Mohammad Shehada Hajjaj, 31; Fawza Saleh Abdul-Rahman Hajjaj, 66; Wa'el Jamal Harb, 32.

July 23: Mohammad al-Kafarna; Mohammad Daoud Hammouda, 33; Osama Bahjat Rajab, 34; Ayman Adham Yousef Ahmad, 16; Bilal Ali Ahmad Abu 'Athra, 25; Abdul-Karim Nassar Saleh Abu Jarmi, 24; Abdul-Qader Jamil al-Khalidi, 23; 'Ala Hamad Ali Khattab, 26; Hasan Abu Hayyin, 70; Abdul-Rahman Abu Hayyin, 26; Mojahed Marwan Skafi, 20; Adnan Ghazi Habib, 23; Mustafa Mohammad Mahmoud Fayyad, 24; Nidal Hamdi Diab al-'Ejla, 31; Rabea' Qassem, 12; Mohammad Abdul-Ra'ouf ad-Dadda, 39; Ahmad Mohammad Darwish Bolbol, 20; Ahmad Nabil Ahmad Abu Morad, 21; Nayef Fayez Nayef ath-Thatha, 19; Nayef Maher Nayef ath-Thatha, 24; Nayef Maher Nayef ath-Thatha, 24; Jihad Hussein Mahmoud Hamad, 20; Rawan Ayman Saoud Suweidan, 9; Naim Juma'a Mohammad Abu Nizeid; Jani Rami Nassr al-Maqat'a, 27; Said Ahmad Tawfiq at-Tawil, 22; Ola Khalil Ali Abu Obada, 24; Do'a Ra'ed Abu Ouda, 17; Amer Abdul Raouf Abu Ozeb, 26; Awad Abu Ouda; Bilal ash-Shinbari; Fatima ash-Shinbari; Falasteen ash-Shinbari; Abed Rabo ash-Shinbari; Ali Sha'boub ash-Shinbari; Souha Musleh; Hamza Ziyada Abu 'Anza, 18; Saddam Ibrahim Abu Assi, 23; Wisam 'Ala Najjar, 17; Mohammad Mansour al-Bashiti, 8; Ali Mansour Hamdi al-Bashiti, 1; Mohammad Riyadh Sha'aban Shabt, 23; Mohammad Naim Salah Abu T'aima, 12; Salem Abdullah Mousa Abu T'aima, 36; Ismail Abu Tharifa;

Zeinab Abu Teir, child; Mohammad Radi Abu Redya, 22; Shama Shahin; Ibrahim Ahmad Shbeir, 24; Khalil Abu Jame'; Husam al-Qarra; Hasan Salah Abu Jamous, 29; Mahmoud Yousef Khaled al-'Abadla, 22; Nour Abdul-Rahim al-'Abadla, 22; Mohammad Farid al-Astal; Ibrahim Omar al-Hallaq, 40; Wael Maher Awwad, 23; Ahmad Mahmoud Sohweil, 23; Issam Ismael Abu Shaqra, 42; Abdul-Rahman Ibrahim Abu Shaqra, 17; Mohammad Ahmad Akram Abu Shaqra, 17; Ahmad as-Saqqa, 17.

July 24: Ra'ed Abu Owda, 17; Yahia Ibrahim Abu 'Arbaid; Mohammad Jihad Matar; Hanan Jihad Matar; Tamam Mohammad Hamad; Mahmoud As'ad Ghaban, 24; Ahmed Abu Jm'ean Hji'er, 19; Amer Abdul-Raouf Mohamed El Azab, 26; Yazid Sa'dy Mustafa al-Batsh, 23;Khalil Nasser Aita Wishah, 21; Ahmad Ibrahim Sa'ad al-Qar'an, 26; Ibrahim Jihad Abu Laban, 27; Ibrahim Sheikh Omar, 36 months; Thaer Ahed Owda Shamaly, 17; Salameh al-Rade'a, toddler; Anas Akram Skafi, 18; Sa'ad Akram Skafi, 18; Khader Khalil al-Louh, 50; Abdel Aziz Nour El Din Noor, 21; Ibrahim Abdullah Abu Aita, 67; Ahmad Ibrahim Abdullah Abu Aita, 30; Jamila Salim Abu Aita, 55; Adham Ahmad Abu Aita, 4; Mohammad Ibrahim Abu Aita, 32; Hadi Abdul-Hamid Abdul-Fatah Abdul Nabi, 3; Abdul-Hadi Abdul-Hamid Abdul Nabi, 2; Abdul-Rahman Mahmoud Abdul-Fatah Abdul Nabi, 1; Bilal Zayad 'Alwan, 20; Majed Mahmoud Mohammad Hamid, 28; Ahmad Rif'at Ar-Roqab, 23; Salman Salman al-Breem, 27; Mohammad Hasan Abdul-Qader al-Astal, 43; Ismael Mohammad al-Astal, 48; Ahmad Mohammad Ismael al-Astal, 20; Mahmoud Mohammad Ismael al-Astal, 19; Mohammad Saleh Mohammad al-Astal, 18; Malak Amin Ahmad al-Astal, 24; Tha'er Omran Khamis al-Astal, 30; Milad Omran al-Astal, 29; Mohammad Omran Khamis al-Astal, 33; Ahmad Thaer Omran al-Astal, 33; Amin Thaer Omran al-Astal, 3; Nada Thaer Omran al-Astal, 5; Mohammed Ibrahim Abu Daqqa, 42; Akram Ibrahim Abu Daqqa, 50; Rasmi Mousa Abu Reeda; Mohammad Radi Mahmoud Abu Reeda, 22; Mohammad Abu Yousef; Ahmad Qdeih; Rami Qdeih; Badr Hatem Qdeih, 13; Anas Hatem Suleiman Qdeih, 7; Hanafi Mahmoud Abu Yousef, 42; Mohammad Suleiman an-Najjar; Ismail Hassan Abu Rjeila, 75; Nafeth Suleiman Qdeih, 45; Nabil Shehda Qdeih, 45; Baker an-Najjar, 13; Shadi Yusef an-Najjar; Mohammad Ahmad Najjar; Anwar Ahmad Najjar; Anwar Ahmad Abu Daqqa; Sami Mousa Abu Daqqa; Adli Khalil Abu Daqqa; 'Atef Kamal Mahmoud Abu Daqqa, 54; Shoeban Moussa Abu Hiya, 64; Ahmad Abdul-Karim Ahmad Hasan; 'Ola Abu Aida, 27; Mohammad Ismael Khader; Mohammed Rateb Abu Jazr, 25; Hisham Mohammad

Farhan Abu Jazr, 23; Mohammed Farhan Abu Jazr, 48; Shadi Suleiman Kawar'e, 31; Ashraf Ibrahim Hasan Najjar, 13; Mahmoud Jihad Awad Abdin, 12; Ahmad Talal Najjar; Mohammad Samir Abdul-Al an-Najjar, 25; Mahmoud Abdo an-Najjar; Sana' Hasan Ali al-Astal; Nabil Mahmoud Mohammad al-Astal, 12; Ashraf Mahmoud Mohammad al-Astal; Mahmoud Suleiman al-Astal, 17; Mahmoud Jihad Awad Abdin, 12; Amir Adel Khamis Siam 12; Issam Faisal Siam, 24; Mahmoud Silmy Salim Abu Rowaished, 49; Mohammed Yousef Mansoub Al-Qadi, 19; Yasmin Ahmed Abu Moor, 27; Mohammad Suleiman Nimr 'Oqal, 34; Laila Ibrahim Zo'rob, 40.

July 25: Maram Rajeh Fayyad, 26; Eid Mohammad Abu Qteifan, 23; Hamed al-Bora'ey; Husam Mohammad Najjar; Sha'ban Abdul-Aziz al-Jamal; Mohammad Wisam Dardouna; Ala' Joudy Khader; Shaima' Hussein Abdul-Qadder Qannan (pregnant), 23; Mohammad Issa Khaled Hajji, 24; Hasan Hussein al-Howwari, 39; Hosam Rabhi; Mohammad Ahmed Abu Wadiya, 19; Hani 'Adel Abu Hassanein, 24; Rasha Abed-Rabbo 'Affana, 28; Mohammad Abdel Nasser Abu Zina, 24; Abdul Majeed al-Eidi, 35; Walid Sa'id al-Harazin, 5; Tareq Ismail Ahmad Zahd, 22; Salama Abu Kamil, 26; Ahmad Mahdi Abu Zour, 25; Naji Bassem Abu Ammouna, 25; Imad Adnan Mohammad Abu Kamil, 20; Tamer Bassam Mohammad Abu Kamil, 19; Mohammad Yassin Siyam, 29; Yousef Kamal Mohammed al-Wasify, 26; Mohammad Matar al-'Abadla, 32; Mohammad Ibrahim al-Khatib, 27; Mohammad Samir Najjar, 25; Rasmiyya Salama, 24; Suleiman ash-Shawwaf, 21; Ali Mohammad Ali Asfour, 58; Eyad Nassr Sharab, 24; Najat Ibrahim Hamdan an-Najjar, 42; Sharif Mohammad Salim Abu Hasan, 25; Mohammad Khalil Hamad, 18; Mandouh Ibrahim ash-Shawaf, 25; Osama Salim Shaheen, 27; Hamada Suleiman Abu Younis; Mohammad Kamel an-Naqa, 34; Kamaal Kamel an-Naqa, 35; Yassin Mustafa al-Astal, 38; Yosra Salem Hasan al-Breem, 65; Abdul-Aziz Salah Ahmad Hassanen, 15; Abdul-Hadi Salam Ahmad Abu Hassanein, 9; Abdul-Hadi Salah Abu Hasanen, 9; Hadi Salah ed-Deen Abu Hassanen, 12; Salah Ahmad Hassanen, 45; Adnan Shahid Ashteiwi Abdeen, 35; Mazin Abdeen, 23.

July 26: Ikram Ahmed Tawfiq al-Shanbari, 23; A'ed Mahmoud Ahmad al-Bura'i, 29; Mohammad Ibrahim Ahmad az-Zweidi, 30; Ala' Maher Juma' Tamtish, 19; Abdullah 'Ayesh Salam Ermeilat, 39; Abdul-Karim Ali Abu Shanab, 40; Aziza 'Atiyeh Mohammad Abu Shanab, 77; Naim Abdul Aziz Abu Zaher, 36; Husam Abdul-Ghani Yassin, 17; Ismael Abdul-Qader al-Kojok, 54; Mohammad Said Hosni as-Saqqa, 20; Islam

Ibrahim an-Naji, 19; Mohammad Ahmad Matar al-Abadla, 32; Yosra Salem Hasan al-Breem, 56; Mohammad Khalil Mohammad al-Breem; Ibrahim Salman Qabalan, 34; Mohammad Ahmad Abu Wadia, 19; Eman Hasan ar-Roqab; Bara' Mahmoud ar-Roqab, 11; Jona an-Najjar; Ekhlas Najjar; Amna an-Najjar; Majed Sameer an-Najjar, 19; Khalil Mohammad an-Najjar, 59; Ghalia Mohammed an-Najjar, 56; Ahmad Khaled Mohammad an-Najjar, 14; Eman Salah Mahmoud an-Najjar, 23; Sumayya Harb Yousef an-Najjar, 50; Kifah Samir Hasan an-Najjar 23; Rawan Khaled Mohammad an-Najjar, 17; Husam Hussein an-Najjar, 7; Samir Hussein an-Najjar, 2; Moa'taz Hussein Samir an-Najjar, 6; Ulfat Hussein Samir an-Najjar, 4; Ikhlas Sameer Hussein Abu Shahla, 30; Amir Hammoudeh Khaled Abu Shahla, 3; Amira Hammoudeh Khaled Abu Shahla, 1; Islam Hammoudeh Abu Shahla, 4; Bassam Khaled Abu Shahla, 44; Riham Fayez al-Breem, 19; Abdul-Hamid Mohammad Abdul-Hamid Al-Maghrabi, 31; Abdul-Majeed Abdullah Abdul-Majeed al-A'ady, 36; Hamad Mohammad Ala Sheikh Salim, 30; Mohammad Rafiq Said al-Ayeer, 30; 'Amro Abdul-Hakim as-Sheikh Khalil, 25; Shadi Kamal Ramadan Yassin, 22; Mohammad Issam Deeb Abu Dalfa, 25; Walid Said Nassr al-Ijlah, 7; Osama Issam Fawzi 'Azzam, 23; Abdullah Ibrahim Abdullah Abu Leila, 51; Ahmad Walid Nasrallah Samour; Hasan Abdullah Mustafa al-Athanna, 59; Hasan Zaki Hasan at-Tahrawy, 23; Omar Ismail Ali Quz'aat, 18; Rami Faisal Matar as-Shishi, 31; Mohammad Abdul Hamid; Ghassan Yousef Salem Abu Dabakh; Khadra Ibrahim Salman Abu Bleimy, 55; Nour Mohammad Salameh Abu Dbagh, 13; Ahmad Ramzi Mohammad Abu Qadoos, 13; Maisara Anwar Suleiman dar-Azzeen, 6; Mohammad Anwar Suleiman dar-Azzeen, 13; Mohammad Abdul-Hamid Mohammad Shaat, 29; Raja' Hamad Mohammad ad-Daghme, 36; Sami Abdullah Ahmad Judeh, 18; Husam Abdul-Atif Raady, 42; Mohammad Ibrahim Sobhi al-Arheir, 30; Wala' Mohammad Ali al-Qayedh, 15; Isam Mohammad Saleh Shamaly, 29; Mohammad Abdul-Nassar Ali Abu Zeina, 20; Mosab Salah al-Aab Abu al-A'ata, 20; Ibrahim Aish Abed Abu Ghneimah, 27; Ismail Aish Abed Abu Ghneimah, 24; Fadel At-Tawaneh; Arafat Salem Abu Oweily, 27; Abdul-Rahman Ouda at-Tilbani; Mohammed Salameh Mohammed Abu Khousa, 75; Salman Mohammed Ahmed Sama'na, 30; Do'a' Sani Ibrahim Sama'na, 11; Mohammed Sa'id Sha'ban Baba, 40; Mohammed Rafiq Sa'id Alareer, 30; Hassan Fathi Ahmad Alareer, 39; Sami Fathi Ahmed Alareer, 50; 'Abdul Karim Fathi Ahmed Alareer, 34; Fathi Sami Fathi Alareer, 20; Khaled Yousef Mohammed Badwan, 48; Azmi

Khaled Yousef Badwan, 16; 'Abdul Rahman Ziad Hassan Abu Hain, 28; Mohammed 'Essam Dib Abu Balta, 28; Mahmoud Ra'ed Mahmoud al-'Eish, 23; Fadi 'Abdul Qader 'Abdul Malek Habib, 31; Farid Abdul-Khader Abdul-Malik Habib, 38; Adham Majed Yousef Dhaher, 18; Mohammad Mahmoud Rajab Hajjaj, 32; Mohammad Ahmed Kamel Abu al-'Ata, 32; Jihad Mahmoud Hamed al-Hilu, 59; Siham 'Ata al-Hilu, 57; Mohammad Jihad Mahmoud al-Hilu, 29; Tahreer Jihad Mahmoud al-Hilu, 20; Najiya Jihad Mahmoud al-Hilu, 15; Ahmad Jihad Mahmoud al-Hilu, 27; Hidaya Talal al-Hilu, 25; Maram Ahmad Jihad al-Hilu, 2; Abdul-Kareem Ahmad Jihad al-Hilu, 1; Karam Ahmad Jihad al-Hilu, 5 months; Ayman Anwar Salem Burai'em 39; Munther Talal Abdul-Karim Nassar, 33; Tamer Talal Abdul-Karim Nassar, 24; Ala' Abdul-Rahman Mohammad Nassar, 25; Taher Ismail Abdul-Rahman Nassar, 18; Sharif Rafiq Mohammad al-Hamdin, 26; Ala' Khaled Najib al-Yaziji, 21; Mohammad Mahmoud Sa'id Abu al-'Ata, 28; Mohammed Riad Sha'ban Shabet, 25; Abdul-Jawad Ali Abul-Jawad Al-Houm; Ehab Sa'dy Mohammad Nassr, 22; Mohammad Abdullah Hussein al-Jawajri; Wisam Sofyan Omar al-Kilani, 27; Mazin Adnan Salman Abdin, 25; Salah Eshtewy Ibrahim Adbin, 42; Suleiman Zaki 'Abdul Mawla al-Dardissi, 27; Ahmad Shawqi Mohammad Sa'ada, 37; Mohammed Ibrahim Hamdan Abu T'aima, 25; Ra'ed Khalil Hamdan Abu T'aima, 33; Mamdouh Mallahi Suleiman Abu Naja, 24; Ayman Akram Ismail al-Ghalban, 22; Jihad Naji Abu 'Aamer, 22; Rabah Rashed Mosallam Fayad, 40; Fadi Mahmoud Sa'd al-Masri, 22; Eyad Yousef al-Sadi, 24; Salem Mustafa al-Hadhidi, 18; Wassim Nasser 'Abdu Shurrab, 22; 'Ali Mohammed 'Ali al-Astal, 32; Fawzi Ahmad Abu Amsha, 67; Na'ma Mohammad Hussein Abu Amsha, 64; Wassim Salah Abu Riziq Al-Masri; Saed Munir Shida Abu Khater, 19; Amar Mustafa Rashid Hamdouna, 22; Tariq Mohammad Moehsin al-Ajrami, 25; Hamza Mazin Khalil Madhi, 23; Ismail Younis Abdullah Khalla, 21; Abdul-Rahman Yusef Ahmad Saadat, 24; Khaled Abdullah Mahmoud Adwan, 30; Osama Mohammad Nassr al-Kafarneh, 50; Khaled 'Ata Mohammad Abu Shehadeh, 23; Hani 'Adel Mohammad Abu Hashish, 23; Mohammad Ahmad Abu Dawabe', 19; Mohammad Ali Khalil Saidam, 17; Ibrahim Mohammad Awad Barak, 19; Bilal Bassam Salem al-Masri, 21; Anwar Abdul-Khader Hasan Younis, 2; Arafat Salem Ahmad Abu Oweily, 27; Mohammad Fayez Sha'ban al-Sharif, 23; Mahmoud al-Sharif, 24; Hossam Mohammad Suleiman Abu Ghneifi, 18; Ghassan Taher Suleiman Abu Kamil, 25; Ismail Abdul-Jawad Ismail Abu Sa'ada, 26; Mahmoud Riyadh Abdul-Khader Miq'dad, 22; Mazin

Yusef Suleiman Abu Joerban, 31; Shaker Ahmad Shaker al-Jamal, 46; Faisal Fa'eq al-At-Toame, 31; Hazem Yusef Abdul-Rahman al-Moebid, 34; Abdullah Nabil Abdul-Khader al-Batsh, 21; Sharif Jalal Hasan al-Karshali, 27; Mohammad Arafat Saleh Khalil al-Ghamare, 33; Abdul-Raziq Shoeban Abed Ommar, 27; Amjad Nahedh Ala' al-Sarefy, 22; Adham Majed Yousef Daher, 18; Hamza Hassan Mahmoud Halas, 25; Ahmad Mousa Ahmad Ahl, 75; Mohammad Hussein Hasan al-Nasri; Mahmoud Husam Mohammad Mansour, 22; Mosab Mustafa Rajeb Ali, 20; Mo'amin Mustafa Mahmoud al-Kasha; Eyas Ahmad Mohammad Abu Ouda, 28; Nidal Khaled Mohammad Khalil, 20; Nader Majdi Abdul-Rahman Qassim, 30; Eman Ibrahim Suleiman al-Ghandour; Salmad Hamad Salmad al-Amour, 32; Rifat Nabil Ramadan Oweida, 27; Ashraf Qassim Mansour Wafi, 25; Baha Rafiq Oweida, 36; Ahmad Barham Oleiman Abu Daqqa; Taysir Mohammad Aish an-Najjar; Hisham Abdul-Karim Ahmad Abu Mour; Salim Salaam Abu ath-Thoum, 87; Mohammad Ahmad Khaled Hassouneh; Nidal Ahmad 'Issa Abu al-'Asal, 27.

July 27: Ikram ash-Shinbari, 23; Yusef Jamil Sobhi Hammouda, 16; Ibrahim Khalil ad-Derawi, 27; Ala Nahedh Matar, 26; Hazem Fayez Abu Shammala, 33; Ahmad Abu Sweirej, 23; Mohammad Abu Haroun, 29; Fadi Baraka (child); Baha' ed-Deen Ahmad Sa'id; Yousef Abed Shehada al-Masri, 24; Jalila Faraj Ayyad; Essam Ibrahim Abu Shab, 42; Imad Jami al-Abed al-Bardaweel, 44; Issam Abdul-Karim Abu Sa'ada; Hussein Hasan Abu an-Naja, 65; Khaled Abdul-Sattar Samhoud; Mohammad Siyam, 15.

July 28: Samih Jebriel Jneid, 4; Mohammad Abu Louz, 22; Bissan Eyad Abu Zeid; Abdul-Hadi Abu Zeid, 9; Ahmad Abdullah Hasan Abu Zeid; Widad Ahmad Salama Abu Zeid; Sham'a Wael Abu Zeid; Mariam Marzouq Abu Zeid; Falasteen Mohammad Abu Zeid; Abdullah Nidal Abu Zeid; Mohammad Jom'a Shaat, 30; Mohammad Fadel al-'Agha, 30; Marwa Nader al-Agha; Ahmad Nader Al-Agha; Donia Nader al Agha, 13; Seham Najjar, 42; Abdul-Samad Mahmoud Ahmad Ramadan, 16; Ayman Adnan Mousa Shaker, 25; Issa Kamel Abdul-Rahman Mousa, 61; Salem Mousa Badawi al-Far, 59; Ramzi Hussein Ahmad al-Far; Salem Mohammad al-Far; Hanan Salem al-Far, 14; Azza Abdul-Karim Abdul-Rahman Al-Faleet, 59.

July 29: Naji Ahmad al-Raqqab, 19; Ramy Khaled al-Raqqab, 35; Mahmoud Osama al-Qosas; Shadi Abd al-Kareem Farwana; Mustafa

Abd al-Samiee al-Ubadala; Yahiya Mohammad Abdullah al-Aqqad, 49; Mohammad Ata Najjar, 2; Rafif Ata Najjar, 3; Waddah Abu Amer; Ahmad Suleiman Ahmad Abu Amer; Mohammed Ahmad Abu Amer; Marwa Ahmad Abu Amer; Marah Ahmad Abu Amer; Yasser Ahmad Abu Amer; Suleiman Ahmad Abu Amer; Moha Hajjaj Abu Amer; Zaher Ahmad Najjar, 6; Soheil Hasan Nassar; Anis Abu Shammala; Soheila al-'Ejel, 70; Mo'nes Ahmad; Tahrir Nasr Jaber, 15; Mos'ab Ahmad Sweih, 17; Nariman Khalil al-Agha, 39; Ali Mohammad Abu Ma'rouf, 23; Dr. Bashir al-Hajjar; Samir al-Hajjar; Hana' Na'im Balata; Doa' Na'im Balata; Esra' Na'im Balata; Mariam Na'im Balata; Yahia Na'im Balata; Sahar Motawe' Balata; Naim Nathmi; Yusef Emad Qaddoura; Huna Emad Qaddoura; Mohammad Musa Alwan; Mariam Khalil Ruba, 70; Hani Abu Khalifa; Baha' ed-Deen Khatib; Mary Dheir, 12;Tasneem Dheir, 8; Ezzat Dheir, 23; Turkeyya Dheir, 80; Yasmeen Dheir, 25; Ayman Samir Qeshta, 30; Ismael Shahin, 27; Baha' ed-Deen al-Gharib; Ola Baha' ed-Deen al-Gharib; 'Ola Baha' ed-Deen Khatib; Suleiman Mos'ad Barham al-Hishash, 30; Jamal Ramadan Lafi, 50; Karam Abu Zeid, 1.

July 30: Odai Yahia Zaki Abu Jneid, 19; Abdul-Jalil Mohammad Kamel Abu Shodoq, 35; Jamal Shihda Abu Shodoq, 40; Taiseer Sababa, 22; Wisam Dardouna; Mustafa Ahmad Abu Jalala; Asma' Abu al-Kaas, 16; Mayar Jamal Abu Musbeh, 9; Mohammad Tayseer Abu Hazaa', 25; Maisara Mohammad at-Ta'ban, 35; Ali Ahmad Shahin; Ammar Suleiman Ali al-Masdar, 31; Hamza Yasser Mohammad Mheisin, 23; Husam Mohammad an-Najjar; Sha'aban Abdul-aziz al-Jamal; Alaa' Joudy Khader; Mohammed Mazen Moussa Foda; Ahmad Abdulkarim Hannoun; Saadi Saadi Faraj; Hussein Saeed Kar're'ra; Hamdi Sadi Abu Zour; Abdulkarim Hussein El-Selk; Aahed Ziad Al Gharabli; Abdulaziz Ibrahim El-Beltagy; Lena Ala'a El-Selk; Abdulaziz Mohammed El-Selk; Abdel Halim Mohammed El-Selk; Moataz Bassam Deeb; Mahmoud Mohamed Ragab; Moaaz Khaled Tayeh; Malak Jalal El-Selk; Amina Mohammed El-Selk; Layan Nael El-Selk; Abdullah Fayez Fayad 23; Suhaib Salleh Salama 23; Ibrahim Yusuf al-Astal 35; Sojoud Abdul-Hakim Oleyyan, 11; Mohammad Ezzat Abu Sweireh, 34; 'Aed Zaqqout; Issam Jaber al-Khatib; Sa'id Abu Jalala; Taiseer Hammad; Lu'ay al-Feery; Bassem Khaled Najjar; Tha'er Khaled Najjar; Osama Mohammad Sohweil; Bilal Midhat al-'Amoudi; Abdullah Midhat al-'Amoudi; Mohammad Mousa Ghaban; Ramadan Khader Salman; Alaa' Khader Salman; Ali Ahmad Shaheen; Rami Barakat; Adel Mohammad Abu Qamar; Ahmad Mohammad Yassin al-Majayda; Ali Mahmoud al-Astal,

23; Khaled Salim al-Astal, 26; Mohammad Salim al-Astal, 26; Ramzi
Ibrahim al-Astal, 21; Odah Ahmad al-Astal, 25; Ahmad Mahmoud
Suleiman al-Astal, 26; Ahmad Ibrahim Ali al-Astal; Khalil Ibrahim Ali
al-Astal; Ezzedddin Jabr Mohammad al-Astal; Mohammad Mahmoud
al-Astal; Mohammad Abdul-Sattar al-Abadla, 21; Fahd Mahmoud Jaber
al-Agha, 23; Abdul-Aziz Hosni Abu Hajras, 23; Omar Awad al-Breem;
Kamal Ahmad Al-Breem, 57; Jihad Salah Mohammed al-Breem, 28;
Mariam Ahmad Hejazi; Salah Hejazi; Sabha Ibrahim Hejazi; Ibrahim
Mousa al-Ghalban; Ismael Mahmoud al-Ghalban; Ahmad Suleiman
Abu Amer; Mohammad Ahmad Abu Amer; Marwa Ahmad Abu Amer;
Marah Ahmad Abu Amer; Yasser Ahmad Abu Amer; Suleiman Ahmad
Abu Amer; Mona Hajjaj Abu Amer; Jihad Salah Mohammad Al-Breem,
25; Zeinab Abu Jazar; Iftikhar Mohammad Shahin (Abu Zrei'ey), 50;
Jamalat Mahmoud Dheir; Mahmoud Dheir; Arwa Mahmoud Dheir;
Salama Mahmoud Dheir; Mahmoud Salama Mahmoud Dheir; Yamen
Omar Salama Mahmoud Dheir; Shorouq Ramadan Mohammad Abu
Jazar; Aassem Ahmed Baraka, 25; Ahmad Khalil Abu 'Anza, 32; Shadi
Abdullah Abu 'Anza, 38; Ali Mahmoud Abu 'Anza, 27; Ahmad Abdullah
Abu 'Anza; Mohammad Suleiman Baraka; Anwar 'Adel Abu Nasr, 20;
Ismael Walid Abu Nasr, 18; Hussein Mohammad Abu Rezeq, 36; Walid
Shihda Marzouq Moammar, 51.

July 31: Kamal Abdul-Karim al-Louh, 32; Ibrahim Abdul-Karim al-
Louh, 29; Khaled Nasr al-Louh, 46; Amaal Abdul-Karim al-Masri, 48;
Ilham Yahya al-Louh, 27; Suleiman Baraka, 31; Aref Baraka, 58; Ahmed
al-Loah, 22; Baraa' Yousef, 19; Hamza Fa'ek Ahmad al-Haddad, 20;
Ibrahim Asa'ad Ahmad al-Haddad, 21; Mohammad Ammar Sharaf, 10;
Mohammad Daher; Mohammed Ra'fat Na'eem; Husam Ra'fat Na'eem;
Majdi Mohammad Ahmad Fseifis, 34; Mohammad Juma' an-Najjar,
32; Hani Abdullah Abu Mustafa; Hanan Yusef Abu T'aima; Mahar an-
Najjar; Mahmoud Fouad an-Najjar; Samih Kamal Abu al-Kheir, 63;
Othman Fawzi 'Abdeen, 17; Abdullah abu Shabab 20; Alaa' 'Alweh, 22;
Ahmed Salim Abdin; Mohamed Ahmed Hamad; Mahdiyya Suleiman
Omar Abu Louly, 58; Tha'er Naji al-Amour, 22; Mohammed Yousef Al-
Abadla, 21; Siham al-Ham, Khan Younis; Mohammad Adel Ashour;
Renad Ashraf Ashour; Abeer Nahed al-'Ata; Naima Darwish Abu Shouq;
Zaher Tawfiq Abu Maktoum; Ama' Rafat al-'Asa; Hasan Nassr Zaqqout;
Labibeh Abu Shouqa, 23; Maha Abdul-Nabi Salim Abu Hilal; Fadel
Nader Almeghari, 27; Atiyyeh Salameh al-Hashash, 68.

August 1: Souad Ali Al-Bahri, 60; Samal Nail Al-Barawi, 8 months; Hasan Abdul-Majid al-Bayyoumi; Abdul-Malek Abdul-Salam al-Farra, 58; Osama Abdul-Malek al-Farra, 34; Emad Abdul-Hafeth al-Farra, 28; Awatef Ezzeddin al-Farra, 29; Mohammad Mahmoud al-Farra, 12; Lojein Bassem al-Farra, 4; Yara Abdul-Salam al-Farra, 8; Nadine Mahmoud al-Farra; Abdullah Awad al-Breem; Mohammad Suleiman al-Breem; Maisoun Ra'fat al-Breem; Raed Abdul-Latif al-Qarra; Sami Suleiman al-Madani; Husam Suleiman al-Madani; Ahmad Salim Abdin; Mohammad Ahmad Hamad; Mousa Hamad Abu 'Amran; Hilal Eid Abu 'Amran; Ismael Zuheir Mohammadein, 26; Maher Ja'far Hajjaj, 54; Wajih Sha'ath; Fadi Al-Qawasmi; Ali Barbakh; Shadi Mohammad Jom'a Abu Daher, 29; Ahmad Mohammad Hassanein; Basil Diab al-Basyouni; Mohammad Reziq Hassanein, 20; Ahmed Wisam Al-Abeed, 4; Osama Abdul-Malik Abu Mualla, 37; Atif Sohail Kandil, 24; Nihad Mohammed Yasin, 24; Faiz Tareq Yassin, 16; Hassan Ismail Yassin, 32.;Aseel Sha'ban Gheith, 3; Sufian Farouq Gheith, 35; Farouq Gheith, 65; Ahlam No'man Zo'rob, 18; Sabiha Zo'rob, 55; Amir Ra'fat Zo'rob, 7; Shahd Ra'fat Zo'rob, 10; Odai Ra'fat Zo'rob, 7; Khaled Ra'fat Zo'rob, 8; Rawan Nath'at Siyam, 12; Su'ad No'man Zo'rob, 34; Yousef Darbieh, 25; Mousa Ibrahim Abu Hazir; Atef Zamili; Joseph Jameen Sheikh Eid; Yousef Jaber Drabiah; Ibrahim Sulayman Al-Masri, 50; Nadia Yousef Al-Masri, 45; Ibrahim Al-Masri, 6; Mohamed Anas Arafat, 4 months; Anas Ibrahim Hamad, 5; Sabri Shaykh Al-Eid, 35; Mohammed Khalid Al-Aloul, 30; Ibrahim Mostafa Ghaneem; Amna Azamaly; Yahya Abd Al-Karim Lafi; Musa Mohamed Abu Omran; Hilal Eid Abu Omran; Salama Mohamed Al-Zamaly; Nuha Jamal Abu Ziyada; Taiseer Ali Moamir'; Hussein Salaam Al-Jaafari; Yousra Mohamed Abu Hazir; Ataf Hamad Al-Mahmoum.

August 2: Haitham Yasser Abdel Wahab, 16; Mohamed Issa Ashaar; Hossam Yassin Abu Naqira, 20; Mousa Yasin Abu Naqira; Ola Bassam Al-Nairab; Arwa Mohamed al-Nairab; Mariam Hasan Abu Jazzar, 60; Fida Yousef Abu Suleiman, 23; Maha Raed Abu Suleiman; Mohammad Rami Abu Suleiman; Ahmad Rami Abu Suleiman; Lama Rami Abu Suleiman; Jana Rami Abu Suleiman; Sadia Abu Taha, 40; Mohammed Abu Taha, 27; Youssef Abu Taha; Rezeq Abu Taha, 2 months; Muhammad Hassan Qeshta; Ahmed Shtewi Qeshta; Yahya al-Nems; Hazem al-Nems; Mohammad al-Nems; Osama Abu Nakirah; Mousa Mohammad Ahmad Abu Rajila, 25; Salma Suleiman Mohammad Radwan, 86; Ibrahim Abdel-Hakim Daoud al-Zaqzouq, 22; Mohammad Foaz Ibrahim Abu Rajilah, 26; Hazim Khaled Abdel-Maadi Awda'; Mohammad Fouad Al-Dedda,

28; Issa Saadi Ashaar, 40; Yasser Yousef Abu Dbagh, 20; Amro Tareq Hasan Qandil, 17; Wael Nihad Sayyed, 23; Mohammad Taiseer Hasan Qandil, 20; Hamdi Mohammad Abdul-Aziz Ayyad; Shadi Hamdi Mohammad Ayyad; Yousef Daoud Abu Madi, 65; Hassan Yousef Abu Madi; Karim Yousef Abu Madi 24; Amin Yousef Abu Madi, 5; Hathifa Abu Teir; Nabil al-Najjar; Kamal Abu Teir; Ahmad Abu Teir; Yahya Jamal Musa Shabat, 29.

August 3: Ahmad Qassem; Qassem Qassem; Fares Abu Jazar, 2; Maria Abu Jazar, 2; Amani Abu Jazar, 23; Issa Sha'er; Saed Mahmoud al-Lahwani; Mohammad al-Hour, 30; Nasrallah al-Masry; Mohammad Ismael al-Ghoul; Wael Ismael al-Ghoul; Ismael Mohammad al-Ghoul; Asma' Ismael al-Ghoul; Hanadi Ismael al-Ghoul; Khadra Khaled al-Ghoul; Ismael Wael al-Ghoul; Malak Wael al-Ghoul; Mustafa Wael al-Ghoul; Remas 'Atwa al-'Attar (Khattab); 'Atwa Suleiman Khattab, 64; Mohammad 'Atwa Khattab; Suleiman 'Atwa Khattab; Nevin Suleiman Khattab; Turkiyya Mahmoud 'Okal, 60; Elham Mohammad Mahmoud 'Okal, 34; Mahmoud As'ad Mohammad 'Okal, 18; Mahmoud Mohammad Na'im 'Okal, 10; Mohammad Abu Rajal; Sami Abdullah Qishta'; Sami Ismael Abu Shaouf; Ahmad Khaled Abu Harba'; Mohammad Mosa'ed Qishta'; Hazem Abdel-Baset Hilal; Amr Tariq Abu al-Rous; Ahmad Kamal al-Nahhal; Yousef Akram Skafi; Tareq Sa'id Abu al-Rous; Munir Abu Daba'a; Hatem Abdul-Rahman Wahdan, 50; Seniora Wahdan, 27; Jamila Jamal Wahdan; Amira Ahmad Khattab; Rajab Abdul-Rahman Sharafi, 10; Mahmoud Abdullah Sharafi, 26; Najah Rajab Sharafi, 48; 'Ahed Badran; Abdul-Karim Najm; Bilal Abdul-Karim Najm; Ahmad Abdul-Karim Najm; Raghd Najm; Soha Najm; Shimaa' Wael Qassim; Rowan Ahmed Majdalawi, 7; Mohammad Ahmad Majdalawi, 6; Ras Hadi Majdalawi; Mahmoud Abdel-Hadi Majdalawi; Abdullah Majdalawi; Khalil Mohammad Ramadan Abu Daba'a, 42; Qassim Mahmoud Qassim, 40; Mohammad Sa'dy Ahmad, 37; Basil Walid at-Tala'a, 23; Abdullah Soheil Abu Shawish, 24.

August 4: Dia' ed-Deen Mohammad al-Madhoun, 23; Ahmad Banat, 22; Hamada Khalil al-Qaaq; Ahmad Khaled al-Qaaq; Suleiman Mohammad Ma'rouf; Zaher al-Andah; Abdul-Nasser al-Ajjoury; Abdul-Hai Salama al-Qreinawi, 45; Mohammad Sabri Atallah, 21; Raghd Mas'oud, 7; Daniel Abdullah Abu Mansour, 44; Abdul-Nasser Ajjouri; Ashraf Mashal, 25; Fadi Madhi, 23; Aseel Mohammad al-Bakri, 8; Saher Talal Abu Mohsen, 23; Aseel Saleh Hussein Abu Mohsen, 18; Ebtisam Hammad al-Mahmoum, 18; Hiba Mustafa al-Mahmoum, 7; Obada Mustafa al-Mahmoud, 3; Abdullah Hussein Mousa Mubarak, 50; Mahmoud Zaki Lahham, 25; Ahmad Abdul-Halim Mohammad al-Astal, 26; Walid Darabiyyah; Amro Mohjez; Mohammad Saleh Shemaly, 60; Mohammad Fawzi Bhar, 22; Mohammad Hosni Sukkar, 20; Mohammad Amjad Awida', 12; Amal Amjad Awida', 5; Karam Mahrous Dahir, 24; Ibrahim al-Masharawi, 30; Ebtisam al-Bakri, 38; Mahmoud Zaki al-Laham, 25; Ahmad Abdel-Halim Mohammad al-Astal, 26; Fayez Ismail Abu Hamad, 34; Saleh Ahmad al-Ghouti, 22.

August 5: Nida Raed 'Oleywa, 12; Sha'ban Suleiman ad-Dahdouh, 24.

August 7: Mohammad Jom'a Najjar, 32.

August 8: Ibrahim Zoheir ad-Dawawsa, 10; Mahmoud Mohammad Abu Haddaf; Suleiman Samir Abu Haddaf; Mahmoud Khaled Abu Haddaf; Ahmad Na'im 'Okal, 22.

August 9: Moath Azzam Abu Zeid, 37; Nidal Badran, 34; Tareq Ziad Abdullah, 25; Abdul-Hakim Suleiman al-Masdar, 65; Moath Akram al-Masdar, 19; Aaya Nour ash-Sha'er, 13.

August 10: Ahmad Mohammad Atiyya al-Masri, 17; Ahmad Mohammad Atiyya al-Masri, 14; Anwar Mustafa Za'anin, 17; Saqer Abdullah Reehan, 25; Amani Abed al-Bakara, 35; Ehsan Hussein Kaware', 24.

August 11: Maida' Mohammad Aslan, 45; Mohammad ar-Roumy.

August 13: Camille Simon, 37; Bilal Mohammad Sultan, 27; Taiseer Ali al-Houm, 40; Hazem Abu Morad, 38; Ali Shihda Abu Afsh; Deema Klob; Kamal ad-Daly, 26.

August 19: Omar Mohammad Jarghoun; Abdullah Abed-Rabbo, 20.

August 20: Mohammad al-Louh, 21; Ahmad Rabah ad-Dalo, 20; Nabila Eid al-Louh (pregnant), 35; Farah Ra'fat al-Louh; Maisara Ra'fat al-Louh; Mustafa Ra'fat al-Louh; Ra'fat Moustafa al-Louh, 32; Ahmad Mustafa al-Louh, 21; Mohammad Mustafa al-Louh, 21; Sami Hasan Ayyad; Zaki Suleiman ar-Ra'ey, 54; Nour Mohammad Abu Haseera, 2; Sufian Abu Mheisin, 49; Mustafa Sufian Mheisin, 31; Darwish Mheisin, 52; Mustafa Rabah ad-Dalo, 14; Wafa' Hussein ad-Dalo, 48; Widad Deif; Ali Deif (child); Mohammad Imad al-'Abeet, 16; Saher al-'Abeet, 11; Haitham Ramadan al-'Awour, 20; Abdullah Salah Safy, 33.

August 21: Srour Mohammad Tamboura, 36; Hasan Tamboura, 13; Iman al-Louah; Raed al-'Attar; Mohammad Barhoum; Hasan Hussein Younis, 75; Amal Ibrahim Younis; Saba Rami Younis, 4; Ahmad Nasser

Kallab, 17; Natheera Kallab; Aisha Atiyya; Jom'a Matar, 27; Omar Abu Naddi, 22; Marwan Mohammad Abu Shallouf, 29; Ibrahim Essam Hammad, 22; Abdul Rahman Saad Abu Shallouf, 31; Mohammad Abu Shammala; Abdullah Tareq ar-Reefy (child); Omar Nasr ar-Reefy (child); Mohammad Ziad ar-Reefy (child); Nassr Ziad ar-Reefy, 35; Mohammad Talal Abu Nahl; Rami Abu Nahl; Haitham Tafesh; Abed Talal Shiokh; Mohammad Ahmad Abbas Abu al-Omarain, 45; Issam Mohammad al-Hosni, 26; Mahmoud Talaat Shreiteh, 14; Bashir Ahmad Shreiteh, 35; Sarah Mohammad Deif, child; Hamdan Salem Hadayed, 40.

August 22: Mahmoud Nasser Qashlan, 24; Yassin Hamed Abu Hamad, 22; Ismael Mosallam Abu Bteihan, 75; Ahmad Qassem Al-'Abadla, 59; Mousa Ahmad Al-'Abadla, 23.

August 23: Hussein Khaled Ahmad, 8; Nisreen Ahmad; Suheir Abu Mdein; Hadi Hayel Abu Dahrouj, 3; Abdullah Hayel Abu Dahrouj, 4; Hayat Abed-Rabbo Abu Dahrouj, 49; Hoda Mohammad Abu Dahrouj, 27; Hayel Shihda Abu Dahrouj, 26; Mahmoud Osama Mahmoud Abbas Abu al-Omarain, 28; Mohammad Sabr al-'Ejla, 64; Abdel-Rahman Hadayed, 25; Salah Isleim.

August 24: Mohammad Ibrahim al-Louqa, 21; Adam Ahmad Khattab, 26; Mahmoud Ahmad al-'Attar, 30; Yahia Saber Abu al-'Omarein; Bader Hashem Abu Mnei', 18; Mohammad Tal'at al-Ghoul, 30; Zeinab Bilal Abu Taqiyya, 18 months; Mohammad Wa'el al-Khodary, 17; Yahia Abu Daqen, 27. Osama Abu Mustafa Jouda, 7; Mohammad Abu Mustafa Jouda, 8; Tasneem Abu Mustafa Jouda, 14; Raghad Abu Mustafa Jouda, 13; Rawiya Abu Mustafa Jouda, 40; Mo'ayyad al-A'raj, 3.

August 25: Yassin Ibrahim al-Biltaji, 23; Farhana Ibrahim al-'Attrar, 48; Raddad Ahmad Tanboura, 78; Hani Mohammad Yassin, 20; Bassem Hassan Hijazi, 36; Ahmad Taysir Fahmi al-Daali, 28; Saad Bassem aj-Jour, 21; Osama Mohammad Shbeir, 25; Abdullah Murtaja.

August 26: Mohammad Mo'in Abu 'Ajwa; Hasan Omar as-Awwad; Shadi 'Oleiwa, 26; Salem Mohammaden, 26; Mohammad Abdul-Rahman Thaher, 49; Samer Midhat Hamad, 24; Mohammad Majdi Za'anin; Yousef Ghannam; Mohammad Saleh ar-Ribaty, 18; Ahmad Kamel Jarboa', 26; Omar Husam al-Breem (child); Mohammad Husam al-Breem (child).

August 29: Mohammad al-Ma'sawani, 22; Widad Abu Zeid.

September: Bassem 'Ajjour, 55; Ziad ar-Reefy, 9; Nasser Abu Maraheel, 42; 'Etaf Mohammad 'Ajrour; Mahmoud Suleiman Sheikh Eid; Mohammad Ibrahim ar-Reyati, 22; Rahaf Abu Jame', 5; Samira Hasan al-Louh, 53; Abdul-Fattah abu Salmiyya, 72; Anas Taiseer al-Hinnawi, 22; Ayman Ziad Abu Jibba, 23; Abdullah Jibril Abu Aser, 24; Mohammad Riyadh Abu Aser, 24.

October: Jamal Abu Lebda, 50; Arafat Suheil Tafesh.

Notes

Introduction

1. Rania Khalek, "Israel 'Directly Targeted' Children in Drone Strikes on Gaza, Says Rights Group," Electronic Intifada, April 17, 2015, http://bit.ly/1BmT8xd. See also Breaking the Silence, *This is How We Fought in Gaza: Soldiers' Testimonies and Photographs From Operation "Protective Edge,"* http://bit.ly/1F1BKVv

2. Institute for Middle East Understanding, "50 Days of Death & Destruction: Israel's "Operation Protective Edge." September 10, 2014. http://bit.ly/1xTBcgo

3. The expression regarding putting Gaza on a diet was articulated by Israeli government advisor Dov Weisglass; see Media Lens, "Put the Palestinians on a Diet," Information Clearinghouse, November 17, 2010, http://bit.ly/1DI7afX.

4. Food Security Sector, *Report of the Rapid Qualitative Emergency Food Security Assessment (EFSA), Gaza Strip,* October 2014, http://bit.ly/1KwPZDd

5. Mouin Rabbani, "Israel Mows the Lawn," *London Review of Books* 37, no.15 (July 31, 2014), http://bit.ly/1rtE14c.

6. For more on these massacres, see Joe Sacco, *Footnotes in Gaza: A Graphic Novel* (New York: Metropolitan Books, 2010).

7. Jean-Pierre Filiu, "The Twelve Wars on Gaza," *Journal of Palestine Studies* 44, no. 1 (Autumn 2014), pp. 52-60.

8. Ali Abunimah, "Video Analysis Pinpoints Israeli Killer of Palestinian Teen," *The Electronic Intifada*, November 21, 2014, http://bit.ly/1qJPy0q

9. Mouin Rabbani, "Institutionalised Disregard for Palestinian Life," *London Review of Books*, July 9, 2014, http://bit.ly/ VK2hl8

10. Rashid Khalidi, "Collective Punishment in Gaza," *The New Yorker*, July 29, 2014, http://nyr.kr/1lSQLKv

11. Yusef Munayyer, "Israel/Gaza Cease-fire Dynamics Breakdown," Jerusalem Fund Blog, February 5, 2014, http:// bit.ly/WuwftG

12. Palestine Center, "Israeli Ceasefire Violations in Gaza and World Silence," Jerusalem Fund Blog, December 7, 2012, http://bit.ly/1rohenH

13. Ben White, "What a 'Period of Calm' Looks Like in the Occupied Territories," Al-Jazeera, February 22, 2013, http:// bit.ly/1zTogG6

14. Mona El Farra, "Unknown Child #6: Horrible Tales From My Days at the Red Crescent Clinic," Middle East Children's Alliance, July 30, 2014, http://bit.ly/1FOFZCg

15. Ali Abunimah, "How Many Bombs Has Israel Dropped on Gaza?" *The Electronic Intifada*, August 19, 2014, http://bit. ly/1n6GdIl

16. UNDP, *Detailed Infrastructure Damage Assessment, Gaza, 2014*, http://bit.ly/1EfZp28

17. Ali Abunimah, "Israel Student Union Sets up "War Room" to Sell Gaza Massacre on Facebook," Electronic Intifada, July 14, 2014, http://bit.ly/1jrPGhc. See also Abunimah, "Israel Setting up 'Covert Units' to Tweet, Facebook Government Propaganda," *The Electronic Intifada*, August 13, 2013, http:// bit.ly/1BpdmX1

18. Irene Calis, "Beyond the Apartheid Analogy: Time to Reframe Our Palestinian Struggle," al-Shabaka, January 13, 2015, http://bit.ly/1KwREZu

19. Adam Horowitz, "Video: Diane Sawyer Misrepresents Photo of Gazans in Aftermath of Israeli Bombing as Israeli Victims of Palestinian Missiles (updated)," *Mondoweiss*, July 9, 2014, http://bit.ly/1LI63Pz

20. United Nations Office for the Coordination of Humanitarian Affairs, Occupied Palestinian Territory: *Gaza Emergency Situation Report (as of 4 September 2014, 08:00 hrs)*, http://bit.ly/1qhkyT4

21. Norman Finkelstein, *Beyond Chutzpah: On the Misuse of Anti-Semitism and the Abuse of History* (Berkeley and Los Angeles: University of California Press, 2008).

22. According to Salon, "Within eight minutes, Rihanna deleted her tweet. Howard apologized, stating, "Previous tweet was a mistake. I have never commented on international politics and never will," and Gomez followed up her "Pray for Gaza" Instagram post with, "And of course to be clear, I am not picking sides." Remi Kenazi, "Tweet and Delete: On Gaza, Celebrity Courage—and Cowardice—Over Social Media," *Salon*, July 31, 2014, http://bit.ly/1RjPsWh

23. Dave Zirin, "On Dwight Howard and #FreePalestine," *The Nation*, July 17, 2014, http://bit.ly/1zNXajv

24. Robert Mackey, "Professor's Angry Tweets on Gaza Cost Him a Job," *New York Times*, September 12, 2014, http://nyti.ms/1J5zFHI

25. Sherene Seikaly, "Palestine as Archive," Stanford University Press Blog, August 1, 2014, http://bit.ly/1uP3N5e

26. Mya Guarnieri, "The Blockade on Gaza Began Long Before Hamas Came to Power," *972mag*, June 29, 2011, http://bit.ly/1ILmVE8

27. Ibid.

28. Ari Shavit, "Top PM Aide: Gaza Plan Aims to Freeze the Peace Process," *Haaretz*, October 6, 2004, http://bit.ly/1kBiaoA

29. Gisha, *Disengaged Occupiers: The Legal Status of Gaza*, January 2007, http://bit.ly/1FTmRFf

30. Mohammed Samhouri, *Gaza Economic Predicament One Year after the Disengagement: What Went Wrong?* Middle East Brief no. 12, November 2006, http://bit.ly/1ySlraO

31. Robin Wright, "Rice Cites Concerns for Palestinians, but Low Expectations Mark Visit," *Washington Post*, October 5, 2006, http://wapo.st/1HtRdci

32. Gisha, *Restrictions on the Transfer of Goods to Gaza: Obstruction and Obfuscation*, January 2010, http://bit.ly/1EuG74y

33. Tim McGirk, "One Year Since Israel's Offensive, Gaza Still Suffers," *Time*, December 28, 2009, http://ti.me/1GAaOLQ

34. Muna Dajani, "Drying Palestine: Israel's Systemic Water War," al-Shabaka, September 4, 2014, http://bit.ly/1FASss5

35. Lena Odgaard, "Gaza Farmers Struggle in War Aftermath," al-Jazeera, October 7, 2014, http://bit.ly/1v5PKHO

36. Rashid Khalidi, "Collective Punishment in Gaza," *The New Yorker*, July 29, 2014, http://nyr.kr/1lSQLKv

37. "Eight months after Gaza war, 'not a single home has been rebuilt'—UN agency," UN News Centre, April 23, 2015, http://bit.ly/1R1pswP.

Chapter 1: Everyone Is a Target: The Human Toll

1. Page 51 (photo): Euro-Mid Observer for Human Rights, "Israeli Assault on Gaza in Numbers," August 28, 2014, http://bit.ly/1BNtmSF

Chapter 2: Destitute by Design: Making Gaza Unlivable

1. "50 Days of Death & Destruction: Israel's 'Operation Protective Edge,'" Institute for Middle East Understanding, http://bit.ly/1xTBcgo. See also "Report: Rebuilding Gaza to Cost $7.8 Billion," Ma'an News Agency, September 4, 2014, http://bit.ly/1G6o0mR.

2. Bloodlust in Israel: "Flatten Gaza, Send It Back to Middle Ages, They Need to Die," RT, November 19, 2012, http://bit.ly/1K4xVgK

3. Page 73 (photo): Euro-Mid Observer for Human Rights, "Israeli Assault on Gaza in Numbers," August 28, 2014, http://bit.ly/1BNtmSF

4. Page 81 (photo): The estimated number of amputees is provided in Mohammed Omer, "Prosthetic Limbs: A fresh start for War Wounded Gazans," *Middle East Eye*, December 8, 2014, http://bit.ly/1wlb0YB

5. Page 117 (photo): Euro-Mid Observer for Human Rights, "Israeli Assault on Gaza in Numbers," August 28, 2014, http://bit.ly/1BNtmSF

Chapter 4: Gaza Burns, the World Responds: Analysis and Commentary

1. Page 153 (photo): The description comes from "Shujaiyya: A Moonscape Strewn with Bodies," Ma'an News Agency, July 20, 2014, http://bit.ly/1FfRjWl. The number of those killed that day is from "Names of Palestinians Killed in the War on Gaza since 8 July," International Middle East Media Center, October 11, 2014, http://bit.ly/1mYswQn

2. Chris McGreal,"Capture of Soldiers Was 'Act of War' Says Israel," *Guardian*, July 13, 2006, http://bit.ly/1GICFLe.

3. Why They Died: Civilian Casualties in Lebanon during the 2006 War, Human Rights Watch, vol. 19, no. 5(E), September 2007, p. 13, www.hrw.org/sites/default/ files/reports/lebanon0907.pdf.

4. "Israel Warns Hizbullah War Would Invite Destruction," Ynet, October 3, 2008, http://bit.ly/1eim8l9.

5. Avi Shlaim, *The Iron Wall: Israel and the Arab World* (New York: W. W. Norton, 2001), p. 101.

6. "Netanyahu: Hamas Is Islamist Extremism Like al Qaeda, ISIS," NBC News, July 22, 2014, http://nbcnews.to/1fdsuCn. See also euronews, "Netanyahu & Ban Ki-moon Joint Conference on Gaza Offensive (Recorded LIVE Feed)," www.youtube.com/watch?v=zbpB50MQnQE, at the 12:30 time stamp.

7. Joshua Mitnick,"Israel Does About-Face Over Hamas-ISIS Tweet," *Wall Street Journal*, updated August 22, 2014, http://on.wsj.com/1KTzD75.

8. "PM Netanyahu Meets with British Foreign Secretary Hammond," Israel Ministry of Foreign Affairs, July 24, 2014, http://bit.ly/1IgttZq.

9. William Youmans, "Israel's Mixed Message on the Threat of Hamas' Rockets," Al Jazeera America, July 29, 2014, http://bit.ly/1qJ0hrc.

10. Youmans,"Israel's Mixed Message," July 29, 2014.

11. Andrea Germanos, "Mounting Civilian Casualties an 'Image Problem' for Israel," Common Dreams, July 27, 2014, www.commondreams.org/news/2014/07/27/mounting-civilian-casualties-imageproblem-israel.

12. See, for example, "Israeli Forces Use Palestinian Child as Human Shield in Gaza," Defense for Children International Palestine, August 21, 2014,http://bit.ly/1ToyCaA.

13. Katherine Connell, "Netanyahu: Hamas Wants 'to Pile Up More and More Dead Bodies of Palestinian Civilians,'" *National Review Online*, July 27, 2014, http://bit.ly/1IgtSv8.

14. Charles Krauthammer, "Moral Clarity in Gaza," *Washington Post*, July 17, 2014, http://wapo.st/1jDCuFR.

15. "Netanyahu: Israel Seeks 'Sustainable Quiet' with Gaza," CNN, July 21, 2014, http://cnn.it/1rDiGCZ.

16. Giora Eiland, "In Gaza, There Is No Such Thing as 'Innocent Civilians,'" Ynet, August 5, 2014, http://bit.ly/1kkmJEn.

17. Thomas L. Friedman, "Israel's Goals in Gaza?" *New York Times*, January 13, 2009, http://nyti.ms/1MXnoW1.

Chapter 6. 51 Days Later, and Counting: The Untenable Status Quo

1. Arundhati Roy, "Power Politics" (Excerpts), Third World Traveler (Blog), http://bit.ly/1C18lTG

2. Page 267 (photo): Information about the losses incurred to the fishing industry as a result of Israel's assault appear in Mohammed Omer, "Gaza Fishermen Demand End to Blockade," Aljazeera, August 9, 2014, http://bit.ly/1IOfrjZ

Afterwords

1. Page 277 (photo): The number of displaced is from "Gaza Crisis: Facts and Figures," United Nations Office for the Coordination of Humanitarian Affairs, October 15, 2014, http://bit.ly/1n4buAk

Names of the dead

The names of 1,614 individuals killed by Israeli forces during its 51-day assault in July–August 2014 have been confirmed by the Palestinian Ministry of Health and are taken from "Names of Palestinians Killed in the War on Gaza since 8 July," International Middle East Media Center, October 11, 2014, http://bit.ly/1mYswQn. (The names with an asterisk have not yet been confirmed by Ministry of Health.) Individuals listed after August 26 died from injuries sustained during the assault or from unexploded ordinance. For a more personal look at the victims, see www.beyondthe-number.org.

Bibliography

Abunimah, Ali. *The Battle for Justice in Palestine*. Chicago, IL: Haymarket Books, 2014.

Abu Saif, Atef. "Eight Days in Gaza: A Wartime Diary." *New York Times*, August 4, 2014, http://nyti.ms/1ag0hZp.

Abu Saif, Atef, ed. *The Book of Gaza: A City in Short Fiction*. Manchester, UK: Carcanet Press, 2014.

Alareer, Refaat, ed. *Gaza Writes Back: Short Stories from Young Writers in Gaza, Palestine*. Charlottesville, VA: Just World Books, 2014.

Al Mezan Center for Human Rights. *Bearing the Brunt Again: Child Rights Violations during Operation Cast Lead*. Gaza, Palestine: Author, 2009, http://bit.ly/1DtUPip.

Anderson, Tom and Therezia Cooper. *Besieging Health Services in Gaza: A Profitable Business*. Corporate Watch, 2014, http://bit.ly/1P7oUXS.

Barir, Idan. "Why It's Hard to Believe Israel's Claim That It Did Its Best to Minimize Civilian Deaths." Huffington Post, August 13, 2014, http://huff.to/1oNjOUM.

Baroud, Ramzy. *My Father Was a Freedom Fighter: Gaza's Untold Story*. London: Pluto Press, 2010.

Berlin, Greta, and William L. Dienst, MD. *Freedom Sailors: The Maiden Voyage of the Free Gaza Movement and How We Succeeded in Spite of Ourselves*. Free Gaza, 2010.

Blumenthal, Max. *The 51 Day War. Ruin and Resistance in Gaza*. New York: Nation Books, 2015.

Breaking the Silence, *This is How We Fought in Gaza: Soldiers' Testimonies and Photographs From Operation "Protective Edge,"* http://bit.ly/1F1BKVv

Chediac, Joyce, ed. *Gaza: Symbol of Resistance.* World View Forum, 2011.

Chomsky, Noam. "The Real Reason Israel 'Mows the Lawn' in Gaza." *Alternet,* September 9, 2014, http://bit.ly/ZgPoRr.

Chomsky, Noam and Ilan Pappe. *Gaza in Crisis: Reflections on Israel's War Against the Palestinians* (Frank Barat, editor). Chicago, IL: Haymarket, 2010.

Cooper, Therezia, and Tom Anderson. *Gaza: Life Beneath the Drones.* Corporate Watch, 2015, http://bit.ly/1y5U4tI.

Eid, Haidar. "The Rape of Gaza." *Aljazeera,* July 31, 2014, http://bit.ly/1uPYYsd.

El-Haddad, Laila. *Gaza Mom.* Charlottesville, VA: Just World Books, 2010.

El-Haddad, Laila and Maggie Schmitt. *The Gaza Kitchen: A Palestinian Culinary Journey.* Charlottesville, VA: Just World Books, 2013.

Erakat, Noura. "Five Israeli Talking Points on Gaza—Debunked." *Jadaliyya,* July 26, 2014, http://bit.ly/1CtUwQQ.

Filiu, Jean-Pierre. *Gaza: A History.* Oxford University Press, 2014.

Finkelstein, Norman G. *"This Time We Went Too Far": Truth and Consequences of the Gaza Invasion* (Revised and Expanded). New York: OR Books, 2010.

Gilbert, Mads and Erik Fosse. *Eyes in Gaza, Revised* (Trans. Guy Puzey and Frank Stewart). London: Quartet Books, 2013.

Hass, Amira and Maxine Nunn. *Drinking the Sea at Gaza: Days and Nights in a Land Under Siege.* London: Picador, 2000.

Hroub, Khaled. *Hamas: Political Thought and Practice.* Washington, DC: Institute for Palestine Studies, 2014.

Human Rights Watch. "Witness Accounts and Additional Analysis of IDF Use of White Phosphorus." March 25, 2009. http://bit.ly/1xMhhkl.

Kattan, Victor. "The Gas Fields off Gaza: A Gift or a Curse?" Al-Shabaka, April 24, 2012, http://bit.ly/1NFs4k5.

Levy, Gideon. *The Punishment of Gaza.* New York: Verso, 2010.

Lock, Sharyn, with Sarah Irving. *Gaza: Beneath the Bombs.* New York: Pluto Press, 2010.

Makdisi, Saree. *Palestine Inside Out: An Everyday Occupation.* New York: W.W. Norton, 2008.

Munayyer, Yousef. "Gaza Cease-Fire Dynamics Explained: What Cease-Fire Will Work?" *The Jerusalem Fund Blog,* July 15, 2014, http://bit.ly/1zdLFAI.

Omer, Mohammed. "Butchery in Rafah: The Dead Are Kept in Vegetable Refrigerators." *Middle East Eye,* August 2, 2014, http://bit.ly/1oizzhj.

Rose, David. "The Gaza Bombshell." *Vanity Fair*, April 2008, http://vnty. fr/1Mez22a.

Roy, Sara. *The Gaza Strip: The Political Economy of De-development.* Washington, DC: Institute for Palestine Studies, 1995.

Roy, Sara. *Failing Peace: Gaza and the Palestinian-Israeli Conflict.* London: Pluto Press, 2007.

Sacco, Joe. *Footnotes in Gaza: A Graphic Novel.* New York: Metropolitan Books, 2010.

Sourani, Raji. "Why a Gaza Ceasefire Isn't Enough." *The Electronic Intifada*, August 3, 2014, http://bit.ly/1s3eBXP.

Suliman, Mohammed. "From Gaza: I Would Rather Die in Dignity Than Agree to Living in an Open-Air Prison." Huffington Post, July 28, 2014, http://huff.to/1k4tPwC.

Tait, Robert. "Hundreds of Thousands of Children Shell-Shocked after the War in Gaza." The Telegraph, January 28, 2014, http://bit.ly/1CMv0rc

United Nations Office for the Coordination of Humanitarian Affairs. *Gaza Humanitarian Situation Report—The Impact of the Blockade on the Gaza Strip: A Human Dignity Crisis* (December 15, 2008), http:// bit.ly/1xUzJaT.

United Nations Office for the Coordination of Humanitarian Affairs. *Between the Fence and a Hard Place* (August 2010), http://bit. ly/1jVoCHd.

UNRWA. *Gaza in 2020: A Liveable Place?* Jerusalem: Office of the United Nations Special Coordinator for the Middle East Peace Process, 2012, http://bit.ly/1f5Mgwx.

Weizman, Eyal. *The Least of All Possible Evils: Humanitarian Violence from Arendt to Gaza.* New York: Verso, 2012.

About the Contributors

Sharif Abdel Kouddous is an independent journalist based in Cairo. He is a *Democracy Now!* correspondent and a fellow at The Nation Institute.

Ali Abunimah, a cofounder of the *Electronic Intifada*, is the author of *The Battle for Justice in Palestine* (2014) and *One Country: A Bold Proposal to End the Israeli-Palestinian Impasse* (2007).

Shahd Abusalama, 23, is a Palestinian artist, a blogger from Gaza, currently working on her MA in Media and the Middle East at University of London, SOAS.

Mahmoud Alarawi is an artist and a graphic designer who is interested in oil painting, sculpture, and three-dimensional graphic design.

Refaat Alareer is the editor of *Gaza Writes Back: Short Stories from Young Writers in Gaza, Palestine.*

Sarah Algherbawi is a writer who worked with the International Solidarity Movement.

Sarah Ali is a Palestinian from the Gaza Strip who is currently working on a master's degree in English Literature at Durham University (UK).

Rami Almeghari is the editor-in-chief of the Gaza-based Palestinian Information Service, part-time lecturer on the media at Islamic University of Gaza, and a contributor to the *Electronic Intifada*.

Lina H. Al-Sharif writes poetry and is currently working on a master's degree in creative writing at Lancaster University.

Tom Anderson is a boycott, divestment, and sanctions activist and researcher. He has volunteered with various solidarity groups in Palestine and is the coauthor of *Targeting Israeli Apartheid: A Boycott Divestment and Sanctions Handbook*, published by Corporate Watch.

Rina Andolini is a UK citizen who has been living and working in solidarity with Palestinians in Gaza since 2014.

Mohammed Asad is a photojournalist who lives in Shuja'iya. His photograph "Unbreakable," of a Gaza girl whose face was badly scarred by Israel's 2014 bombing, won the Grand Jury prize in the photography competition organized by the United Nations Office for the Coordination of Humanitarian Affairs in the Middle East and North Africa.

Zeina Azzam, a writer and educator, is the executive director of The Jerusalem Fund/Palestine Center in Washington, DC.

Hana Baalousha, a Palestinian from Gaza, has a degree in English language from the Islamic University of Gaza, taught Arabic as a foreign language in the UK, and recently relocated to the United States. She is currently a stay-at-home mom of two little girls.

Farah Baker is a high school student in Gaza.

Ramzy Baroud, a PhD scholar in People's History at the University of Exeter, is the Managing Editor of *Middle East Eye*, the founder of PalestineChronicle.com, and the author of *My Father Was a Freedom Figher: Gaza's Untold Story* (Pluto Press).

Ayah Bashir, an Al-Shabaka policy member, holds a Master's degree in Global Politics from the London School of Economics and Political Science (LSE). She is a member of the steering committee of PACBI (The Palestinian Campaign for the Academic and Cultural Boycott of Israel), the Gaza-based organizing committee for Boycott, Divestment and Sanctions (BDS) against Israel, and One Democratic State Group.

Hatem Bazian, PhD, is a senior lecturer and cofounder of al-Zaytuna College.

Diana Buttu, a Canadian-Palestinian human rights lawyer and analyst based in Palestine, is a frequent commentator on Palestinian affairs and has appeared on major international news outlets including BBC, Al Jazeera, and CNN, among others. She was a legal adviser to Palestinian negotiators in 2000–2005.

Jonathan Cook, winner of the Martha Gellhorn Special Prize for Journalism, is the author of many books, including *Israel and the Clash of Civilisations: Iraq, Iran and the Plan to Remake the Middle East* (Pluto Press) and *Disappearing Palestine: Israel's Experiments in Human Despair* (Zed Books).

Therezia Cooper is a boycott, divestment and sanctions activist and researcher. She has volunteered with various solidarity groups in Palestine and is the coauthor of *Targeting Israeli Apartheid: A Boycott Divestment and Sanctions Handbook*, published by Corporate Watch.

Belal Dabour, a recently graduated doctor in Gaza, Palestine, blogs at belalmd.wordpress.com.

Allison Deger is the assistant editor of *Mondoweiss*.

Mariam Elba is a writer on social justice in the United States and the Middle East, particularly Egypt.

Nour ElBorno did not find poetry; poetry found her when she was a child, and ever since she could not be anywhere without inspiration in her heart and a pen in her hand.

Laila El-Haddad was *Al Jazeera English*'s online correspondent in Gaza from 2003 to 2006. Originally from Gaza, she now lives in Maryland, where she works as a writer, media activist, and public speaker.

Sharif S. Elmusa is a scholar and poet who taught for many years at the American University in Cairo, Egypt, and is the author of several publications, including *Flawed Landscapes: Poems, 1987-2008.*

Richard Falk is an Albert G. Milbank professor emeritus of international law at Princeton University and a research fellow at the Orfalea Center of Global and International Studies at the University of California at Santa Barbara. He was the United Nations special rapporteur on Palestinian human rights from 2008–2014

Lynda Franken (the pseudonym of Linda de Veen) is a Dutch national and former journalist at the *Palestine Monitor* who is a project coordinator at EIRENE NL.

Ron Gerlitz is the co-executive director of Sikkuy, the Association for the Advancement of Civic Equality.

Nathalie Handal is a Palestinian writer. Her latest collection, *The Invisible Star*, is the first contemporary collection of poetry that explores the city of Bethlehem and the lives of its exiles in such broad geographic spaces.

Chris Hedges is the author of 12 books, including *Death of the Liberal Class* and *War is a Force that Gives Us Meaning*.

Yousef Al-Helou, a Palestinian journalist in London, is a Reuters fellow at Oxford University.

Ruairi Henchy is an Irish writer and journalist with a special interest in Palestine.

Trevor Hogan is an Irish solidarity activist.

Kim Jensen is a Baltimore-based writer, educator, and activist whose books include *The Woman I Left Behind, Bread Alone*, and *The Only Thing that Matters*.

Hatim Kanaaneh, MD, MPH, a retired public health physician who practiced in Arrabeh, is the author of *Chief Complaint: A Country Doctor's Tales of Life in Galilee* (2015) and *A Doctor in Galilee* (2008).

Rania Khalek is an independent journalist reporting on the underclass and marginalized.

Rashid Khalidi is the Edward Said Professor of Arab Studies at Columbia University and the editor of the *Journal of Palestine Studies*. He was an adviser to the Palestinian delegation at the Madrid-Washington Palestinian-Israeli negotiations of 1991–93. His most recent book is *Brokers of Deceit*.

Sami Kishawi, a Palestinian American currently studying biology and human rights as an undergraduate at the University of Chicago, heads the University of Chicago's Students for Justice in Palestine and serves on the executive committee of American Muslims for Palestine–Chicago chapter. His blog, *Sixteen Minutes to Palestine*, reports about everyday living in the occupied territories.

Joseph Massad is professor of modern Arab politics and intellectual history. He is author of the forthcoming book *Islam in Liberalism* (University of Chicago Press).

Eman Mohammed is a photojournalist documenting the Israeli-Palestinian conflict.

Maureen Clare Murphy, a solidarity activist based in Chicago, is the managing editor of the *Electronic Intifada* and has covered cultural production for the site since 2003.

Ahmad Nafi is a contributor to *Middle East Monitor* and is currently working on a masters degree in Middle East Politics at the School of Oriental and African Studies. His research interests include Islamic thought and political society in the Middle East.

Mouin Rabbani is a Senior Fellow with the Institute for Palestine Studies and co-editor of *Jadaliyya* (www.jadaliyya.com).

Esther Rappaport is a clinical psychologist practicing independently in Tel Aviv. She is an anti-occupation activist with the Coalition of Women for Peace and a member of its board, as well as an activist with Psychoactive— Mental Health Professionals for Human Rights.

Ned Rosch is an activist and yoga instructor who lives in Portland, Oregon.

Samah Sabawi is a Palestinian writer originally from Gaza.

Omar J. Sakr is an Arab-Australian poet whose work has been published in many literary journals, including *Meanjin*, *Overland*, *Cordite Poetry*, and *Carve Magazine*.

Steven Salaita is a scholar, activist, and author of several books.

Rosa Schiano is a volunteer with the International Solidarity Movement

Michael Schwartz is a Distinguished Teaching Professor, Emeritus, of sociology at Stony Brook State University, and the author of many books and articles on popular protest and insurgency, corporate dynamics, and political policy, including *War Without End: The Iraq War in Context*.

Nadera Shalhoub-Kevorkian is the Director of the Gender Studies Program at Mada al-Carmel and is a professor at the Faculty of Law, Institute of Criminology and the School of Social Work and Public Welfare at the Hebrew University of Jerusalem.

Alaa Shamaly is a photographer and photojournalist who lives in Gaza.

Bushra Shanan is a Hebron-based graphic designer.

Charlotte Silver, an independent journalist in the San Francisco Bay area, was previously based in the West Bank.

Beth Staton is journalist whose work has appeared in Al Jazeera, *Palestine Monitor*, Salon.com, *Newsweek*, and *Middle East Eye*.

Patrick O. Strickland, an independent journalist who focuses on human rights and social justice issues, is a regular contributor to *Al Jazeera English*, *AlterNet*, and the *Electronic Intifada*.

Mohammed Sulaiman is a Palestinian from Gaza, currently working on his PhD in Australia. He has a master's degree in Human Rights from London School of Economics. Mohammed's work has appeared on the *Huffington Post*, Al Jazeera English, openDemocracy, the *Electronic Intifada*, and other publications. Mohammed also worked for Al Mezan Center for Human Rights in Gaza.

Lena Khalaf Tuffaha is an Arab-American poet of Palestinian, Jordanian, and Syrian heritage.

Ezz Al Zanoon is a freelance photographer based in the Gaza Strip. His work has appeared in many publications and outlets, including *The Guardian*, APA, *Time*, *BuzzFeed*, *El Mundo*, and Reuters.

Acknowledgments

This project would have never happened were it not for the persistence of our wonderful publisher, Helena Cobban, and her trusted associates, Diana Ghazzawi and Ida Audeh. They set us straight where we flailed, and pushed us up when self-doubt threatened to derail us. Summarizing the cruelty of what happened was a burden that we felt we were not up to. How do we do justice to the victims? How can we compete (and should we) with so many compelling works on the topic? Ultimately, our humble goal was to be a venue for those who would speak up, educate others, inspire change towards justice and equality in Palesitne. Thank you, Ida especially, for reminding us of this important obligation, and to our families, for being our sounding boards and being our bedrocks of support.

A special thanks goes to the numerous contributors who allowed their excellent writing and art to be included in this book. Your work will serve as a record and testament. We would also like to acknowledge the invaluable contributions of the photographers—Mohammed Asad, Ezz Al Zanoon, Eman Mohammed, and Alaa Shamaly—whose enthusiasm and generosity inspired and humbled us. Many of them either declined payment or request nominal fees, asking only that their work move people to action.

And finally, our humble thanks to the people of Gaza for trusting us to convey your story to the world.

About the Editors

Refaat Alareer, editor of and contributor to *Gaza Writes Back*, is an academic living in Gaza. He received his M.A. in Comparative Literature from the University College of London (U.K.) and is currently working toward his Ph.D. in English Literature at the Universiti Putra Malaysia, though this has been interrupted by the travel restrictions on Gazans. He has also been teaching world literature, comparative literature, and both fiction and non-fiction creative writing at the Islamic University of Gaza since 2007.

Alareer is interested in emerging Palestinian writers and works very closely with many of them to help them develop their creative writing skills. His book, *Gaza Writes Back*, is a compilation of short stories written in English by young Palestinian writers living in the Gaza Strip. It shows a different side of the struggle to create a free Palestine, since it includes fictional work and is written by young people; it is Gaza's creative reaction to Israel's aggression, which eventually culminated in Operation Cast Lead in 2008-2009.

Laila El-Haddad is an award-winning author, public speaker, and parent-of-three from Gaza City. She is the author of *Gaza Mom: Palestine, Politics, Parenting, and Everything In Between* and co-author of the critically acclaimed *The Gaza Kitchen: A Palestinian Culinary Journey*. Through her work as a journalist, documentarian and media activist, she provides rare insight into the human experience of the region.

From 2003-2007, El-Haddad was the Gaza correspondent for the Al Jazeera English website and a regular contributor to the BBC and the *Guardian* as well as radio correspondent for Pacifica's Free Speech Radio News. During this time, she co-directed two Gaza-based documentaries for Tourist with a Typewriter Productions, including the award-winning film *Tunnel Trade*.

She has been published in the *Baltimore Sun*, *Washington Post*, *International Herald Tribune*, *The New Statesman*, *The Daily Star*, *Le monde diplomatique*, and has appeared on CNN, NPR, and Al Jazeera. She was also featured in *Anthony Bourdain's Parts Unknown* episode "Jerusalem, the West Bank, and Gaza" as his guide in the Gaza Strip.

A graduate of Duke and Harvard, she currently makes her home in Columbia, Maryland with her husband Yassine Daoud, and their three children.